THE MAKING OF BIHAR AND BIHARIS

The Making of Bihar and Biharis

Colonialism, Politics and Culture in Modern India, c. 1870-1912

NARENDRA JHA

MANOHAR
2012

First published 2012

ISBN 978-81-7304-967-5

Published by
Ajay Kumar Jain *for*
Manohar Publishers & Distributors
4753/23 Ansari Road, Daryaganj
New Delhi 110 002

Typeset by
Ajay Arts
New Delhi 110 002

Printed by
Salasar Imaging Systems
Delhi 110 035

To the memory of
my father late T.N. Jha
and my brother-in-law late K.K. Jha
who were both alive and much involved
when this study began

Contents

Preface

This book analyses one of the earliest and pioneering (pioneering for providing both the blueprint and inspiration for later movements such as the demand for the creation of Andhra Pradesh) identity movements in the history of modern India. It examines how the natives of Bihar which till 1912 was administratively-speaking merely a geographical expression, a way of describing certain districts included within the Presidency of Bengal, came to acquire a consciousness of having common interests and a common identity centred around the territorial-historical symbol of 'Bihar' during the last three decades of the nineteenth century and early years of the twentieth century and launched a movement for its separation from Bengal (including of those areas which now constitute the state of Jharkhand). It argues that the making of modern Bihar was also the making of Biharis. It demonstrates and reaffirms the fluid and dynamic nature of identity formation which has now been exemplified by the separation of Jharkhand in the year 2000 where people a hundred years back had felt pride in announcing their Bihari identity. Though maintaining that identities—regional or national or of any other variety—are essentially constructions, it reiterates that they do need certain raw materials, some objective bases lying in their culture, language or history for this construction. Identities cannot be conjured out of nothing. It strongly refutes the negative connotations associated with the term 'regionalism' arguing that regionalism and nationalism are essentially similar phenomenon.

I first took up the subject for study while writing my M.Phil. dissertation and then as a Ph.D. thesis entitled 'Regional Identity and Consciousness: A Study of Bihar, *c.* 1870-1912' at the Centre for Historical Studies at the Jawaharlal Nehru University, New Delhi out of which this book has emerged. In the course of the research and writing of this book I have accumulated a long list of debts. My foremost debt is to my supervisor Prof. K.N. Panikkar who both advised and encouraged me to study this topic and guided me through the entire course of research and writing of the thesis. He was generous with his time and advice. I am equally grateful to the authorities of C.M. College, Darbhanga and L.N. Mithila University, Darbhanga for having granted me study leave for this research and for awarding me a short-term UGC Teacher Fellowship for its completion. I am thankful to the UGC for approving this award. I am also obliged to the ICHR for having granted me Junior Research Fellowship for some time.

I am indebted to the librarians and staff of the National Archives of India, Nehru Memorial Museum & Library, Jawaharlal Nehru University Library, Centre for Historical Studies Library (JNU), Sahitya Akademi Library, Indian Council of Historical Research Library, all at New Delhi; the Bihar State Archives, Sinha Library, Bihar Rashtra Bhasha Parishad Library, K.P. Jayaswal Reseach Institute Library, Khuda Baksh Oriental Public Library, Patna College Library, all at Patna; Maharaja Kameshwar Singh Library (L.N. Mithila University) and C.M. College Library, both at Darbhanga for the help rendered in my research. I have benefited greatly from the advice I received from a number of scholars such as Profs. Surendra Gopal, Hetukar Jha and Ratneshwar Mishra. I take this opportunity to thank them all. My colleagues at the Centre of Historical Studies had been generous with their advice, support and encouragement. I recall with pleasure the help rendered by Dhirendra Dangwal, P. Ranjan and above all Senu Kurien George. I must express my gratitude to a number of my present and former colleagues at the C.M. College for their constant encouragement and support. In particular I would like to mention the names of Bishwambhar Jha, Rajanand Jha, I.N. Jha and Avani R. Singh.

The work of typing the first draft was done by Tushar Mishra and the final draft by Rajeevji. I am grateful to both of them.

My thanks are above all due to my family members and relatives who have stood by me over the years. Especially supportive have been my mother, my two elder brothers Rajendra Jha and Bhupendra Jha. My brothers-in-law U. Jha, V. K. Jha, R. K. Jha and my sisters Bibha did and Rekha have provided unwavering support and encouragement through the years. During my visits to Delhi I have continued to enjoy the hospitality of Kshitish Mishra, Amit Mishra and Vinayachal Jha. During the entire period of research I had to live away from my wife Neeta and my daughters Pragya and Maitreyi, who bore my absence with grace. There is no way I can thank them well enough for what they have done. They are going to be the happiest persons to see this book in its present form. Neeta also helped me with the work of proof-reading the text. I am greatly thankful to Shri Ramesh Jain for taking up the study for publication and to Siddharth Chowdhury for the editorial help rendered by him.

The responsibility for all errors of fact or interpretation are solely mine.

Darbhanga NARENDRA JHA

Glossary

Amil	:	Revenue Officer.
Amla	:	Officer.
Ashraf	:	Higher of the two social divisions among Indian Muslims.
Babu (Baboo)	:	A title of respect but in the nineteenth century the English used it pejoratively to refer to educated Indians. In Bihar used in a similar sense for Bengalis.
Bhaat	:	Boiled rice.
Cutchery	:	Generic term for revenue office; office of administration; court house.
Darbar	:	A public audience held by a native prince or by a high-ranking British official.
Daroga	:	Police officer.
Deagdan	:	Fireplace.
Diwan	:	A native minister of the revenue department and chief justice in civil cases within his jurisdiction; officer-in-charge of revenue and finance.
Diwani	:	Functions of a diwan; revenue and fiscal administration.
Farman	:	Grant or letter royal patent.
Faujdar	:	Properly a military commander or a military governor of a district; local or provincial executive officer.
Faujdari Adalat	:	Criminal jurisdiction court.
Kalasasthapana	:	The ceremony of filling the earthen pots.
Kanwar	:	A stick made of bamboo for carrying sacred water which is to be poured on idols of gods.
Kayastha	:	A clerical caste, most numerous in northern India and Bengal.

Khichri : Pulse and rice boiled together.
Khirki : Window.
Madrasa : A secondary school or college for Muslims.
Maktab : Muslim primary school.
Mofussil : The country stations and districts as opposed to principal towns.
Mangini : Betrothal.
Mouja : Village.
Mukhtear : Legal petition-writer.
Munsif : The lowest grade of judge under British government in India.
Ohda : Post.
Pandit : Learned men, teachers of Sanskrit and allied languages.
Pargana : Administrative division.
Pyaju : Onion.
Qazi : A judge trained in Islamic Law, though often the title was inherited as a name by men with no such training.
Ratjagga : The night-watching and rejoicing by ladies especially before a marriage ceremony in the family.
Ryot : Cultivator, peasant.
Sabha : An assembly, usually of Hindus.
Sarkar : Administrative division of a territory during the Muslim rule corresponding to a division under British rule.
Suba : Province of the Mughal empire.
Sherestadar : Head native officer in a collector's office or court of justice.
Teli : A large oil-pressing and trading caste in Bihar and elsewhere.
Vaisya : The third *varna* whose traditional means of subsistence were trade, agriculture and the keeping of cattle.
Zamindar : Landholder, paying revenue to the government directly; under the British rule the holder of a right of property in land.

Introduction

जै हो विहार माता महिमा अपार तेरी।
तेरे ही गोद मांही श्री मैथिली ने खेली।
चाणक वो बुद्ध गौतम सब ही यहीं हुवे हैं।
भक्तों में जो शिरोमणि प्रह्लाद जी हुवे हैं।
सन्तानों में तेरे ही हुवे, शेरशाह भी नामी।[1] (1911)

[Glory be to you, Mother Bihar,
Your greatness is boundless.
It is in your laps that,
Shree Maithili (Sita) played.
Chanakya and Gautama Buddha,
Were all born here.
So was Prahlad,
The greatest of the devotees.
It was among your sons that
Sher Shah too became famous].
(Translation mine)

The Beharis are a sturdy, loyal people. . . .[2] (1911)

The people of Behar are Hindustanees, speaking the same language, and in their manners, & c. identical with the forty or fifty millions of Hindustanees, who inhabit the North-West Provinces, Oude and parts of the Central Provinces, Rajpootana & c.[3] (1873)

The song of celebration at the Beharee Students' Conference and the two observations made by the British colonial rulers at a gap of nearly forty years from each other encapsulate and articulate the essence of a process that had been unfolding in Bihar in the last three decades of the nineteenth century and the first decade of the twentieth century—the process of development of a group consciousness and identity around the symbol of Bihar—a process by which *Hindustanis* living in Bihar became *Biharis*. Here we are confronted with all the trappings of an identity movement—the personification and deification of a territorial entity, an intense search and a formidable build-up of the most glorious historical tradition possible, even if not always backed by evidence. One may note, for instance, that at least one historical figure whose name figured in the song with which we have opened this study, Gautama Buddha was born in Nepal (Lumbinigrama) and died in Uttar Pradesh (Kushinagar). Bihar was no doubt the region where he attained enlightenment but he gave his first sermon in Uttar Pradesh (Sarnath). Uttar Predesh certainly has as much claim on him as Bihar.[4] But then to forget and getting its history wrong, as Ernest Renan had so perceptively observed in the late nineteenth century, are essential features in the making of a nation.[5] The present study is an attempt to understand this process.

Though India, since Independence, has witnessed a number of movements based on the consciousness of a common regional identity, seeking the creation of a state for the given regional people within the Indian Union, even the colonial period experienced a number of such movements. A by-product of administrative arrangements and uneven development of different regions under the colonial rule which made possible the domination of interests of one group of people by another regional group, those movements aimed at protection of political, economic and cultural interests of the disadvantaged group and in the process firmed up the feelings of a common identity. These emerged forth in different parts of the country and enjoyed a mixed share of good and bad luck.

While in the south the struggle of the Andhra people for a separate statehood could attain success only after the country became independent, a similar struggle by the people of Bihar and Orissa came to a successful end during the colonial period itself. A complex of factors contributed to the creation of a separate province of Bihar along with Orissa in 1912, both of which were till then included in the Bengal Presidency. These were the growth of regional consciousness during the last three decades of the nineteenth century, the resultant emergence of a demand for a distinct political status for the region and the movement launched by the Bihari leaders to achieve that objective and lastly the political considerations of the colonial government.

The present study is an attempt to understand and analyse all this. The study of the growth of regional nationalism and the making of a regional identity proceeds on the very explicit understanding that the making of Bihar and Biharis were interwoven processes and we cannot understand the one without accounting for the other.

The movement for the creation of a province of Bihar, though the earliest of its kind in India, was not by any means unique. Territorial-historical regions have been among the major symbols along with language and religion around which group identities have emerged. It was not unique in yet another sense. Like many other regional movements, it too elicited two kinds of responses. These need to be explained.

The phenomenon of the emergence of regional consciousness accompanied by the demand of a distinct political status for the region has been generally viewed in two contrasting lights.

Many scholars and most political leaders, with the obvious exception of those leading such movements, tend to look at these with apprehension—as threats to the maintenance of territorial integrity of nation-states. Geertz, for instance, found regionalism as 'being especially troublesome in geographically heterogeneous areas'.[6] In its own time the Bihari movement was routinely criticized and vilified as being an anti-national one by some leading lights of the national movement, especially those from Bengal. The arguments advanced by them appear far too familiar today and very predictable too. On a note of condescension it was said that the Biharis were ignorant people, incapable of evaluating their own interests, and in fact, in demanding a separate Bihar for themselves they were playing into the hands of colonial rulers, who were only interested in driving wedges among Indian people to weaken the national movement (whose major aim then was to prevent and later nullify the partition of Bengal). Another argument was that the movement diverted the energy of the people away from the mainstream national movement and was indeed a mere camouflage to conceal the real aims of its leaders to have an area all for themselves where they could enjoy the loaves and fishes of power. We shall examine at a more appropriate place the validity or otherwise of such arguments. What needs to be pointed out now, however, is the interesting fact that one can discern in such criticism the traces of the Brown man's burden—civilized Indians taking upon themselves the onerous burden of helping other Indians on to the right path. What comes in as something of a surprise is the reply to such criticisms given by the Bihari leaders, which we shall discuss later in the study, which anticipate many of the arguments and conclusions of social scientists, that such movements tend to give rise to resurgence and reassertion of groups who are left behind or marginalized[7] and that acceptance and accommodation of regional demands does not necessarily weaken national unity or prevent economic growth.[8]

Bihar's was the earliest instance of the success of an identity movement when the British granted a separate statehood to Biharis and explicitly accepted the argument that it was essential for proper growth of the people there. The success of the struggle encouraged a host of other people to make similar demands.[9]

Unfortunately and also surprisingly this important and pioneering movement, pioneering for being the first of its nature chronologically and for being based on and presenting an ideological blueprint on the basis of which a sustainable nation-state could be created in India, has failed to draw the kind of attention of social scientists it so richly deserved.

The number of published works on the theme is quite limited and even those that exist suffer from some lapses. *The Creation of Modern Bihar*,[10] the pioneering and by far the most authoritative and most oft-referred study, thus devoted itself mainly to the struggle for separation of Bihar from Bengal and in the process accepted uncritically the existence of both 'Bihar' and 'Biharis'. Once these were accepted as 'givens' not much attention was paid to the emergence of educated groups or to the role of colonial rulers, both of whom were the principal agents, who reconstructed 'Bihar' and constructed the 'Biharis'. Some articles and chapters in different books on Bihar's history do offer critical insight into the subject but these have generally a limited scope.[11]

There is a need then to take a more comprehensive look on those eventful years and to fill a gap in the available literature identified by Paul Brass more than 35 years ago—the absence of a study on the development of group identity in Bihar (as also in

Uttar Pradesh).[12] A plethora of insightful studies in different disciplines of social science dealing with the themes of nationalism, regionalism, formation of group identities, etc., during the last 30 years have made it possible to look at these phenomena more critically. It is time then to take a look at these works to prevent terminological inconsistencies which might creep up in our work, as they have tended to in even the more incisive of such studies, and to properly situate ourselves, in other words, to prepare a clear and safe road map for our intellectual journey.

NATIONALISM, REGIONALISM, AND IDENTITY FORMATION

Definitions

The need for such a roadmap becomes evident the moment one begins to ask a methodologically relevant and theoretically important basic question—whether the growth of political consciousness among the people of Bihar and their struggle for a distinct political set-up should be treated as an instance of the growth of nationalism or regionalism there? That affirmative answers indeed would be forthcoming in both the directions can be safely predicted if we go by the clues offered by the existing literature on the subject. In fact, it is not uncommon to find the same movements being studied under different rubrics—nationalism, nationality formation, regionalism and regional nationalism (by those who want to play safe) depending upon the thematic and ideological orientation of scholars. The quest for a united Orissa for one scholar represents Oriya nationalism, for another it is an outcome of growing regional consciousness.[13] Though it stands to reason that nomenclatures may change over time with changing political scenario, as for instance those who spoke of Bengali regionalism[14] in Pakistan would now most likely speak of Bengali nationalism, what comes as a real surprise is that on occasions the same movement has been given different names in the same text. Thus while Brass says at one place that the Sikhs come closest among all the ethnic groups of north India to satisfying the definition of a nationality or a nation, he treats the demand of a Punjabi Suba as an instance of regionalism.[15] Does all this mean that they are essentially similar or even the same phenomenon as was argued by Schwartzberg who suggested, 'At the scale of the nation-state regionalism takes the form commonly known as nationalism'.[16] We may probe a little further to find out if this assertion can be substantiated from other sources. Though there is no unanimity of opinion on the precise meaning of nationalism which has received far more attention of historians and other social scientists than the other term (regionalism) which is presently under our discussion, we still find that there is a remarkable similarity in the way they have been defined irrespective of whether they have been seen as a state of mind, an ideology or a movement.[17] Thus if Akzin sees nationalism as 'the consciousness of belonging to a nation coupled with an active urge to perpetuate and strengthen national bonds by various including political means',[18] Schwartzberg says the same about regionalism. For him it is 'the awareness which people commonly have of "belonging" to a particular region, naively-given or instituted, their sense of identification with it and loyalty to it. . . .'[19] We find this similarity of view continuing even in the writings of those who maintain that these 'isms' are in the ultimate analysis grounded on certain objective bases, for the bases so identified by them happen to be the same ones in both the cases. It is best to quote Brian Jenkins and Spyros Sofos who maintain that nationalism needs something,

> on which to feed some 'raw materials' of collective identity. The potential ingredients of this are diverse—a common language, a shared history or culture, religious particularism, a sense of territorial, ethnic or 'racial' distinctiveness, and/or assertion of opposition to other communities, or indeed the existence either in the past or in the present of some political identity—a state or subordinate administrative unit.[20]

Interestingly *The Encyclopaedia of the Social Sciences* finds the same ingredients necessary for regionalism. Its definition is fairly instructive in that even while treating regionalism as a movement against any exaggerated and oppressive form of centralization it argues that regionalist problems should not be viewed solely from the point of political control or governmental administration.

> Regionalist problems arise only when there is a combination of two or more such factors as geographical isolation, independent historical

traditions, racial, ethnic and linguistic peculiarities and local economic or class interests. It is different from mere sectionalism in that it is not exclusively based on regional economic or class interests, but involves certain ethnic factors such as cultural, traditional or linguistic peculiarities which provide a basis for what is often termed as sub-nationality.[21]

Should we conclude then that it is merely a matter of choice as to which term to use to describe a particular phenomenon or we need to make and maintain some distinction between the terms? In our opinion Schwartzberg's observation quoted above, offers a way out of this terminological impasse. We need to look at the stated or implied aims of a movement, or the scale at which it operates. Myron Weiner substantially endorses Schwartzberg's view when he reserves the term regionalism for those movements in which an ethnic group identifies itself with a given territory within the country and seeks to create a state within it.[22]

Following them we are now in a position to answer the question asked at the beginning of the discussion. The growth of political consciousness in Bihar in so far as it led to a struggle for a separate statehood within India should be treated as an instance of growth of regionalism and it would be so done in the present work. This growth of regional consciousness and the formation of a regional identity would also be treated as the making of a nationality. This follows both Brass[23] and Akzin.[24] The second reason for not using the term 'nationalism' in the study, although using insights from studies on nationalism and also believing that they are essentially the same phenomenon, is that Bihari leaders and intellectuals did not portray Bihar as a 'nation' and did not seek to create a nation-state.

Perspectives

Given that Bihar witnessed the growth of regionalism and the emergence of a Bihari identity in the last 30 years of the nineteenth century and early years of twentieth century, how is this particular and similar other phenomenon to be analysed and explained? A host of questions stare us in the face. How do we define a region? Does the mere presence of some objective characteristics distinctive of a region—language, culture, history and others—ensure the emergence of a regional identity or is it an outcome of a more complex process of construction and imagination made possible by a multiplicity of factors and do all of these play an equally important role in the genesis of regionalism or is their importance and salience both variable and context-specific? Studies done on regionalism and nationality movements in India, seeking to answer some of the questions posed above, have been guided and informed by different perspectives conveniently labelled as Marxist, primordialist, constructionist, modernist, etc., and, needless to say, these studies have not always asked the same questions.

Except for the primordialist approach and it does not have many adherents, many common strands of thought, assumptions and arguments run in other approaches. It would be useful to take a brief look on these studies.

The Marxist social scientists were among the earliest to look at the question of emergence of nationalities. However, this perspective on the emergence of nationalities and the growth of regionalism though insightful in certain ways has been marred because of an early tendency to valorize the national movement.

An early Marxist work related the problem of nationalities to the uneven nature of the growth of nationalism in India. It viewed the growth of nationalism in India as the result of conditions created by the British conquest and the action of the forces accompanying these. As neither the conquest nor the penetration of new forces occurred simultaneously, the conditions making for the growth of national consciousness also matured unevenly, with some areas and communities becoming politically conscious earlier than others. Subsequently, however, a number of factors like further economic development leading to the growth of industrial and commercial classes, increase in the number of educated people, growth of provincial literature aroused these provincial groups, 'dormant nationalities', like the Biharis, Oriyas, etc. The desire to lead a free corporate life made them demand a reconstitution of existing provinces so that these might correspond to linguistic groups. However, this desire did not challenge the concept of a single Indian state as the demand was never for a sovereign political identity.[25]

The analysis, though illuminating the context under which movements for distinct political status emerged, overlooked the fact that in the generation of such nationality consciousness among different provincial social groups, a perceived domination of their interests by a more developed nationality whose members had migrated to their areas played a crucial role, a factor to which Partha Chatterjee and Myron Weiner drew our attention. Partha Chatterjee argued that a colonized country often had more than one identifiable nationality. Because of their imperial connection the economic and political interests of the first nationalists usually ranged throughout the country. However, with the spread of nationalist consciousness among a wider strata of the population, the inevitable lopsidedness of the colonial economic development could create an awareness of uneven development within the people of the country and could give rise to separatist nationalism aimed not so much against the colonial rulers but against the allegedly more advanced ethno-cultural community.[26]

Even more problematic in this perspective is the later tendency to see the term 'regionalism' in a pejorative sense, to treat it as a divisive phenomenon and to make an unnecessary distinction between regionalism and the democratic notions of linguistic-cultural regions or linguistic states, whose cultural and economic interests are to be protected and promoted. Equally difficult to accept has been the assertion that as modern economy and politics compel people to organize on the basis of wider collective identities if such organization does not occur on the basis of nation and class it would occur on some other bases such as religion, sect, language, region, etc.[27] That one can have a number of identities not necessarily competing with one another is too well known to require exemplification. In India, too, the growth of regional and national consciousness often went together and the same people were often involved in regional and national politics. Bihar provides a number of instances to substantiate this assertion.

Bihari leaders like Mahesh Narayan and Sachchidananda Sinha who were actively involved in the region's struggle for a distinct identity also participated in the sessions of the Indian National Congress. In fact, Hindi literature of 1870s, a period when voluntary associations for the welfare of 'Bihar' were being set-up and also of 1880s shows a high sense of national consciousness. Here we may give a few instances.

A poem, 'Bharat ki Dasha' (The state of India) by Lakshmi Prasad, whose period of writing extended from 1875 to 1890 and whose poems were published regularly in *Bihar Bandhu* (a Hindi weekly) in 1876, gained wide popularity around that time. It spoke about the pathetic and desolate state of the country under the colonial rule,

> जहाँ मन्दिर थे खड़े बाँ हैं कांटे उपजे
> बस्तियाँ बस गयीं श्रगाल खर और शुकर से।
> याँ के लोगों की दशा कैसी थी क्या कोई कहे,
> लेखनी का हिया फट जाय जो लिखने बैठे।[28]

> Thorns have grown where once temples stood
> and jackals, asses and pigs have formed colonies.
> It is very difficult to speak of the past (flourishing)
> condition of the country and even the heart of the pen
> would burst if it (he) starts writing of this.
>
> (Translation mine)

A second instance may be given of a Hindi play *Sajjad Sumbul* written around 1880 by Keshav Ram Bhatta. The hero of the play Sajjad remains worried about the state of the country. While walking in a garden he feels anguished by the fact that between 7 and 9 p.m. only the white people could walk there. He holds his countrymen responsible for this state of affairs. He is desirous of seeing trade and commerce prosper in the country. Going further, in the course of a fight he not only beats an English police officer and abuses him but also announces that Indians are no longer afraid of the white skin. Sajjad would be happy to see his country become independent but is afraid that Indians would not be able to preserve freedom.[29]

The point we are trying to make here is that very often emergence of regional and national consciousness took place simultaneously. As the above two examples would show, intellectuals in Bihar like elsewhere in India clearly perceived the economically and politically dominating nature of the colonial rule and tried to grapple with this political reality and were thus in tune with developments taking place elsewhere.[30] Interestingly Keshav Ram Bhatta was also the founder of the Bihar Upkar Sabha. By arguing that regional and national consciousness emerged simultaneously very often, we do not mean to deny that at certain periods of time greater salience was given to the 'region'.

The primordial perspective though holding the same negative opinion on regionalism as the Marxist perspective is largely concerned with the way identities come into being. The perspective, presented at its unambiguous best by Clifford Geertz, holds regionalism to be a primordial phenomenon. The basic argument is that every person carries from birth attachments based on factors like assumed blood ties, race, language, religion, custom and region and the power of the 'givens' of place, tongue, blood, looks and way-of-life to shape an individual's notion of who, at bottom, he is and with whom, indissolubly, he belongs is rooted in the non-rational foundation of personality.[31] The identity, in this perspective, then assumes an ineluctable and immutable reality, inexorable too, being beyond the control of reason.

The perspective is a persuasive one to a certain extent. The attachments based on the above-enumerated factors often provide a basis for the formation of social and political groupings for some people. However, they do not always do so because some attachments are variable and national (regional) identification and what it is believed to imply, can change and shift in time, even in the course of quite short periods.[32]

The approach also does not take note of the fact that there is a wide range of variation in the structure and characteristics of many factors which are supposed to anchor our identity and a group's language, religion and even its territory may undergo change as the group's consciousness develops. The perspective, then, is not backed by realistic sociology nor is it very historically grounded. A number of scholars have called attention to these shortcomings.

As against the primordial perspective, an overwhelming number of scholars argue that communities and identities are constructs, some even going to the extent of terming these (communities, nations) as imaginary constructions. Implied within it is the contention that objective markers like language, history, etc., which are used to distinguish a people, a region or a nation are not in any essential sense 'given' and their mere presence need not ensure the ultimate emergence of a community or a nationality and that both nationalism and regionalism are dynamic and contingent phenomena.

Schwartzberg, in an extremely insightful article, draws attention to this dynamic nature of both region and regionalism. Starting from the definition that a region is a perceived segment of space-time continuum different from others on the basis of one or more defining characteristics, which could be natural, political, cultural, etc., he builds his theory on other bases for the recognition of regions. Regions could thus be 'naïvely given', 'instituted' or 'denoted'. A 'naïvely given' region is one which is recognized as a meaningful territorial entity by the people who live there and/or by other people to whom it is of some concern [e.g. Mithila, Tamil Nadu, India (for many centuries)] while 'instituted' regions are created by human agency as distinctive and discrete units limiting the areal extent of operation of certain functions, e.g. West Bengal, etc.

His crucial argument is that 'naïvely given' and 'instituted' region are mutually interrelated through the medium of regionalism and their boundaries may change accordingly. Thus while the instituted regional reality affects and gradually alters peoples' naïve perceptions of spatial reality, the naïve perceptions of people as well as those of scholars and leaders, who help mould the popular view, may give rise first to inchoate regional consciousness and ultimately to pressures so strong as to force an alteration in existing institutionalized regions which come to be regarded as unrealistic, inefficient or unjust.[33] This theory then both alerts against any uncritical, teleological reading of such movements and asserts like Anderson the significance of territorial underpinning of nations.[34]

Bernard Cohn presents a variation on largely the same axis of arguments. In his opinion, too, regions are far from fixed things when any historical perspective is taken and they are difficult, if not impossible, to define by objective criteria. The growth of regionalism is not spontaneous but dependent upon the presence of certain conditions.[35]

It is by way of extension of Cohn's arguments and also drawing on the insight of Karl Deutsch's work that a comprehensive theory of identity formation and growth of regionalism in a constructive perspective has been developed by Paul Brass. This theory emphasizes the need of certain requisites for the transformation of an objectively different group of people into a subjectively self-conscious community. The first two of the requisites are the existence of a set of symbols of distinctiveness to be utilized as per need and an elite willing to choose, transmit and standardize those symbols for the group. The third requisite, identified by Brass, is a socially mobilizing and mobilized population to whom symbols of group identity can be transmitted. These include literates, town dwellers, newspaper readers, persons employed in non-agricultural occupations and the like. And the last requisite is the existence of one or more groups from whom the group in question is to be differentiated. Brass argues that it is the perception of objective differences between the groups and particularly the perception of uneven rates of social change, which provides a catalyst to the development of group consciousness. Regarding the crucial role of the government, Brass argues that in the decisions and policies they make and in the general strategy they follow, they influence the development of group consciousness and the patterns of group conflict. He also suggests that political organizations and voluntary associations play a critical role in the shaping of group identity. They do not arise spontaneously to reflect the demands of a natural group but often precede the existence of a widespread sense of group identity.[36]

It is a persuasive thesis. A number of theoretical as also empirical works on the themes of nation, nationalism and nationality formation lend support to the arguments of Brass. Gellner, for instance, refers to the use as 'raw material' of the cultural, historical and other inheritances from the pre-nationalist past in the making of a nation.[37]

The impact of education and urbanization and the role played by educated elites in promoting nationalism in former colonies is too well documented to merit illustration. Equally passé would be the observation that identities are grounded in difference. Lastly, students of Indian history are all too familiar with the role of government in fostering elements of identity consciousness. However, even this comprehensive formulation is open to criticism. It leaves out two generic agents or catalysts of group formation and maintenance, identified by Gellner. These are will, voluntary identification and adherence on the one hand, and fear, coercion and compulsion on the other. Also, one finds difficulty in accepting in entirety, the argument regarding symbol selection, standardization and transmission. The process, rarely, if ever, is so elaborate or planned. Identities may not always be constructed by deliberate design. At times, they get constructed almost imperceptibly. The distinction needs to be kept in mind. The people who established Behar Literary Society in 1873 might have been simply interested in promoting education in Bihar as they claimed. The choice of the name Behar could not have been fortuitous but one can safely suggest that they were not engaged in the task of constructing a regional identity. This, however, is not to deny their ultimate importance in the growth of regional consciousness in Bihar.

Though not a unified body of thought and containing a wide array of social scientists, the modernization perspective, in the main, holds that nation understood as a community of people as also nationalism/regionalism are ultimately the products of the process of modernization. Gellner is the most distinguished proponent of this perspective and his arguments have a familiar ring about them.

He argues that in the early periods of industrialization those entrants into the new order, who come from cultural and linguistic groups different from that of the ruling stratum and advanced areas, suffer considerable disadvantages (treated as rustics living in slums). However, the cultural/linguistic distance and the ability to differentiate themselves from others turns out to be positively advantageous for the formation of communities. These people, as they learn in their dealings with the outside world, the differences between dealing with someone who understands and sympathizes with their culture and one who is hostile to it become aware of their culture and develop love for it, whereas earlier they had taken it for granted and were not conscious of it. Uprooted from their native places they come across other exploited people speaking the same or similar dialects while the better-off speak some different ones. Out of this contrast and with some help from journalists and teachers a sense of community, a 'nation' of these people is born.[38] While Gellner notes one aspect of modernization, industrialization, as being extremely crucial for the formation of a community, in a very interesting study Myron Weiner draws attention to another aspect or consequence of modernization process, inter-ethnic migration, as being crucial for the rise of many regional movements. He also brings to our notice the important question of employment and its powerful significance in defining a group and giving rise to such movements.

Weiner argues that the process of modernization by providing incentives and opportunities for mobility creates the condition for increased internal migration. This situation is created because the development process is an uneven one. Historical and cultural factors enable some ethnic groups to move ahead more rapidly than others. The more advanced groups then move into places, which require the knowledge and skills they have. But when the backward groups (regions) produce their own educated class, who aspire to move into jobs held by migrants in civil service, as teacher in local schools, as clerks, etc., they start viewing the migrants as blocks to their mobility and a situation of conflict is built-up, and it may result in the emergence of anti-migrant political movements. An ethnic (regional) group may perceive that separate statehood is the only way of legitimizing its claims for a separate cultural identity. Weiner suggests that it is not easy to separate the issue of cultural identity from the struggle over access to jobs. Migration, in his view, precipitates self-awareness both on the part of the indigenous population and migrants, as they are able to contrast their cultural differences with one another.[39]

Yet another perspective, most notably associated with the name of Benedict Anderson, considers nation as an imagined political community and nationalism a cultural artifact of a particular kind. In this analysis of the growth of national consciousness and nationalism, emphasis is laid on the important roles played by the growth of print-capitalism, emergence of national languages and books and newspapers. He argues that print languages laid the foundation of national consciousness in three distinct ways. Firstly, they unified fields of exchange and communication. Now millions became capable of comprehending one another via print and paper. Secondly, print capitalism gave a new fixity to languages, which in the long run helped to build that image of antiquity so central to the subjective idea of the nation. Thirdly, certain dialects closer to each print-language came to dominate their final forms. Thus languages of power were created like the King's English or High German, which were elevated to a new political-cultural eminence. He also draws attention to the critical roles played by census, map and museum, all brought into existence by the colonial state, in generating nationalism in colonies. Like Schwartzberg, Anderson too underscores the importance of the creation of fixed administrative units and shows how over time they develop a firmer reality. In the growth of nationalism in South American colonies one of the significant causative factors, in his opinion, was the fact that these had been administrative units from the sixteenth to the eighteenth century. He argues that though original shaping of these units was to some extent arbitrary and fortuitous, marking the spatial limits of particular military conquests, but over time they developed a firmer reality under the influence of geographic, political and economic factors.[40] In an important revision of this thesis, Glenn Bownan, while admitting that all ideas of community are imaginary constructions in so far as people create communities rhetorically through thinking that some people are 'like' themselves while others are 'unlike' them, argues that the 'mass ceremony' of reading newspapers, so central in Anderson's analysis, does not by itself lead to the discovery of a national identity. Rather a national identity is constituted by discovering a set of concerns the reader recognizes as his or her own within a text or texts. This can happen only when the reader already has some prior sense of his/her own identity. That identity provides the 'subject' with means of recognizing and evaluating antagonisms.[41] This perspective, too, encompasses many of the elements of other perspectives.

Before pooling at one place the arguments and insights from the above discussion we need to know if all the objective structural bases of an identity play an equally important role in the genesis of identity movements or the different bases become salient in different situations. One scholar has argued that geographical boundaries, although clung to, are not central to the growth of regionalism. They are symbolic and need economic and political props from time to time for their retrieval from hazy memories of the people. History and language are given more importance. History buttresses regionalism by way of cultural heritage, folklore, myths and symbolism.[42] Language has been seen as a major mark of group identification. As an expression of shared life, thought structures and value patterns it has the potential to unite people emotionally and make them work to improve their common destiny.[43] One scholar while writing about the growth of regional consciousness in Assam and Orissa has shown how the language factor was significant in the growth of such consciousness. Thus the concern for Assamese was part of a larger concern for Assam. And again like the Assamese language, which acted as a cementing force in Assam, Oriya provided the base for the emergence of a similar consciousness in Orissa during the second half of the nineteenth century.[44] Even Hobsbawm who refuses to accept language as a criterion of nationhood and argues that national languages are almost always semi-artificial constructs and occasionally invented and 'are the opposite of what nationalist mythology supposes them to be, namely the primordial foundations of national culture and the matrices of the national mind', admits that French was essential to the concept of France and that the only basis for Italian unification was the Italian language.[45] Obviously there is no getting away from admitting the critical importance of language in generating national and regional identity movements. No wonder, Deutsch who finds that criteria like language do not appear to be essential to the unity of a people offers an insight as to how they can become important in certain contexts. Thus

> language similarities or differences may be unimportant in the lives of two peasant villages isolated from each other; they become more important when the sons of their peasants go to compete for jobs in the same industrial or mining areas; and very important when their grandsons begin to compete with each other as shopkeepers or as candidates for white-collar jobs.[46]

THE PREMISES

While drawing on the insights provided by the different studies, this study seeks to situate itself broadly within the constructionist framework and is firmly anchored on the central thesis that Bihar, in large measure, and Biharis, almost in entirety, were made during the colonial period and there was nothing foregone or inevitable in the course of events that made all this possible. We enter the history of Bihar around 1870, when the first glimmerings of regional consciousness become visible, and trace the course of events till 1912, the year in which Bihar got a distinct political identity of its own.

The principal propositions and arguments of the study are worked out in six chapters and a conclusion.

The first proposition of the study is that the region of Bihar possessed certain objective characteristics which make for a region and could help the making of a regional identity. These consisted of distinct historical traditions and also distinct ethnic-cultural and linguistic features. There also existed a naïve perception of a regional identity. However, these naïve perceptions were further augmented through the growth of political consciousness and historical construction, through articulation and assertion and lastly through the institutional measures of the government. Thus we believe that a process of region-in-making also took place in Bihar.

Another proposition of the study is that it was the British rule and its accompanying effects, which created the context both for the articulation of ideology of regional nationalism and the launching of a struggle for a separate political identity by the people of Bihar.

The study is of the firm view that growth of English and vernacular education and the emergence of new social groups played a critical role in the process of regional identity formation in Bihar. In an atmosphere of growing political consciousness they could become more aware of Bihar's distinctiveness and could also provide both the leadership and the constituency for the transmission and reception of the messages of that identity. They were also to take the lead in articulating the grievances of Biharis and championing their various interests.

We also believe that the British perceptions regarding Bihar's society and its distinct needs and the resultant policy decisions greatly influenced the process of regional identity formation. In our view, there was a dialectical relationship between the governmental policies and decisions, on the one hand, and people's own perceptions and articulations of regional consciousness, on the other hand. It was this factor that made possible the birth of the demand

'Bihar for Biharis'. Further we are of the opinion that various public associations and societies arose only partly to reflect the demands of an already existing Bihari political community. A more important role was played by them in creating that community. Similarly, the newspapers by articulating the various grievances of the people helped to politicize the socially mobilizing population and spread among them the consciousness of a common identity. Works of literature also played a role in fostering regional consciousness.

A further premise of this study is that the consciousness of a common regional identity was mainly confined to the middle class, and particularly those living in the urban areas. The movement for a separate political identity also appears to be largely a middle class affair, providing both the leadership and the support base. However, it does not appear to be a case of a narrow political elite trying to mobilize people to secure its own selfish ends like high government posts or other important positions, but seems to have emerged out of a feeling of relative deprivation and appears firmly anchored on the belief that Bihar's personality would not flower unless it was given a separate political identity of its own. We examine this theme in detail. We also believe that the movement was not against national interests and, in fact, was a manifestation of growing political consciousness emerging all over India during that period.

THE CHAPTERS

The first chapter discusses the pre- and early colonial history, society, culture and polity of Bihar and the early impact of imposition of colonial rule on these aspects. This discussion is meant to enable us to find out as to what extent Bihar was a 'region' and what necessary objective attributes needed for the construction of a regional identity did it possess before the British intrusion. The analysis of the impact of colonial rule on these aspects is intended to bring out the colonial context of the emergence of a regional identity in Bihar.

The second chapter looks at the progress and spread of education and formation of new social groups like those of lawyers and journalists in Bihar. The major focus is on the spread of English education, especially at higher levels, and seeks to identify which groups, castes/communities were being educated. The major conclusion of this chapter is that it was the equal participation of both Hindu and Muslim literati class in education that made possible the assertion of rights of Bihari people as a whole and when they tried to seek preferential treatment in the matter of jobs, as against the perceived domination of the Bengalis, they did not demand preference in the name of communal or caste identities.

The third chapter discusses British perceptions, attitudes and policies regarding Bihar and their impact on the formation of a regional identity there. The British government in the nineteenth century became ever more convinced of the importance of knowledge and information for purposes of administration and good government. The growing awareness about the distinctiveness of Bihar, its society and its needs led the government to take some important decisions which helped to concretize Bihar as a reality and to foster a sense of common identity among the people—by categorizing Biharis as a group, by partly creating new urges in them and directly and indirectly encouraging them to unite and organize themselves for the satisfaction of these urges. The government was also partly responsible for determining the character of that identity.

But if the government was a major agent in the construction of a regional identity in Bihar it was not the only one.

The fourth chapter analyses the role of public associations and societies, newspapers and intellectuals to locate the internal dynamic of the construction and articulation of regional identity in Bihar. In the local political discourse of the period Bihar itself was set-up as a major symbol and other symbols, although at times contradictory, were developed defining a Bihari identity. Myths were also constructed to explain Bihar's degraded condition.

The next two chapters are devoted to the analysis of Bihar's struggle for a distinct identity. The fifth chapter traces the beginning and early phase of this struggle. It focuses on the roles of leaders of the movement like Dr. Sachchidananda Sinha and Mahesh Narayan. The methods through which the demand was put forward as also the arguments backing this demand are looked into. It also discusses how the people of Chota Nagpur came to proclaim their Bihari identity. The government responses are examined throughout.

The sixth chapter takes note of those political and administrative developments between the years 1906-12, which contributed to the emergence of a Bihari identity. Thus it looks into the later phase of Bihar's search for identity and the ideological moorings of the movement. It traces the stages through which the separation of Bihar was accomplished paying special attention to the role of the government in the process.

The seventh chapter summarizes the findings of the study and seeks to identify the factors that could undermine the ongoing process of further concretization of a Bihari regional identity.

NOTES

1. Part of the opening song sung at the Beharee Students' Conference in 1911. See *The Beharee,* 22 September 1911, for the full text of the song.
2. See the despatch from the Government of India to the Secretary of State for India, August 1911, in India Home (Delhi) A Progs, December 1911, nos. 8-11.
3. *Report on the Administration of Bengal, 1872-73*, Calcutta, 1873, p. 102.
4. See R.R. Diwakar (ed.), *Bihar Through the Ages*, Calcutta, 1959, pp. 138-42 and R.C. Majumdar, H.C. Raychaudhari and K.K. Datta, *An Advanced History of India* (rpt.), Madras, 1985, pp. 82-3. Such inventions of symbols and traditions were certainly not peculiar to Bihar. Similar phenomenon have been noted to be in existence in different parts of the world. For an incisive look see E.J. Hobsbawm and Terence Ranger (eds.), *The Invention of Tradition,* Cambridge, 1983.
5. See Partha Sarathi Gupta, 'Identity-Formation and Nation-States: Some Reflections', Presidential Address, Indian History Congress, Fifty-Ninth Session, Patiala, 1998; also see E.J. Hobsbawm, *Nations and Nationalism since 1780: Programme, Myth, Reality,* Cambridge, 1990, p.12.
6. Clifford Geertz, 'The Integrative Revolution: Primordial Sentiments and Civil Politics in New States', in C. Geertz (ed.), *Old Societies and New States*, New York, 1963, p. 113.
7. Sajal Basu, *Regional Movements: Politics of Language, Ethnicity, Identity,* New Delhi, 1992, p. xi.
8. Paul R. Brass, *Language, Religion and Politics in North India* (henceforth *Language, Religion*), Cambridge, 1974, p. 19. Also see Madhu Sudan Mishra, *Politics of Regionalism in India with Special Reference to Punjab,* New Delhi, 1988, pp. 16-17.

9. See K.V. Narayan Rao, *The Emergence of Andhra Pradesh,* Bombay, 1973, for the growth of a similar movement.
10. V.C.P. Chaudhary, *The Creation of Modern Bihar*, Patna and Darbhanga, 1964.
11. See A.P. Jha, 'Political History of Bihar (1859-1912)', in K.K. Datta (ed.), *The Compreheshive History of Bihar* (henceforth *CHB*), vol. III, pt. I, Patna, 1976. Also see M.K. Basu, 'Regional Patriotism: A Study in Bihar Politics' *Indian Historical Review*, vol. III, no. 2, 1975.
12. Brass, *Language, Religion*, p. 21.
13. See the title of Nivedita Mohanty's book, *Oriya Nationalism: Quest for a United Orissa, 1866-1936*, New Delhi, 1982. Also see Sudhir Chandra, *The Oppressive Present: Literature and Social Consciousness in Colonial India*, New Delhi, 1992, pp. 149-52.
14. See the article by M. Rashiduzzaman entitled, 'East-West Conflict in Pakistan: Bengali Regionalism, 1947-1970', in A.J. Wilson and D. Dalton (eds.), *The States of South Asia*, New Delhi, 1982.
15. Brass, *Language, Religion*, pp. 277, 319. Brass is in good company here. Hobsbawm in a similar vein talks of Catalan nationalism/regionalism at different places in the same text. See his *Nations and Nationalism*, pp. 107, 140.
16. J.E. Schwartzberg, 'Prolegomena to the Study of South Asian Regions and Regionalism', in R.I. Crane (ed.), *Regions and Regionalism in South Asian Studies: An Exploratory Study,* Duke University, Durham, 1966, p. 95.
17. Of course, there are social scientists who do not see nationalism in such terms. John Breuilly, for instance, does not accept that nationalism is a state of mind or the expression of national consciousness or a political doctrine or as representing the interests of a national group. For him it is merely a form of politics and politics is about power. See John Breuilly, *Nationalism and the State*, Manchester, 1982, pp. 1-2. Max Weber's views are remarkably similar, for him too national consciousness was not in anyway dependent upon objective ethnic and linguistic factors and the key factor was participation in the process of deciding on the power status of one's state. See G. Aloysius, *Nationalism without a Nation in India*, New Delhi, 1997, p. 8.
18. Benjamin Akzin, *State and Nation*, London, 1964, p. 46.
19. Schwartzberg, 'Prolegomena', p. 95.
20. Brian Jenkins and Spyros, A. Sofos, 'Nation and Nationalism in Contemporary Europe: A Theoretical Perspective', in Brian Jenkins and Spyros, A. Sofos (eds.), *Nation and Identity in Contemporary Europe,* London and New York, 1996, p. 11.

21. Edwin R.A Seligman (ed.), *Encyclopaedia of the Social Sciences*, vol. XIII, New York, 1924, pp. 208-9.
22. Myron Weiner, *Sons of the Soil: Migration and Ethnic Conflict in India*, New Delhi, 1978, p. 296.
23. Paul Brass uses the term 'nation-state' for a nation, which achieves political independents and 'nationality' or 'nation' for ethnic groups whose political goals do not necessarily include separate sovereignty. He also considers nationalism as a sub-type of the process of identity formation. See Brass, *Language Religion*, pp. 9-11 (including fns.).
24. B. Akzin uses slightly different words to convey essentially the same thing. See his *State and Nation*, p. 29, fn.
25. See A.R. Desai, *Social Background of Indian Nationalism*, Bombay, 1989 (rpt.).
26. See Partha Chatterjee, 'Bengal-Rise and Growth of a Nationality', *Social Scientist*, vol. IV, no. 1, August 1975, p. 70. Also see Myron Weiner, *Sons of the Soil* (entire text).
27. See Bipan Chandra, *Communalism in Modern India*, New Delhi, 1984, p. ix and fn., p. 22 and fn. and p. 124.
28. B. Varma and K. Sharma 'Nayan' (eds.), *Hindi Sahitya Aur Bihar* (Hindi), vol. IV, Patna, 1984, p. 286.
29. Keshav Ram Bhatta, *Sajjad Sumbul* (Hindi), Calcutta, 1904 (rpt.).
30. See K.N. Panikkar, *Culture, Ideology, Hegemony: Intellectuals and Social Consciousness in Colonial India,* New Delhi, 1995, for a discussion of the growth of anti-colonial consciousness in India.
31. Geertz, 'The Integrative Revolution', pp. 108-10 and 128.
32. See Paul R. Brass, *Ethnicity and Nationalism: Theory and Comparison*, New Delhi, 1991, pp. 69-71, for a critique of the primordial perspective. Also see Michael Igantieff, *Blood and Belonging: Journeys into the New Nationalism,* London, 1993, pp. 4-5.
33. Schwartzberg, 'Prolegomena', pp. 89-98.
34. B. Anderson, *Imagined Communities: Reflections on the Origin and Spread of Nationalism*, London, 1989, p. 54. Hobsbawm makes a similar point. See his *Nations and Nationalism*, p. 138.
35. Bernard S. Cohn, 'Regions Subjective and Objective: Their Relation to the Modern Indian History and Society', in R.I. Crane (ed.), *Regions and Regionalism*, pp. 22-33.
36. Brass, *Language, Religion*, pp. 28-44. Brass' study has been greatly influenced by Karl W. Deutsch's *Nationalism and Social Communication: An Inquiry into the Foundations of Nationality,* Cambridge, Massachusetts, 1953, 1966 (rpt.). The arguments regarding the important role of the government is fairly common. Bernard Cohn, in this connection, gives an example from the colonial

period of Indian history. He argues that the British first by choosing and then by enshrining in books, government regulations and teaching materials helped in the standardization of languages like Hindi, Urdu and Bengali in such a way that educated people could read the same materials throughout the region. Regional languages thus got a primacy that they may not have had before. Thus conditions for the growth of regionalism were laid. See B. Cohn, 'Regions Subjective and Objective', pp. 25-6.

37. E. Gellner, *Nations and Nationalism*, New Delhi, 1986, p. 49.
38. Ibid., pp. 59-62.
39. See Weiner, *Sons of the Soil*, for this argument.
40. See Anderson, *Imagined Communities*, full text.
41. Glenn Bowman, ' "A Country of Words": Conceiving the Palestinian Nation from the Position of Exile', in E. Laclau (ed.), *The Making of Political Identities*, London, 1994, pp. 138-70.
42. Iqbal Narain, 'A Conceptual Analysis in the Indian Context', in A. Majeed (ed.), *Regionalism: Developmental Tensions in India*, New Delhi, 1984, p. 25. Karl Deutsch in his study of the origins of nationality, however, finds difficulty with the notion of community of histories and memories and argues that 'Instead of being automatically united by a shared history, men at least under certain conditions cannot share the historical events through which they live, unless they are already in some sense united. To explain a nation as a result of the shared experiences presupposes already this ability to share experience, which is the very thing that cannot be taken for granted.' Karl W. Deutsch, *Nationalism and Social Communication*, p. 19. Deutsch does not appear sensitive to a social reality that history is always an integral part of social consciousness.
43. Ibid. (Narain, 'A Conceptual Analysis'), p. 25.
44. See Chandra, *The Oppressive Present*, pp. 146-9.
45. Hobsbawm, *Nations and Nationalism*, pp. 54-60.
46. Deutsch, *Nationalism and Social Communication*, p. 174.

CHAPTER 1

Pre- and Early Colonial Bihar

Bihar, termed 'the heart of India'[1] by an observer, when finally constituted as a province along with Orissa in 1912 covered an area of 1,13,000 sq miles and contained a population of 35,000,000 people.[2] A land-locked province, as it became after the splitting off of Orissa in 1936, it consisted of two distinct physical units of roughly equal size—the Gangetic plain and the Chota Nagpur plateau.[3]

Did this regional entity contain the elements—the objective bases—on which a consciousness of common identity could develop or be built-up? And if at all the bases did exist what was the context in which the issue of identity acquire its salience? The first question may be answered by taking a close look into the history and political geography of the region. A study of the cultural–linguistic aspects of the society as also its structure would be equally revealing. An analysis of the early impact of the colonial rule would supply answer to the second question. The present chapter seeks to tackle both these questions.

HISTORY OF THE REGION

History, as seen in the introductory chapter, has always supposedly played a crucial role in fomenting regional/national identities and the region of Bihar was exceptionally fortunate in this respect. The history of the region was especially aflush with symbols on which an awareness of common identity could be built-up. Events of the past had become historical legends and passed into popular consciousness.

No one could probably fail to notice this rich legacy. Early in the nineteenth century Walter Hamilton noted, 'Buddhists and Jains both agree in placing within the limits of South Bahar and its immediate vicinity the locality of the death and apotheosis of the last Buddha as well as of the last Jina.'[4] A mid-nineteenth-century gazetteer elaborating further said that it was universally acknowledged that the court of kings of Magadha 'now the province of Bahar was one of the most brilliant that ever existed'.[5]

By the beginning of the twentieth century the history of the region had been nearly fully established.

> The province of Behar is known to us from very early times. The ancient kingdom of Magadh comprised the country now included in the districts of Patna, Gaya and Shahabad. Its capital was at Rajagriha, some thirty miles north-east of Gaya. North of the Ganges was Videha or Mithila, which included the modern districts of Darbhanga, Saran, Champaran and Muzaffarpore; the south of the latter district constituted the small kingdom of Vaisali. To the east lay Anga, including Monghyr, Bhagalpore and Purnea, as far as the Mahananda river. . . . It was in Magadha that Buddha developed his religion and that Mahavira rounded the cognate creed of the Jains. Soon after Buddha's death, a Sudra, named Nanda. . . . founded a new dynasty. He made his capital at the confluence of the Sone and the Ganges near the modern Patna. Chandra Gupta, a contemporary of Alexander the Great, overthrew this family and founded the Maurya dynasty. . . . His grandson Asoka, established a hegemony over the whole of Northern India including a great part of Bengal and Orissa. He was the greatest protagonist of Buddhism and sent his missionaries to every known country. In the fourth century the Gupta dynasty rose to power. Their capital also was at Patna and their supremacy was acknowledged by the kings of Bengal and Kamrupa.

The above quotation is from a quotation used in a pamphlet in 1906 demanding the separation of Bihar and was significantly taken not from any standard textbook of history but from a government source—E.A. Gait's *Report of the Census of the Lower Provinces, 1901.*[6] Significant yet again is the fact that though it very accurately summarizes the glorious ancient history of the region, it contains a very interesting contention,which is historically inaccurate. We do not know the province of Bihar from ancient times. In fact, no such region existed during the ancient period and no such name was known to the ancient Indians.[7] Everything about this version of history and its use is important. But we shall come to that later. What is important is to recognize the fact that the region decidedly had a glorious history in the ancient period.

It was noted by O'Malley about the Patna district. 'No district in Bengal has such an ancient and eventful history as Patna. This history stretches back for 2,500 years and centres around Rajgir, Patna and Bihar (Biharsharif) which have all been at different times famous capitals.'[8]

The medieval history of the region though not so picturesque, not abounding in big names (we may note the solitary reference to a medieval figure, that of Sher Shah from this period as compared to five from the ancient period in the song with which we opened this study), was significant from other points of view. The political geography of the region, as one unit, was shaped during this period and the name 'Bihar' fastened on to this unit, providing the people living therein with the biggest historical symbol of all. Both the processes were long-drawn affairs and were initiated by a Muslim invader, Bakhtiyar Khalji, in the thirteenth century. It is in the *Tabaqat-i-Nasiri*, a historical work written by Minhaj in the second half of the thirteenth century AD that it has been found that the word 'Bihar' was used to denote the name of a place. Minhaj, while recording the origin of the name of Bihar as a territorial unit, said that Bakhtiyar Khalji attacked *Hisar-i-Bihar* (Bihar fort), captured it and pillaged it. It was actually a fortified monastic educational institution of the Buddhists and was situated near modern Biharsharif. According to the author the conquerors came to know that the whole of the fortress and city was a *madrasa* (college) which in the Hindvi language was called *vihara.* Khalji called the entire area around Biharsharif as Bihar. Later, in the medieval period the term 'Bihar' began to be used for southern Bihar as distinct from northern Bihar. Iltutmish tried to constitute Bihar as a separate province but the attempt did not prove to be very enduring. However, the first half of the fourteenth century proved an eventful period regarding the shaping of the political geography of Bihar. In AD 1324 Tirhut, which had till then maintained a separate tributary status, was annexed to Delhi sultanate following the final attack by Ghiyas-ud-din Tughlaq. The Tughlaq rule was firmly established over north and south Bihar and the region thus acquired a new political status and, in fact, Bihar was mentioned as one of the provinces of the empire by a fourteenth-century Arab writer Ibn-i-Fadlullah al-Umri in an extremely valuable account of the political, social and economic conditions in India during the reign of Muhammad bin Tughlaq (1325-51). However, in the wake of the disintegration of the Tughlaq empire many regional kingdoms sprang up and different parts of Bihar came under the control of the Sultanates of Delhi, Lakhnauti and Jaunpur. A very important, though short-lived, phase in the history of the region came in the early sixteenth century when the son and successor of Dariya Khan Nuhani, who had been appointed as the *hakim* of the *vilayat* of Bihar by Sikandar Lodi, Bahar Khan made a dash for carving out an independent principality. About 1524 he assumed the title of Sultan Muhammad and got the *khutba* read and coins struck in his name as the ruler of the Nuhani kingdom of Bihar. The *khutba* was read in his name for more than two years. Interestingly Babar has referred to him as *Bahar Khan Behari* (emphasis added) providing the first instance when a person was thus identified by the territorial entity of Bihar.[9] However, the process of creating a more enduring political identity for the region, though of a subordinate sort, reached its culmination in the sixteenth century when a son of Bihar, Sher Shah, succeeded in unifying under one administration different parts of the region such as Monghyr and Bhagalpur, South Bihar and Tirhut with its capital at Patna and Akbar finally in 1575 constituted Bihar as a suba.[10] The suba was divided into 7 sarkars and 199 parganas. The sarkars were as follows: Champaran, which included modern Bettiah and Motihari; Saran which included Manjhi and Narhan; Hajipur which included Begusarai; Tirhut which covered a large part of the old kingdom of Mithila and included Darbhanga; Rohtas which included Arrah, Sasaram and Rohtas; Bihar, the largest of the seven sarkars of the suba, covered the greater part of the old districts of Patna, Gaya and northern parts of the old districts of Hazaribagh, Ranchi and Palamau (by old districts is meant districts of Bihar state in the 1960s. In the 1970s and 1980s many of them were split up and now some form part of the Jharkhand state); Monghyr formed the eastern and south-eastern portion of the suba and included Bhagalpur and also covered a portion of the area of the Santhal Parganas.[11] The division between the subas of Bengal and Bihar was marked by a stone wall running from the Ganges to the hills.[12]

The might of the later Mughal kings ensured both its endurance and expansion. The suba by the second half of the seventeenth century had come to include large areas of Chota Nagpur.[13] It is apparent that during the Mughal period Bihar had come to include a large part of the area which were to remain under it till the separation of Jharkhand.

Arguably it was the fashioning of this territorial entity which made it possible for the later colonial administrator—historians as also native intellectuals to think of 'Bihar' as existing since time immemorial. Even those not interested in articulating its antiquity made use of its existential identity. Two medieval Hindi poets Prabal Shah of Bhojpur and Bhudhar Mishra of Monghyr respectively thus chose to introduce themselves through this territorial identity.

> सूबा मधय बिहार के, नगर भोजपुर नाम[14]
>
> (I belong to the town of Bhojpur which is situated in the middle of suba Bihar)
>
> (Translation mine)
>
> सूबा नाम बिहार है, गढ़ मुंगेरि निज धाम[15]
>
> (I belong to fort Monghyr which is in the suba Bihar)
>
> (Translation mine)

Bihar enjoyed political and administrative unity for almost two hundred years before the British established their rule. The crystallization of its territorial identity was aided by the fact that till the end of the reign of Aurangzeb the province had independent and occasionally even princes as governors. It was only towards the end of his reign, in AD 1703, that Azim-us-Shan was given Bihar as an appendage to Bengal governorship. However, there were independent governors even after that. Fakhr-ud-Daula (1724-34), for instance, was an independent governor.[16] In fact, attempts were made by a succession of governors to establish themselves locally in the years 1700 to 1740, though to no avail.[17] Though Alivardi became governor of all the three eastern provinces—Bengal, Bihar and Orissa—in 1740,[18] the distinct administrative identity of Bihar did not die out. It becomes evident from the fact that in 1765 when the Mughal emperor conferred Diwani of

Bengal, Bihar and Orissa on the East India Company, three separate *farmans* were issued for the three provinces.[19] Bihar, at this time as would be evident, also included Chota Nagpur.[20]

Though the suba was an administrative convenience, it developed a firmer reality over a period of time under the influence of political and administrative factors.[21] Economic factors, too, began to play their role in sustaining and strengthening this identity. In a persuasive study, R.G. Hambly has argued that every suba headquarter of the Mughal state functioned as a regional capital, servicing the subadar's court and administration attracting entrepreneurs to exploit its commercial potential and acting as a magnet for local political and cultural life.[22] That Patna played a similar role for Bihar is easy enough to see in the growth of the city. The city of Patliputra that had suffered a decline in importance after the Gupta period once again started regaining its former eminence. By the early seventeenth century it had emerged as one of the largest cities in the Mughal empire with an estimated population of about two lakh people.[23]

It was this politico-administrative identity of Bihar, which was to be submerged with the arrival of the British. This event was also to inaugurate the modern period of the region's history. It was the submergence of this identity that was to provide the local people the powerful myth of neglect and deprivation of the region by the colonial rulers. The whole process (of submergence) happened over a period of time. The British initially took care to recognize the distinct politico-administrative status of Bihar and special arrangements were made for the collection of revenue from the region. In 1781, for example, the whole of Bihar was settled with the Diwan of the Company, Kalyan Singh, who had the high sounding official title of 'Roy-Royen of Subeh Bihar'.[24]

The English till the Charter Act of 1833 maintained control over the whole of the Lower Provinces of Bengal including Bihar, Orissa and Assam as well as the entire region in upper India up to Delhi (including modern U.P.) from Calcutta and it was only in 1836 that the Upper Provinces were formed into a separate administration. However, Bihar was not included in the Upper Provinces for purely administrative reasons.[25] With this separation it got more firmly tied up with Bengal and became what popularly came to be known as its 'appendage' as we shall see later in the study. Its sheen was completely outshone by the aura of Bengal—the chief province of the imperial power. The wheel of fortune had now turned against Bihar and its people.

Bihar, as this narrative makes clear, had witnessed two hundred years of political and administrative unity before the arrival of the British. Its rich history was to play a major role in engendering regional consciousness and was called to aid in demanding a separate politico-administrative identity for the region as we have seen above. The colonial rulers had perhaps inadvertently aided in the process of appropriating in the name of 'Bihar' the entire history of this part of the country. The mistake, committed by Gait noted earlier in the chapter, certainly must have strengthened the claim of Bihar of having a glorious history. The memory of the great past was to add poignancy and force to the quest for identity. Furthermore the politico-administrative unity and uniformity provided by the Mughals contributed to the emergence of a society, where at the level of the upper classes, people shared many common features of life.

CULTURE AND SOCIAL STRUCTURE

The society that evolved in Bihar after the long contact with the Muslims was imbued with a new culture that hinted towards syncretism. In different spheres of life common patterns of behaviour emerged.

Dress was one such sphere. Early in the nineteenth century, Francis Buchanan noted that Hindu men of rank in Patna and Bihar districts on high occasions adopted the Muhammadan dress.[26] The same dressing habits prevailed in Bhagalpur and Purnea districts too, where in the higher ranks of Hindus, even pandits, on occasions of great ceremony, adopted in a large measure the Muhammadan dress. Very significantly this pattern was noticeable only in those parts of the district that belonged to Bihar.[27] W.W. Hunter, almost half a century later, found the same pattern to be in existence. 'On State occasions, such as when their attendance is required at court, Hindus and Muhammedans dress alike.' On such occasions the headdress consisted of a flat turban (*pagri*) or occasionally of one twisted-round the head (*muretha*), while loose drawers took the place of *dhoti*. People used a looser robe over the *chapkan* (long, tight-fitting coat), and shoes of English shape took the place of country slippers.[28] One would not have been able to tell apart a pandit from a sheikh or a Rajput from a Pathan.

True for men. True for women. While most of the Muslim women in ordinary dress used the Hindu petticoat or wrapper, Rajput women used long drawers like the Muslim ladies.[29]

And if they dressed alike, they did not marry too differently either. The Muslims had adopted many customs from the Hindus. The reason probably was that the converts had retained some of these customs as part of their heritage. Though this offended the purist and the orthodox, however, the practices were difficult to be given a go by.[30]

Ahsan-ul-Akhlaq, a work written in AD 1781 by a Chisti saint of Rajgir, gave details of what a religious Muslim ought to do and what to avoid. The text also contained a list of customs and ceremonies adopted from the Hindus and therefore were to be given up.

Those related to the marriage ceremony were *ratjagga*, *kalasasthapana* (the ceremony of filling the earthen pots), the *mangini* (betrothal), the ceremony of making *tika* marks on the forehead of the bride and the bridegroom, preparing a *degadan* (fireplace) and the singing of women in chorus around the fireplace, etc.[31] However, the saint's advice to give up these customs fell on deaf ears. Even after a century later, Grierson noted the continued existence of *mangini* and *ratjagga* ceremonies. *Kalsa* was still filled.[32] At marriage the bridegroom often followed the Hindu practice of smearing the bride's forehead with vermilion.[33]

The spirit of acceptance and accommodation was visible in other aspects of life, religious practices, for instance, which were generally supposed to fundamentally divide the Muslims from the Hindus. Keen observers like Buchanan and Hunter did not to fail to notice this. Early in the nineteenth century Buchanan noted, 'The same mutual adoption of each others' religious practices that exist between the Moslems and Hindus of Purnaiya, prevails in

Bhagalpoor.'[34] W.W. Hunter, the author of the *Indian Musalmans*, noted almost sixty years later, 'Muhammedans have conformed to many Hindu practices, so that the distinction between the two religions have ceased to be a marked one'.[35]

The syncretic spirit was most evident at the time of festivals. For the Hindus Muharram and especially Tazia processions were occasions where they could participate as enthusiastically as the Muslims. In 1811 when Buchanan went to Bhagalpur he found the native people so much engaged in the celebration of Muharram that no business was possible. The Hindus were as much engaged as the Muslims.[36]

The Hindu participation continued even later on. In fact, in Patna, in the later half of the nineteenth century the number of Hindu participants in the Tazia procession exceeded that of the Muslims.[37] The Kayasthas of the Hazaribagh district too observed Muslim festivals.[38] Conversely in the nineteenth century, in Patna, Hindus used to invite their Muslim friends to participate in the feast and festivities on the occasion of Holi, Dussehra and Diwali festivals.[39]

The Muslims responded in style and depth. They not only took recourse to idols and made offerings but went beyond these. As late as 1901 the Census Report noted that in Bihar the Muslims joined in the worship of the sun (Chhath festival). In the Santhal Parganas, Muslims were often seen to carry sacred water to the shrine of Baidyanath (at Deoghar) and as 'they may not enter the shrine, pour it as a libation on the outside verandah'.[40] The Muslim participation in two of the holiest religious ceremonies of the Hindus offers the final proof of the syncretic culture prevailing in the region. This cultural-religious fusion had obviously taken a long time in maturing and equally obviously had its roots in the medieval period, when Muslims established themselves in Bihar. This fusion found some very strange expressions.

One family in Nawada (earlier in the Gaya district, now a district headquarter) educated its sons as Hindus and daughters as Muslims.[41] The set of Daryapanthis could be seen as yet another manifestation of this syncretic spirit. A saint famously known as Darya Saheb started it. He belonged to a village in the Bhojpur district and is believed to have died around 1780. His teachings bore the imprint of both Hindu and Islamic influences. He criticized formal worship and maintained that god was the *Satya Purusa* (True Soul). Both Hindus and Muslims were his followers.[42] Though it never became a very popular sect but in a way it reflected the spirit of the times.

The spirit of accommodation and acceptance, thus, marked the spheres of religion and culture of Bihar society. It was to prove crucial in the growth of one Bihari community.

Structurally, the society presented a near uniform pattern. Hindus enjoyed overwhelming dominance in numbers. The percentage of Muslim population was low[43] but they enjoyed a high standing in society. Early in the nineteenth century, Buchanan had noted that in the Bhagalpur district the important people were Muslims.[44] The higher castes among them like the Sayyids, Pathans and Mughals along with the Brahmins, Rajputs, Kayasthas and the merchants (Vaishyas) formed the Ashraf class (that is the noble, respectable class).[45] Later reports presented a similar picture. They mostly belonged to the upper orders and lived in towns.[46]

Among the Hindus, Brahmins and Rajputs enjoyed the highest status in the society. They were the superior castes everywhere in Bihar.[47] The Bhumihar Brahmins enjoyed position below them.[48] The Kayasthas formed the writer class and along with Brahmins and Muslims formed the educated classes.[49]

Ethnically the inhabitants were far more largely of the Aryan stock than in Bengal Proper.[50] The people were more conservative,[51] but not lacking a spirit of acceptance and accommodation as we have already seen.

The caste configuration in Bihar and ethnic attributes of the people did give it the appearance of a distinct region within the Bengal Presidency.[52]

THE LANGUAGE SCENE

The language scene in Bihar had two distinctive features. First, the languages prevalent in the region set it apart from other regions (Bengal Proper and Orissa) within the Bengal Presidency. In 1881 more than 90 per cent people in the Patna and Bhagalpur Divisions and 30 per cent in the Chota Nagpur Division spoke Hindi, Urdu or Hindustani.[53] The second important feature was that in the linguistic evolution of the region, centuries old contact with the Muslims associated with the Arabic-Persian culture had left a lasting impact and as in the case of culture, assimilation and adaptation had been the guiding spirit of this encounter.

This can be clearly seen in two medieval literary works written in Mithila, *Varna Ratnakara* by Jyotirishwara[54] (fourteenth century) and *Kirtilata* by Vidyapati (fifteenth century)[55] which freely used Arabic-Persian words like ***pyaju*** (onion), ***ohda*** (post), ***mouja*** (village), ***adab*** (respect).[56] The sufi saints, on the other hand, equally freely used indigenous words like ***bhaat*** (boiled rice), ***khichri*** (pulse and rice boiled together), ***khirki*** (window), etc.[57]

From adoption of words people moved towards adoption of language. Material interests made for it. During the reign of Sher Shah in the sixteenth century, Persian was recognized as the language of the revenue department. In every pargana one ***kar-kun*** (an official) was appointed to write in Hindi and one to write in Persian.[58] When Todar Mal was appointed minister of finance, he gave an order that all revenue accounts should henceforth be kept in Persian. His order forced the Hindus, if they wished to continue to monopolize the revenue department as they had hitherto done, to study Persian and acquire conversational powers in the language of their rulers.[59]

Its study, therefore, became widely prevalent and in Bihar, too, many Hindus acquired great proficiency in it. Early in the nineteenth century, Francis Buchanan discovered that in the districts of Patna and Bihar (Gaya) many Hindus were taught to read and write the Persian character even before they began Hindi.[60] The Persian language continued to hold sway even in later years. A survey done by William Adam in the 1830s of the existing state of education in two Bihar districts, Bihar (Patna-Gaya) and Tirhut confirmed this. It showed that Persian schools heavily outnumbered Sanskrit schools and the number of students in Persian schools was almost three times greater than those of Sanskrit schools. Most interestingly, Hindu students were in a great majority in these schools.[61] Adam attributed the popularity of Persian schools to the fact that Persian had been language of court and business till very recently.[62]

Obviously Persian was not a commonly spoken language and

would hardly make Bihar a distinct linguistic region. But undeniably at the level of educated elites, it was the common language. It was no wonder that persons like Maharaja Kalyan Singh and Raja Ram Narayan 'Mauzoon' (who occupied the highest offices in Bihar) in the eighteenth century wrote Persian works.[63] What we need to look at is the picture at the popular level. At this level people used Hindi, its allied languages and dialects and also Hindustani.[64] Buchanan mentions about the use of Hindi in Bhagalpur and Purnea districts. In Bhagalpur district those who used the Hindi dialect in common affairs wrote the Nagari character.[65] In Purnea district, Hindi was in use on the right side of the Mahananda River, where the manners of Mithila prevailed.[66] The *Ramayana* of Tulsidas was in use in Patna—Bihar, Bhagalpur and Purnea districts testifying to its wide popularity.[67] Some books, other than this, were also in common use in these districts.[68]

It is apparent that Hindi and its allied forms enjoyed popularity and Hindi character was used in writing. William Adam's survey in the 1830s, too, showed that when viewed in terms of the number of students, Hindi schools were far more popular than even Persian schools in Bihar. Whereas the number of students in Hindi schools in the district of South Bihar was 3,090, the number of students in Persian schools was 1,424. In the district of Tirhut the numbers were 507 and 569 respectively.[69] It shows that in South Bihar Hindi schools were far more popular than Persian schools, while in Tirhut they were almost equally popular.

In the schools set up by the government at Patna and Chapra in the 1830s Hindi classes existed.[70] Similarly, Hindi was taught in the Bhagalpur Hill School.[71] Interestingly, when attempts were made to open schools in the Chota Nagpur area, the post of Hindi teachers was proposed for schools in the Hazaribagh, Lohardagga and Singhbhum divisions (later to be known as districts) while a post of Bengali teacher was recommended for a school in the Manbhum division.[72]

The attempts of the government to provide Hindi teachers for schools in different parts of Bihar in the 1830s shows that there did exist a certain perception in official circles that Hindi was the language of the people in Bihar. As Buchanan's reports in the early years of the nineteenth century show, the official opinion in the later period had some basis to sustain itself.[73]

Another source of linguistic unity was provided by Urdu, also termed as Hindustani very often. It was seen along with Hindi as the language spoken in Bihar.[74] It was also the vernacular language, along with Hindi, taught in schools as also the court language of Bihar.[75] No wonder, many people learnt both Hindi and Urdu. A play *Sajjad Sumbul* written by Keshav Ram Bhatta, who was instrumental in giving Bihar its first Hindi newspaper, had as its hero a Muslim zamindar named Sajjad, who knew Sanskrit. In a tense yet hilarious sequence a Bengali character asks Sajjad to speak the Sanskrit alphabet *ka*, *kha*, *ga*, etc., to ascertain if he (Sajjad) was really the same Sajjad, whom the Bengali character knew. Sajjad cleared the test, of course.[76] That the playwright was not indulging in a flight of fancy is borne out by a number of instances from real life. While thus, the popular Hindi poet 'Roopkala' (real name Bhagwan Prasad *alias* Shree Sitaram Sharan Bhagwan), Braj Bihari Lal and Guru Sahay Lal had their early education in Urdu and Persian, the major Bihari poet of Urdu, Syed Mohammad Ali 'Shad' learnt Hindi and Sanskrit in childhood under a Brahmin teacher.[77]

Bihar, thus, possessed elements of linguistic unity strong enough to be both seen and put forward as a distinct linguistic zone, especially when seen in the background of the fact that it formed part of the Bengal Presidency. It needs to be pointed out, however, that both Hindi and Hindustani were the languages of business and social intercourse of the educated classes. The mass of the people used kindred languages or dialects like Magahi, Bhojpuri or Maithili in their daily lives.[78] Hence, no easy communication across people was possible. It was only after the introduction of Hindi as the medium of instruction in schools, its use as the official language, publication of newspapers,[79] and literary works[80] as also the spread of education that a standardized and widely shared language emerged. However, this development had its roots in the pre- and early colonial period.

This description makes it clear that Bihar possessed the roots on which a structure of a common regional identity could be constructed. However, it was the impact of the early colonial rule that created the conditions and the context under which the people came to feel that they had lost their identity and that their interests were suffering under the existing administrative arrangement. Was there a basis for such a feeling? The following section explores the answer.

EARLY IMPACT OF COLONIAL RULE

The British ruled India for almost two hundred years either directly or as overlords (in the case of princely states) and the country underwent profound changes in every field, social, economic, politico-administrative and cultural-intellectual, during this period. No area and no section of the population was left unaffected. Obviously the content and the contours of this transformation were not wholly determined by the British. The nature and the state of society in different regions also affected the course of transformation but a very significant feature of this (transformation) was that it produced a 'new unevenness of development between different regions'. The balance this time, to quote Anil Seal, 'tilted in favour of the coastal presidencies where British influence had first been felt and where its effects were most intensive'.[81] This also meant a redrawing of the power configuration map between different regions and their people. It then becomes necessary for an analysis of the colonial impact on Bihar, to point out where did the region figure in this map and what conferred power and status on the people in the new era.

The British were no strangers to the region of Bihar when they sought and successfully managed to get the Diwani of the province along with that of Bengal and Orissa in 1765 following their successive victories first in the Battle of Plassey (1757) and the Battle of Buxar (1764). Their commercial intercourse with the region had started way back in 1620, when the first English factory was established at Patna though it was also closed that very year.[82] After 1765 they became the virtual masters of the province and it is their actions as rulers that needs to be studied.

Administrative and Bureaucratic Changes

Soon after assuming the power of government in Bengal, Bihar and Orissa they began refashioning the system of administration, which they had inherited from the Mughals. The old units of administration were gradually dismantled and the element of personnel manning the administrative set-up was changed along with the method of recruitment to the bureaucracy. Undeniably the changes were not introduced at one go. They, in fact, were made over a fairly long period of time but at the end of it all, Bihar and what had been its administrative elite had suffered a body blow. Two blows, in fact, one to their material prospects and the other to their self-esteem.

Though the British took some note of Bihar's distinct identity in the initial years of their rule, as we have seen earlier in the chapter, their decision to do away with the Mughal subas affected it hugely. These subas were subsumed under the much larger administrative units called Presidencies which were headquartered in the port cities of Calcutta, Bombay and Madras. Bihar came to be included in the Bengal (Calcutta) Presidency. Both chance and design led to this decision. Bihar since 1734-5 had been put under the charge of the Bengal subadar.[83] After 1740 Alivardi Khan became virtually an independent ruler of Bengal and Bihar and the latter (Bihar) suffered some erosion of identity.[84] The commercial operations of the Company in Bihar were also overseen by the Calcutta Council, which had come into existence in 1700.[85]

All these factors coupled with the reconfiguring of the administrative map of British India in the post-1833 period, discussed earlier in the chapter, ensured the passing of Bihar under the governorship of Bengal, almost imperceptibly. For a while the name 'Bihar' was retained as the name of a district[86] but later even this practice was given up. It did survive, in a way, but merely as a geographical expression and simply came to imply the two administrative divisions of Patna and Bhagalpur. The government still took decisions in the name of 'Bihar' but orders had to be communicated to the commissioners of both the above-mentioned divisions.[87]

Changes in the system of administration, as mentioned above, gave a severe blow to those associated with the previous administrative system. The Mughals had divided the subas (provinces) into sarkars, which were further subdivided into parganas. Faujdar was the administrative head of the sarkar while amalguzar was the chief revenue officer. In the parganas shiqdar was the representative of the government while the amil oversaw the revenue administration. The pargana qazi took care of civil justice.[88] The British after a number of administrative experiments gradually evolved a system with the districts at its core, and all positions of high pay and power were gradually taken away from Indians and given to the English. In quick succession first Warren Hastings replaced Indian faujdars by English magistrates (1781) and then in 1786 European Collectors were (finally) made responsible for settling the revenue and collecting it in the districts.[89] However, the changes effected by Cornwallis in the Company's government in Bengal greatly affected the element of personnel who managed the administration. Hastings had left criminal administration in Indian hands, but Cornwallis decided to remove the Indian agency. In 1790 all Muslim judges were dismissed and in their place were appointed European covenanted servants as circuit judges.[90] In the revenue administration, in similar fashion, Company's covenanted servants replaced all Indian officers of any consequence.[91] Not only no Indian in future was to be appointed to a post carrying an annual salary of £500 or more[92] but even minor posts like those of sheristadars, accountants and registrars came to be occupied by the English.[93] All this meant a curtailment of the job opportunities for Indians including the people of Bihar who happened to live under the Company's government, but even more serious in their impact were some of the later decisions of the government. After a period of exclusion Indians had again started getting appointments in the officer class and in certain situations their powers were also strengthened. During the administration of the Marquess of Hastings (1813-23), Indians were appointed as munsifs and sadr amins so that justice could be made locally available to the people and the pressure of civil business before the European judges of zila and city courts could be reduced.[94] Once the post of deputy collector came into being, Indians got yet another opportunity to get into it.[95] However, the people of Bihar were not destined to enjoy the fruits of even these concessions, not yet, because the government created huge hurdles for them in the 1830s through two decisions. First in 1835, after much debate and discussion the government finally decided to promote English education and soon, thereafter, in 1837 Persian was abolished as the court language and it was decided to conduct the official work either in English or in the local vernacular. Gradually English education was made the passport to higher appointments open to Indians unlike the period before 1835.

One scholar has shown that before the introduction of English as a regular medium of instruction from 1835, very few of the Indian uncovenanted servants could speak English. No special qualifications were then looked for in an Indian judge beyond general good character, respectability of family, and in Bengal a competent knowledge of the Persian and Bengali languages.[96] It was the educational policy of 1835 and later the abolition of Persian as the court language which hit Bihar as English education was not making much progress there, as we shall discuss in the next chapter. The consequence was that to run the administration the government was obliged to employ in Bihar people from Bengal Proper. In 1857, for example, ten Arts colleges were affiliated to the Calcutta University and most of these were in Bengal.[97] In 1870 there were sixteen colleges in the Lower Provinces. Bihar had just one.[98] In a system of administration where English-knowing people had a decided advantage the people of Bihar were bound to suffer.[99] The second reason was that Bihar was a part of the Bengal Presidency where administration was run from Calcutta and Bengalis, being in closer contact with the English people, had again great advantage.[100] They were employed by the East India Company and sent not only to Bihar but also other provinces.[101] Many Bengalis came to work in the indigo plantations and other commercial concerns, while some came with the East India Company's Military Regiment.[102] When schools imparting English education were started many Bengali teachers taught in these schools.[103] Later also, under the direct rule of the Crown, the Bengalis continued to come and became prominent figures in professions of law and medicine. The story of Bengalis' migration to Bihar was very aptly narrated in a welcome address presented to the Lieutenant-Governor in November 1912, by the Bengalee Settlers' Association. It said

> We count amongst us, families that have settled here from before the commencement of the British rule in Bihar and Orissa and others whose ancestors were introduced into the Province by the British government

on account of the exigencies of public service. There are amongst us also those who have made careers for themselves through the open door of professions, trade and industry.[104]

We shall discuss this theme in other chapters as well. What our basic concern here is to suggest that as a result of the impact of early colonial rule a new unevenness was created within the Bengal Presidency and the result was that a sense of inferiority was built-up among the people of Bihar.[105] Also the colonial rule introduced in significant numbers an outside group—the Bengalis—with a very heightened sense of identity.[106] This was coupled with a superior attitude on their part towards the people of Bihar.[107] Their presence in Bihar provided the people with an important symbol in reference to which they could perceive and construct their own identity. The interests of the people of Bihar also made assertion of a regional identity a necessity.

This discussion makes it clear that during the pre- and early colonial period, Bihar possessed the necessary elements of a regional identity. The people had shared a common historical tradition. Bihar, as a political and territorial unit, had been largely defined. At the level of the educated classes, people shared languages like Persian, Hindi and Hindustani. When viewed in the context that it formed part of the Bengal Presidency, its distinctiveness emerged out even more clearly.[108]

As a consequence of the colonial intrusion a time came when a need emerged to stress this distinctiveness and to give it a political and cultural meaning. This task demanded the presence of elites and intellectuals, and concerted and determined efforts on their part.

NOTES

1. The title of a book by John Houlton, *Bihar: The Heart of India*, Calcutta, 1941.
2. India Home (Delhi) A Progs, December 1911, nos. 5-11. The dispatch dated 25 August 1911, Simla, from the Government of India to the Secretary of State.
3. R.R. Diwakar (ed.), *Bihar Through the Ages* (henceforth *Bihar*) Calcutta, 1959, pp. 23-4 and 632.
4. W. Hamilton, *The East India Gazetteer* (1828), vol. I, rpt. Delhi, 1984, pp. 108-9.

5. E. Thornton, *A Gazetteer of the Territories under the Government of East India Company*, 1858; rpt., Delhi, 1984, p. 84.
6. See Mahesh Narayan and S. Sinha, 'The Partition of Bengal or the Separation of Behar? : An Ideally Perfect Alternative Scheme', Patna, 1906. This author has consulted its typescript copy at the Bihar State Archives Library, Patna, pp. 45-6.
7. Upendra Thakur, 'Bihar: A Geographical Introduction and a Historical Review', in *Bihar: Past and Present*, Patna, 1987, p. 5.
8. L.S.S. O'Malley, *Bengal District Gazetteers, Patna*, Calcutta, 1907, p. 15.
9. See Thakur, 'Bihar: A Geographical Introduction', p. 5, and Q. Ahmad, 'Aspects of the Historical Geography of Medieval Bihar', in S.H. Askari and Q. Ahmad (eds.), *The Comprehensive History of Bihar* (henceforth *CHB*), vol. II, pt. I, Patna, 1983, pp. 3-10, and R.R. Diwakar (ed.), *Bihar*, pp. 398-9.
10. Thakur, 'Bihar: A Geographical Introduction', pp. 7-8, and Diwakar (ed.), *Bihar*, p. 488. However, the year was 1580 according to Ahmad, 'Aspects of the Historical Geography of Medieval Bihar', p. 15.
11. See Ahmad, 'Aspects of the Historical Geography of Medieval Bihar', pp.16-20 and map of the suba Bihar prepared by John Beames in 1885 appended to the chapter. Also see Irfan Habib, *An Atlas of the Mughal Empire*, Delhi, 1982, p. 39 and Political Map of Bihar in 1595, Map no. 10A therein.
12. A.T. Embree draws attention to the critical role boundaries played in the generation of nationalism. He has pointed out that the passage mentioning this fact, regarding the boundary between Bengal and Bihar was omitted without explanation in the edition of *Ain-i-Akbari* edited by Jadunath Sarkar. See his incisive article, 'Frontiers into Boundaries: From the Traditional to the Modern State', in Richard G. Fox (ed.), *Realm and Region in Traditional India*, New Delhi, 1977, pp. 255-80.
13. B.P. Ambasthya, 'Bihar as a Subah of the Mughal Empire I (1614-1660)', in Askari and Ahmad (eds.), *CHB*, vol. II, pt. II, Patna, 1987, p. 134.
14. See Shivpujan Sahay, *Hindi Sahitya Aur Bihar* (Hindi), vol. I, Patna, 1960, p. 84 fn.
15. Ibid., p. 86 fn.
16. Diwakar (ed.), *Bihar*, pp. 493-502.
17. See Muzaffar Alam, 'Eastern India in the Early Eighteenth Century "Crisis": Some Evidence from Bihar', in *The Indian Economic and Social History Review*, 28, I, 1991, pp. 43-71.

18. Diwakar (ed.), *Bihar*, p. 503.
19. Ibid., pp. 62-3.
20. F.B. Bradley-Birt, *Chota Nagpore: A Little Known Province of the Empire*, London, 1903; 2nd edn. 1910, pp. 16-17.
21. Lines of Hindi poems cited above obviously could not have been written in the sixteenth century. Benedict Anderson in his work has shown how administrative units acquire firmer reality under the influence of administrative, economic and other factors. See his *Imagined Communities: Reflections on the Origin and Spread of Nationalism*, London, 1983, pp. 54-7.
22. R.G. Hambly, 'Town and Cities; Mughal India', in Tapan Raychaudhuri and Irfan Habib (eds.), *The Cambridge Economic History of India* (henceforth *CEHI*), vol. I: *c. 1200-c.1750,* Cambridge, 1982, Hyderabad, 1984, p. 441.
23. See Irfan Habib, 'Population', Table 3 in ibid., p. 171.
24. O'Malley, *Bengal District Gazetteers, Patna*, p. 151.
25. See B.B. Misra, *The Unification and Division of India*, Delhi, 1990, p. 171; *Imperial Gazetteer of India (Provincial Series) Bengal*, Calcutta, 1909; rpt., New Delhi, 1984, p. 3; and V.C.P. Chaudhary, *The Creation of Modern Bihar*, Patna and Darbhanga, 1964, p. ii.
26. Francis Buchanan, *An Account of the Districts of Bihar and Patna in 1811-1812* (henceforth, *Patna Account*) in two vols., 1st edn., Patna, 1934; rpt., New Delhi, 1986, vol. I, pp. 279-80.
27. See Montgomery Martin, *The History, Antiquities, Topography and Statistics of Eastern India* (1838) (henceforth *History, Antiquities*) in 4 vols.; Indian rpt., Delhi, 1976, vol. II, pp. 92-3.
28. W.W. Hunter, *A Statistical Account of Bengal* (henceforth *SAB*), 20 vols., London, 1875-7; Indian rpt., Delhi, 1976, vol. XI, p. 100.
29. Buchanan, *Patna Account*, vol. I, pp. 279-80.
30. See Diwakar (ed.), *Bihar*, p. 535.
31. Ibid., pp. 534-5.
32. G.A. Grierson, *Bihar Peasant Life*, Calcutta, 1885, pp. 374-8.
33. *Report on the Census of India 1901*, vol. I, pt. 1, Calcutta, 1903, p. 375.
34. See Martin, *History, Antiquities*, vol. II, p. 108.
35. Hunter, *SAB*, vol. XVI, p. 84.
36. F. Buchanan, *Journal of Francis Buchanan Kept During the Survey of the District of Bhagalpur in 1810-11*, ed. with notes and Introduction by C.E.A.W. Oldham, Patna, 1930, p. 140.
37. Hunter, *SAB*, vol. XI, p. 61. Even in the early years of the twentieth century Hindus continued to participate in Muharram festivals. For example, they used to do so even at Darbhanga, the most important

town of Mithila considered as a very conservative area. See G.M. Mishra, *Kicchu Dekhal Kicchu Sunal* (Maithili), Darbhanga, Saka 1894, p. 147.

38. Ibid. (*SAB*), vol. XVI, p. 76.
39. Surendra Gopal, *Patna in the Nineteenth Century,* Calcutta, 1982, p. 27.
40. *Report on the Census 1901*, vol. I, p. 375. Presently Chhath festival is performed by a large number of Bihari women. It is observed with great purity and caution. Equally popular is the practice of taking holy water from the Ganges river from Sultanganj and after carrying it on foot for about 100 km on a *kanwar* pouring it over the Shivalinga at Baidyanath Dham.
41. Buchanan, *Patna Account*, vol. I, p. 328.
42. Q. Ahmad, 'Islam', in K.K. Datta (ed.), *CHB*, vol. III, pt. II, Patna, 1976, pp. 93-4.
43. In 1872 the Muslims formed 12.4 per cent of the population of Patna district and 11.3 per cent of Saran (*SAB*, vol. XI, pp. 60 and 256). In Monghyr their percentage was 10.1 and in Bhagalpur 9.3 (*SAB*, vol. XV, p. 59 and vol. XIV, p. 77). In Hazaribagh they formed 9.4 per cent of the population and in Lohardagga 4.7 per cent (*SAB,* vol. XVI, pp. 83 and 319).
44. See Martin, *History, Antiquities*, vol. II, p. 100.
45. Buchanan, *Patna Account*, vol. I, p. 265.
46. *Report on the Administration of Bengal, 1872-73*, Calcutta, 1873, p. 103. In Patna almost a half and in Tirhut district, a quarter of all landed proprietors were Muslims, *SAB*, vol. XI, p. 133; vol. XIII, p. 121. A popular saying *Turk, Teli, Tar in Tinon Bihar*, i.e. Bihar is made up of Muslims, oil-pressers and toddy palms, reflected their position in the society. See O'Malley, *Bengal District Gazetteers, Patna*, p. 55.
47. Hunter's *SAB* makes this clear. See vol. XI, pp. 43 and 246-7; vol. XII, p. 184; vol. XVI, pp. 251-2.
48. Ibid. (*SAB*), vol. XI, p. 43.
49. Ibid., p. 248.
50. *Imperial Gazetteer of India (Provincial Series), Bengal*, vol. I, p. 253.
51. A reading of *Reports on Native Papers in Bengal* makes this clear. See especially *RNP (B),* no. 4, 1877; A Hindi novel *Ashcharya Vritanta* by A.D. Vyas published in Samvat 1950, i.e. *c.* AD 1891 also shows how Hindustanis were seen as being more conservative than the Bengalis.
52. The caste of Vaidyas was peculiar to Bengal. Anil Seal, *The Emergence of Indian Nationalism: Competition and Collaboration in the Later*

Nineteenth Century, Cambridge, 1968, p. 40. The Kayasthas in Bihar considered themselves distinct from those of Bengal. See H.H. Risley, *The Tribes and Castes of Bengal*, Calcutta, 1891, vol. I, p. 443.

53. See Seal, *The Emergence of Indian Nationalism*, p. 46.
54. A. Pathak, 'Maithili Literature in Bihar', in K.K. Datta (ed.), *CHB*, vol. III, pt. II, pp. 537-8.
55. See Diwakar (ed.), *Bihar*, p. 444.
56. Ibid., pp. 447-8.
57. Ibid., p. 448.
58. Ibid., p. 555.
59. See, extract from a letter by H. Blochmann, Assistant Professor, Calcutta Madrasa, in Bengal General (Education) A Progs, April 1872, nos. 32-44.
60. Buchanan, *Patna Account*, vol. I, p. 296.
61. See Diwakar (ed.), *Bihar*, p. 715.
62. J.S. Jha, *Education in Bihar*, Patna, 1979, p. 147. Adam's survey was regarding indigenous schools.
63. See Diwakar (ed.), *Bihar*, pp. 541-56.
64. Bihar is officially a Hindi state now. However, Hindi understood synonymously with Khari Boli, is not the mother tongue of the people, who mainly speak Maithili, Bhojpuri, Magahi or tribal languages. This is the view commonly accepted. See 'Hindi Literature in Modern Bihar' by A.N. Sinha in K.K. Datta (ed.), *CHB*, vol. III, pt. II, pp. 503-34; for this generally accepted opinion. The languages spoken in Bihar, i.e. Maithili, Magahi and Bhojpuri, were put under the name *Bihari* by Grierson. See Bhola Nath Tiwari, *Hindi Bhasa*, Allahabad, 1986, pp. 20-7. The term *Bihari* has, however, failed to stick in popular usage.
65. See Martin, *History, Antiquities*, vol. II, p. 102.
66. Ibid., vol. IV, p. 93.
67. See ibid., vol. II, p. 102; vol. IV, pp. 131-2 and Buchanan, *Patna Account*, vol. I, p. 295.
68. Ibid. (Buchanan, *Patna Account*, vol. I), p. 295. and Martin, *History, Antiquities*, vol. II, p.102.
69. Jha, *Education in Bihar*, pp. 141-8.
70. Ibid., pp. 111-21.
71. Ibid., p. 130.
72. Ibid., pp. 134-5.
73. It is interesting to note that after the substitution of English for Persian in 1837 in India and the decision to introduce the Hindustani language in the courts and offices in Bihar a question was raised whether it was to be written in Nagari or in the Persian character (script). It was decided to use the Persian character (script) but at

the same time it was made clear that Nagari 'should eventually become the current characters of the Bihar Districts'. See, K.K. Datta, *Annual Report of the Ad Hoc Regional Records Survey Committee, Bihar (1950-51)*, no other details, pp. 15-18.

74. The use of terms Urdu and Hindustani synonymously was the source of some confusion even during the colonial period. However, a perusal of government records shows that by Hindustani was implied a simpler language than Urdu, of course written in the Persian script. Urdu was seen as being more Persianized. This was on occasions stated though never very explicitly. Not only that, Hindi and Hindustani too were seen as the same language though written in different scripts. See, Bengal General (Education) A Progs, April 1872, nos. 32-44 and Bengal General (Education) A Progs, September 1875, nos. 1-7.
75. See Chapter 3 of this book.
76. Keshav Ram Bhatta, *Sajjad Sumbul* (Hindi), Calcutta, 1904 (rpt). In the preface it is mentioned that it had not been printed since last 21 years. Even prior to that it was only twice printed. The story is based in the year 1874.
77. Shivpujan Sahay and B. Varma (eds.), *Hindi Sahitya Aur Bihar* (Hindi), vol. II, Patna, 1963, pp. 57-94. In fact, 'Shad' not only studied Hindu scriptures such as the *Gita* and the *Ramayana* with the help of one pandit but also translated five chapters of the *Gita* into Urdu verse. See Surendra Gopal, *Patna in the Nineteenth Century*, p. 27.
78. See Bengal General (Education) A Progs, April 1872, nos. 32-44. and Bengal General (Education) A Progs, June 1873, nos. 1-5.
79. Hindi newspapers came to be published from Patna, Bhagalpur, Bettiah, Muzaffarpur and Ranchi. See Chapter 4 of this book.
80. In the second half of the nineteenth century all the districts of Bihar produced people who wrote in Hindi. See B. Varma and K. Sharma, 'Nayan' (eds.), *Hindi Sahitya Aur Bihar* (Hindi), vol. IV, Patna,1984.
81. See Seal, *The Emergence of Indian Nationalism*, pp. 25-6.
82. Ahmad, 'Bihar in Transition', in Askari and Ahmad (eds.), *CHB*, vol. II, pt. II, p. 213. It is interesting to note that the factory of Hugli was started in 1651 and that in Calcutta was not even born in 1620. See R.C. Majumdar, H.C. Raychaudhary and K.K. Datta, *An Advanced History of India*, rpt., Madras, 1985, pp. 630-2.
83. Ibid. (Ahmad, 'Bihar in Transition'), pp. 207, 236 fn. 62.
84. Ibid., pp. 193-211, 241.
85. Majumdar et al., *An Advanced History of India*, p. 632 and J.S. Jha, 'Early European Trading Companies in Bihar', in K.K. Datta (ed.), *CHB*, vol. III, pt. I, Patna, 1976, pp. 60-2.

86. See the title of F. Buchanan's, *An Account of the Districts of Bihar and Patna.*
87. See *Reports on the Administration of Bengal* of 1870s for the use of the terms. However, there was one Bihar Circle in the Education Department. See Bengal General (Education) A Progs, June 1873, nos. 1-5. It needs to be pointed out that the decision to give preference in employment to the people of Bihar was first made applicable in Patna Division only. See Bengal General (Education) A Progs, October 1871, nos. 8-10.
88. J.N. Sarkar, 'Administration in Bihar under the Mughals', in Askari and Ahmad (eds.), *CHB,* vol. II, pt. II, pp. 303-15 and Diwakar (ed.), *Bihar*, p. 512.
89. Majumdar et al., *An Advanced History of India*, pp. 785-9.
90. B.B. Misra, *The Bureaucracy in India: An Historical Analysis of Development up to 1947*, Delhi, 1972, pp. 55-7.
91. Ibid., p. 80.
92. Bipan Chandra, *Modern India*, Delhi, 1971, pp. 108-9.
93. B.B. Misra, *The Indian Middle Classes*: *Their Growth in Modern Times*, London, 1961; Delhi, 1978, p. 177.
94. Majumdar et al., *An Advanced History of India*, p. 793 and B.K. Sinha, 'Administration of Justice, Police, Jails, Revenue, Local Self-Government and Municipalities in Bihar, 1772-1858', in Datta (ed.), *CHB*, vol. III, pt. I, p. 322.
95. Ibid. (Sinha, *Administration of Justice*), pp. 333-4 and (Majumdar et al., *An Advanced History of India*), p. 794.
96. Misra, *The Indian Middle Classes*, p. 181.
97. *Imperial Gazetteer of India (Provincial Series), Bengal*, vol. I, p. 156.
98. *Report on Public Instruction in Bengal, 1869-70*, Calcutta, 1870 pp. 19-23.
99. See Bengal General (Education) A Progs, August 1872, nos. 71-98. Of the 140 Hindu judicial officers in Bengal, Bihar and Orissa in 1858, the number of Bengalis were 133. *The Indian Middle Classes,* pp. 191-2.
100. See *Report on Native Papers in Bengal*, no. 4, 1877. It was also implied in Bengal General (Education) A Progs, August 1872, nos. 71-98.
101. Sudeshna Basak, *Socio-Cultural Study of a Minority Linguistic Group: The Bengalees in Bihar*, Delhi, 1991, p. 29.
102. Ibid., pp. 25-6.
103. Annual Reports on Public Instruction in Bengal make this amply clear.
104. See *The Beharee*, 22 November 1912.

105. Memorials presented to the government in 1870s and newspapers' observations make this clear. See Bengal General (Education) A Progs for 1872 and *Reports on Native Papers in Bengal* for 1877 and other years.
106. The sense of this identity was rooted to some extent in a history, which had seen long periods of regional independence. It was also greatly fostered among the literates by the cultural developments of the nineteenth century. See Sumit Sarkar, *Modern India, 1885-1947*, Madras, 1983, p. 108. In a significant study Sudeshna Basak has referred about various waves of migration of Bengalis in Bihar even prior to the British intrusion. But she points out that there was no attempt on their part to settle in Bihar as an identified group. See S. Basak, *Socio-Cultural Study of a Minority Linguistic Group*, pp. 19-32.
107. See *Report on Public Instruction in Bengal for 1869-70*. Also see *Reports on Native Papers in Bengal* for different years.
108. Thus, for example, was the caste status of the Kayasthas. This differed even within the Bhagalpur district. In areas belonging to Bengal, Kayasthas were regarded as a high caste; in Bihar areas as Sudra. One quarter of Bihari population went to Baidyanath Dham (Deoghar). Few Bengalis did that. In Bihar, Holi was much more celebrated than Durga Puja or Dussehra. In the Bengali part reverse was the case. See Martin, *History, Antiquities*, vol. II, pp. 121-33.

CHAPTER 2

Education and Emergence of New Social Groups

Reflecting on the importance of Patna College, the Director of Public Instruction of Bengal observed:

> . . . no one will question the good it (Patna College) has wrought for Behar, not only in regard to the spread of sound learning and the cultivation of intelligence, but in the practical way of training a body of men fitted to enter the professions or the public service. . . . Patna College is civilizing Behar.[1]

The statement at first sight does appear as an exaggeration, given the fact that the region of Bihar has had a brilliant tradition of learning and had been the home of two renowned universities of yore—Nalanda and Vikramshila. But if seen in a proper context and taken as a representative view, shared alike by colonial administrators and native people, regarding the importance and impact of new education on the people of Bihar during the last three decades of the nineteenth century, it is not devoid of truth. Though in the ancient and medieval periods of Indian history, rulers and nobles had very often supported educational institutions, it was for the first time that a government-sponsored, directed and controlled educational system had been launched in the country. This very fact as also the objective needs of the colonial state, which had largely induced the colonial government to make this momentous foray in the educational field, led to its acquiring a huge utilitarian significance. Education was not only made more accessible but also necessary. It had been possible for a great ruler like Akbar to remain virtually illiterate but even the meanest official or clerk in colonial India had to have some kind of education.[2] Education, however, is not only about jobs. In India, too, the new education also contributed to the creation of new forms of consciousness. The present chapter discusses why and how the spread of education, especially English education during this period and the consequent emergence of new social groups, were crucial factors in the growth of regional consciousness in Bihar.

We begin by looking into the factors which were responsible for the poor progress of education till the 1860s. This is done in order to highlight the context of its ultimate acceptance by the people and to bring out the significance of its spread from around 1870. The second section details this expansion of education and also examines the academic fare that was then offered to the students. The next section tries to find out which of the classes, castes, communities and sub-regions took to it and benefited most from education. The fourth section locates the new social groups which emerged out of it. The general impact of the spread of education is discussed last.

EDUCATION (1835-1870): THE ERA OF HESITANT PROGRESS

Once the colonial government, after a bitter and protracted debate between Orientalists and Anglicists, decided to launch English education and Western knowledge in India in March 1835 efforts were immediately on to open English schools in Bihar too.[3] But these early efforts were not successful more due to the boycott of government institutions than non-appreciation of English education by the people. The history of Patna High School provides an apt example. When the General Committee of Public Instruction decided to start this school, people of Patna refused to let out their houses for it and it had to be perforce started at Alamganj (in Patna), not considered a good site. The school finally opened in August 1835 and had both English and vernacular departments, but even this provision failed to make it popular.[4] Sinister rumours floated regarding the motives of the government in starting the school. More concretely, two other factors, which fuelled hostility, were the Resumption Proceedings, which had impoverished many old aristocratic families and the proselytizing activities of the Christian missionaries.[5] This school, however, managed to survive. A few others were not so lucky. Thus schools started in the early years at Arrah (1837) and Chapra (1839), both district headquarter towns, had to be closed down very soon for want of students.[6] The Bhagalpur School opened in 1837, in spite of having a Persian teacher and provision of monetary incentives to the students, could not make much progress,[7] while the Anglo-Vernacular School, established at Muzaffarpur in 1845, could make some progress only after the introduction of Persian and Arabic and even then, in 1855, the majority of students were of Bengali extraction.[8] The popular indifference also largely contributed to the failure of the Patna Central College experiment. The growing frustration at the non-acceptance of English education at different places gave birth to the idea of providing quality education at one central place by attracting meritorious students from all over the province through the award of scholarships.[9] Accordingly schools at Arrah and Chapra were closed, their headmasters were transferred to Patna School and it was upgraded to the status of a college in 1844, though it was not a college in the present sense of the term. However, even monetary inducements could not attract many students. Even those who joined were of a poor quality.[10] Convinced that the institution was not going to succeed, the Deputy Governor in 1847 decided to reduce it to its former status of an ordinary Zila School till the 'inhabitants of Patna and the Province of Behar came to appreciate the advantages of a liberal education more highly than they have hitherto appeared to do'.[11] Fresh endeavours on the part of education department officials to expand English education continued to face the same difficulties as in the earlier years. When following the Wood's Despatch of 1854 the Inspector of Schools in Bihar, R.B. Chapman, issued a circular to the effect that it was the order of the sarkar that the children should be sent to government schools, the people of Bihar, already aggrieved at an earlier government notification restricting official employment to the English-educated, resorted to passive resistance. Chapman's office was designated as the *Shaitani Daftar* (The Devil's Office) and the people shunned it.[12]

Although Zila Schools came to be established in Arrah, Chapra, Deoghar, Motihari, Chaibasa and Hazaribagh by 1863,[13] the progress of new education till the end of 1860s was not satisfactory. In fact, John Peter Grant, the Lieutenant-Governor of Bengal

(1859-62), while pleading for government action in education in backward areas like Bihar was constrained to call it the 'Boeotia of India'.[14]

However, it would be naïve to pretend that progress of education was hampered only by popular indifference to it. Other factors, equally weighty, were also at work. Lack of suitably qualified native teachers remained a major problem till the early 1870s. This was despite the fact that, by 1868, there were six Normal Schools in operation in Bihar providing training to aspirant teachers. This, however, was not sufficient to bridge the gap between supply and demand. The Inspector of Schools in Bihar, Mr. Fallon, aptly pointed out in 1870:

> The Hindustanis of this province prefer, and the schools generally work better under Hindustani and European or East Indian teachers, who speak their language and have more sympathy with their habits and feelings than Bengali teachers as a rule. But as yet first arts scholars and B.As. are so few in the North-West that their services command a high price in the local market and they are generally unwilling to take employment at a distance on such salaries as we are yet allowed to offer them.[15]

It had resulted in a situation, where to run local higher schools, teachers had to be imported from Bengal but the remedy so conveniently found had an adverse impact on the progress of education in Bihar.[16] The Bengali teachers did not take pains to learn Persian or Arabic.[17] More importantly, they did not command the respect of Biharis as their

> contempt for our uneducated provincials, who are not anglicized and do not speak English, is heartily reciprocated by them on other grounds, which refer rather to differences of race and character. And so, under all the circumstances, it cannot be expected that Bengali teachers should be as successful in Behar, as they ought to be in their own native province.[18]

However, possibly the most important factor, which stood in the way of quick expansion of education, was the absence of proper incentives which would induce people to take to it. In some ways and for a long-time education was not needed at all to secure public employment and hence its non-acceptance. Officials of the education department had been alive to the problem and demanding remedial measures since 1840s. However, measures taken on paper broke down in practice, as these failed to take realities on the ground into consideration. For instance, in 1844, Lord Hardinge in a resolution laid down that preference was to be given in the selection of candidates for public employment to those properly educated in government institutions.[19] However, many of those so educated were not prepared to accept appointments offered to them, which they felt, were not commensurate with their qualifications. The result was that even after seven years of the promulgation of the resolution, no native, educated in the government schools or colleges at Calcutta, had been appointed in any of the offices of Patna Division.[20] The situation did not change for the better even in the later half of the decade. The Inspector of Schools, Bihar Division, A.S. Harrison in his report for the year 1857-8 attributed the unpopularity of English education to the fact that English was not being required for the attainment of highest offices a native aspires to, 'I mean Moonshifships, Deputy Magistracies and Collectorships, Sudder Ameenships and Principal Sudder Ameenships. Hitherto no preference has been shown to candidates possessing some knowledge of English'. He felt that as long as the paths to the 'highest preferment' in the state were opened to natives as freely without an acquaintance with English as with it 'so long will a native refuse to expend (or as he practically finds it, waste) some ten years of his life in acquiring the tongue'.[21] In the 1860s the situation in Bihar was again contrasted with that of Bengal by the Inspector of Schools, Fallon, to drive home the point why government schools were not doing well in Bihar. While analysing the causes of failure of Zila Schools there he pointed out:

> It is needless to pursue the comparison with conditions in Bengal when all the conditions are manifestly less favourable for Behar. Nor is it necessary to do more than allude generally to the large market for English scholarship in Bengal, with its manifold facilities, incentives and rewards which a large market necessarily supplies.[22]

Elaborating the point he argued that while the Bengalis had established themselves in the Railways and the Telegraphs, the Public Service was a close monopoly of the uneducated 'for of 228 appointments to vernacular offices in this province made during the year 1861-62 all but four were conferred on uneducated Natives'.[23]

Obviously in Bihar people could do without education and hence, they did without it. They went for it when they needed it, as we shall see in the next section, but at the end of 1860s Bihar was extremely poorly placed in educational matters as compared to Bengal Proper, with some momentous consequences for the future history of the region.

Table 1 would make the point clear. The figures are for 1871-2.

TABLE 1 : COMPARATIVE FIGURES FOR BENGAL PROPER AND BIHAR IN NUMBER OF SCHOOLS AND STUDENTS FOR 1871-2

Institutions	*Bengal Proper*	*Bihar*
Total Population	36,969,651	23,261,204
Number of Indigenous Primary Schools	6,505	2,828
Number of Government and aided Primary Schools	2,076	126
Number of students in them	55,417	3,456
Number of Government and aided Middle Schools	1,216	138
Number of students in them	58,649	6,591
Number of Government and aided High Schools	95	15
Number of students in them	14,887	2,363

Source: Calculated from *Report on the Administration of Bengal, 1871-72*, p. 215.

Note: The figures for Bihar include figures for Patna, Bhagalpur and Chota Nagpur Division of that period.

This educational backwardness of Bihar was reflected at the college level too. In 1870 Bengal Proper had eight government colleges while Bihar had just one, the Patna College.[24]

But winds of change were already beginning to blow. Education, especially English education, was gradually made almost compulsory by the government of Bengal through a series of measures. In 1863, it was ruled that half of the posts of munsifs, darogas and pleaders would be reserved for those who had passed the university entrance or higher examinations. Next, in 1864, the

High Court ruled that all law examinations would henceforth be in English. In 1866, it was laid down that only Bachelors of Law would be eligible to become munsifs. In 1869, the Lieutenant-Governor recorded a resolution which enjoined strict adherence to the rules circulated in 1865 for the selection of candidates for ministerial appointments. Through it local officials were urged to counteract as far as possible the local influence which could affect the selection of candidates having higher qualification in favour of those having connections in the offices.[25] This gradually forced people to pay attention to it. A preference for appointing better-qualified Bengalis was already initiating a process of exclusion of Biharis[26] and made them pay serious attention to it. The elites of Bihar became conscious of the need to take remedial measures. Winds of change blew from many directions.

EDUCATION SPREADS

The most important factor which finally prompted the people to seek education and thus contributed to its expansion in the region was the desire to find jobs. This report from Shahabad district aptly reflected the popular attitude:

> The cry is still for English and English only. . . . History and Geography not the least bit of use. What is the good of learning the heights of mountains and the lengths of rivers, with the names of ever so many persons and places. Will this knowledge help me to a livelihood? For that after all is man's first want, the world over.[27]

From around 1870 the elites in Bihar started showing a new concern for the promotion of education. This was manifested on various occasions and in different forms but a general desire to enable the Bihari boys to intellectually stand on equal footing with the Bengali boys informed their action. Thus it was reported in 1870 that the zamindar of Sonebursa, Babu Harballabh Narayan Singha, had instituted a scholarship tenable for two years at Patna College. The condition stipulated was that the holder of the scholarship must be a boy belonging, by birth and parentage, to the 'Province of Bihar'. It was intended that such scholarships would enable a large number of persons of the province to pursue university education, without which the difficulty of obtaining public employment was increasing rapidly.[28]

No wonder, any attempted measure by the government which was seen as creating hurdles in the progress of education in Bihar was vehemently opposed by the elites. One such occasion arose in 1872. That year the Lieutenant-Governor of Bengal, Sir George Campbell, broached the idea of removing B.A. classes from the Patna College. The origin of this idea lay in the fact that at the convocation of the Calcutta University, held in March 1872, he had observed that almost all the university candidates from Bihar were Bengalis and came to the conclusion that there were many difficulties in Bihar in the way of cultivation of English literature. It was felt that, as English education had not taken firm root, maintenance of First Arts standard was quite enough. It was made clear that a college could not be kept up and specially protected in Bihar to educate immigrant Bengalis only.[29] However, the news of the proposed reduction resulted in a quick response and leading elites of Patna, both Hindus and Muslims like Nawab Sohrab Jung, Khoda Bux Khan (Khuda Baksh Khan) and Roy Jai Kissen joined hands in making protest against the contemplated measure.[30] How important Patna College, the only institution of higher level in Bihar, was considered by them and why could be seen in the memorial presented to the government by them. It was contended that the intended removal of the B.A. classes from the provincial college at Patna would annihilate the warm zeal and ardour, which was so recently engendered in the 'Behary minds'. The memorialists felt that a firm belief would grow that the 'Government' and their *kismut* (fate) have destined their sons to remain copying clerks and holders of subordinate appointments, while all the honourable and lucrative employment was reserved for their more favoured brethren of Lower Bengal.[31] With almost a note of exaggeration they went on to say:

> From most of the important privileges granted by the Government to the natives of India, the people of Behar would be entirely shut out. The bench and the bar of the High Court at once and for ever will be closed against them; even youths of superior intelligence and energy, solely because they have the misfortune of having been born in Behar, will for a long series of years remain in the lower strata of Government service before they can rise to deputy collectorship and magistracy.[32]

Clearly jolted by the strong protest, the government decided to make a full inquiry into the feelings and wishes of the people on the subject before taking a final decision. The Director of Public Instruction was instructed to see while seeking popular opinion on the subject that 'no small section of the community are allowed to take upon themselves to represent the people of Behar, but that the general feeling among all the classes susceptible of education is ascertained'.[33]

When enquiries were made from the prominent people of Bihar such as Harbans Sahay of Arrah, Moonshee Heera Lal of Chuprah, Moulvie Dulliludin, Deputy Magistrate and others, the contemplated measure was vehemently opposed. A typical opinion came from Syed Zainuddin Hussain Khan, a Deputy Collector, who argued that as the people of Bihar had been making steady progress in the acquirement of knowledge, any check introduced would impede their progress and cool down their ardour. It was made clear:

> The Province of Behar boasts of one college and should that be degraded, no means will be left to the Behar students to compete with their brethren of Bengal in the attainment of high proficiency, and the people will be made to think that they are destined by Government to underserve the highly educated Bengalis by being debarred from those high appointments which require higher education.[34]

Similar feelings continued to run through the decade. No wonder, a few years later a government proposal to abolish some law classes in Patna College was looked upon as a great calamity to the province. A protest memorial maintained that this would close all the avenues of worldly prospects and advancement which were few in number and

> The Beharis would be left to pine away in adversity and obscurity, and to lead a life of drudgery in some petty office, all day and night for a small pittance; while people of the forward province of Bengal would continue to monopolize to themselves all the important offices in the different departments even in the Province of Behar.

The memorialists were clear that 'the prosperity of the province, therefore, in one important respect depends upon the maintenance of these classes'.[35]

It was also believed by people like Imdad Ali (a great promoter of education in Bihar in the 1860s and 1870s) that it was the lack of knowledge on their part, which had reduced wealthy and noble families to the status of beggars and when they would acquire education they would regain the lost glory and the province itself would resume its former enviable and prosperous position.[36] The desire of the people to take to education, especially English education, the willingness of the government to extend a helping hand (they retained the B.A. and Law classes in Patna College) led to a substantial growth of higher education in the 1870s and thereafter. And all this growth took place in the context, which has been mentioned above.

But before education could spread, teachers were needed in large numbers. The paucity of qualified native teachers was sought to be met by establishing Normal Schools for the training of teachers. The first Normal School was established at Patna in 1863. Two years later (in 1865) Normal Schools were established in different parts of the region such as at Chapra, Gaya, Purnea and Bhagalpur. A Normal School was established in 1868 at Muzaffarpur. By 1870 these schools had trained 254 pupil-teachers.[37]

The paucity of textbooks in Hindi was met by the establishment of a textbook committee for Bihar and encouragement of local writers to prepare them. Although the problem could have been partly solved through the translation of Bengali textbooks into Hindi a strong reluctance was shown by the Bihari people in doing this.[38] Aided by these factors there took place a substantial growth at the level of primary and secondary education during the last three decades of the nineteenth century. Tables 2-4 show the increase at all the levels.

At the level of the primary schools the increase in the number of students was proportionately greatest in the Chota Nagpur Division though increase in other divisions was also substantial. This expansion was important because at this level and, in fact, up to the vernacular scholarship, standard teaching was done in Hindi following Campbell's orders.[39]

The new school education differed substantially from that which had prevailed in the early years of the nineteenth century. The most

TABLE 2 : NUMBER OF STUDENTS IN BIHAR IN ALL CATEGORIES OF SCHOOLS AND COLLEGES IN 1871–2

Institutions	Bihar	Chota Nagpur	Total no. in Bihar
Population	19,405,201	3,856,003	23,261,204
Govt. and aided Primary Schools	2,507	949	3,456
Govt. and aided Middle Schools	4,514	2,077	6,591
Govt. and aided High Schools	2,041	322	2,363
Govt. and aided Colleges	84	–	84

Source: Report on the Administration of Bengal, 1871-72, p. 215.

TABLE 3 : NUMBER OF STUDENTS IN DIFFERENT DIVISIONS IN BIHAR IN ALL CATEGORIES OF SCHOOLS AND COLLEGES (1881 TO 1901-2)

	1881	1891	1901-02
Patna			
Primary	1,20,322	1,29,712	1,58,805
Secondary	12,717	16,166	16,849
College	203	298	524
Bhagalpur			
Primary	73,366	75,051	89,928
Secondary	5,470	8,098	9,689
College	–	77	238
Chota Nagpur			
Primary	27,667	53,611	67,545
Secondary	3,014	4,676	6,634
College	–	–	36

Source: Compiled and calculated from *Reports on the Administration of Bengal, Reports on Public Instruction in Bengal and Review of Education in Bengal (1897-98 to 1901-02), Second Quinquennial Report*, Calcutta, 1902.

TABLE 4 : INCREASE IN TOTAL NUMBER OF STUDENTS IN BIHAR (1881 TO 1901-2)

Year	Primary	Secondary	College
1881	2,21,355	21,201	203
1891	2,58,374	28,940	375
1901-2	3,16,278	33,172	798

Source: Compiled and calculated from *Reports on the Administration of Bengal, Reports of Public Instruction in Bengal and Review of Education in Bengal (1897-98 to 1901-02), Second Quinquennial Report*, Calcutta, 1902.

significant contrast was in the nature of contents of education. In the traditional system of education the emphasis was on the study of grammar, law, metaphysics, etc.[40] In the new system even in primary schools, subjects like History and Geography were taught.[41] In the middle schools not only History and Geography but also subjects like Physics, Chemistry, Botany, and Sanitation were taught.[42] These subjects were more calculated to unshackle the minds of the students. The History paper included the history of Bengal and India. Similarly, in Geography, geography of Bengal was taught.[43] The changes also gave a chance to books like *Bihar Darpan* to find a place in the school curriculum.[44] The book containing a biography of some eminent men of Bihar, coming from different parts and different walks of life must not only have familiarized the students with these personalities but also filled them with a sense of pride that they came from a region which was full of great men.[45] The teaching of History and Geography would increase their knowledge of the country and the region. In the first class, *Suchal Shiksha* by Pratap Narayan Mishra was taught.[46] The text made a moving and reasonable plea for recovering pride in being Indian.[47] One book in use in Geography was Shiv Prasad's *Bhugol Hastmalak* (in Hindi).[48] About Bihar it interestingly wrote that in Sanskrit its southern part is mentioned as Magadha and northern part as Mithila.[49] Thus, appropriation of different parts in the name of Bihar was already being done through such works.

ENGLISH EDUCATION

However, it was the growth in the field of English education which was significant. Both the number of such schools and that of students in them increased greatly. From 1871-2 to 1891-2, the number of schools grew four times while those of students six times. By 1897 the increase was even greater. It also appears that the maximum progress was achieved in the Patna Division. Table 5 would make the points clear.

Even more significant was the fact that in Patna Division whereas in 1871-2 there were five government schools with 1,152 students, one aided school with 208 students and two unaided schools with 98 students, by 1891-2 the numbers rose to seven government schools (2,612 students), 10 aided schools (1,809

TABLE 5: ENGLISH HIGH SCHOOLS IN BIHAR 1871-2 TO 1896-7

	1871-2		1875-6		1881-2		1885-6		1891-2		1896-7	
	No. of Schools	No. of Pupils	No. of Schools	No. of Pupils	No. of Schools	No. of Pupils	No. of Schools	No. of Pupils	No. of Schools	No. of Pupils	No. of Schools	No. of Pupils
Patna Division	8	1,458	9	2,101	6	2,503	7	2,403	38	9,130	38	9,506
Bhagalpur Division	5	681	7	1,099	4	1,069	–	995	16	3,254	21	3,918
Chota Nagpur Division	4	204	4	550	4	426	–	662	7	1,184	7	1,184
	17	2,343	20	3,750	14	3,998	7	4,060	61	13,568	66	14,608

Source: Compiled from *Reports on Public Instruction in Bengal (of relevant years) and Review of Education in Bengal (1892-93 to 1896-97), First Quinquennial Report*, Calcutta, 1897, p. XXVIII.

Note: Some discrepancy occurs because while in 1871-2 government aided and unaided schools were included in the Report, in 1881-2 the report did not include the number of aided and unaided schools. The figures for 1891-2 include all categories of higher schools.

students) and 21 unaided schools with 4,709 students. The maximum increase was recorded in the non-aided school category, a telling proof of the spirit of self-help demonstrated by the people of Bihar.[50]

In Bhagalpur Division, too, the same spirit of self-help was evident. In 1871-2 there were four government and one aided school with 629 and 52 students respectively. By 1891-2 there were five government schools with 1,113 students but an impressive increase had taken place in the number of aided and unaided schools and students in them. Now there were four aided schools with 583 students and seven unaided schools with 1,558 students.[51]

By this time good progress had also been made in the field of higher English education. The college which was seen as civilizing Bihar in the early 1880s was established in 1863 with a very small number (in fact, only 5) of students. This was the Patna College, Patna.[52] This maiden venture to promote higher English education in Bihar received liberal financial support from landed magnates from different parts of Bihar, like the Maharajas of Darbhanga and Bettiah.[53] The Muslim elites of Patna like Syed Wilayat Ali Khan[54] and Syed Lutf Ali Khan also made liberal donations.[55]

In 1864 a law class was added[56] and it got a degree college status in 1865-6 by providing instruction up to the B.A. standard.[57] Though the number of students rose to 84 by 1871,[58] its progress was considered slow and in 1872 it was proposed to reduce its status, as we have seen earlier in the chapter. The Lieutenant-Governor wanted to reduce the B.A. classes, if feasible, and to devote all savings to the establishment of a strong physical science and agriculture college with civil service classes in the province of Bihar. Inquiries were made from educated natives and interested persons of Bihar. To their great pleasure and satisfaction the Lieutenant-Governor, in a meeting with prominent people of Bihar at the Patna College, announced that since they were nearly unanimous in preferring to retain the third and fourth year 'Arts' classes he would yield to their wishes.[59]

By 1875 the number of students went up to 90 (out of 1,213 students for the whole of the Presidency).[60] In 1885 the number was 174 (out of 2,722 students for the whole of the Presidency).[61] In 1900 it had 205 students.[62] Till 1887 it remained the only college in Bihar and contrary to the prevailing opinion, the progress of the college was definitely satisfactory. Between 1870 and 1885 the number of college students in the whole of Bengal rose by 100 per cent, in Patna College the increase was 150 per cent.[63] However, the increase was not merely due to the zeal of the Biharis as for many years the college had a larger number of Bengali students than Bihari students. For example, in 1872 out of 79 undergraduate students, 40 were Bengalis and only 37 natives of Bihar.[64]

The government officials soon realized that the number of students depended on the results of the Entrance examination of Zila schools of Bihar. The poor performance in this examination led to the poor presence of the Bihari students in the college.[65] But this situation changed soon and by 1874 they started outnumbering the Bengali students. It was reported by the Principal in 1875: 'In the preceding year the number of Beharis was 48 and of Bengalis 42; while in 1873 the Beharis numbered only 40 and the Bengalis 55. In the early days of the college the classes were chiefly composed of the Bengalis.'[66]

The Principal found these figures interesting as showing that the 'natives of the province are overcoming their distrust of English education, and beginning to avail themselves freely of its advantages . . . the upper classes are no longer keeping aloof either from school or from college'.[67] In 1884 out of 178 students 119 were Biharis and only 59 Bengalis.[68] Thus, over a period of time the Biharis clearly gained ascendance in the college. It attracted students from Chota Nagpur Division too.[69] However, the mere increase in the number of the Bihari students in it does not reveal the true significance of the Patna College for the people of the region.

We have seen earlier as to how the Patna College was seen by the people of Bihar as the major weapon through which they could fight their way out of the Bengali domination in services even within Bihar (their own region) and achieve a status of parity with them. Any attempt to belittle its status was fought with emotional fervour.

Gradually the desire for higher English education spread to other parts of Bihar, too. Not surprisingly, in the second most important town of Bihar, Bhagalpur, was established the Tej Narayan Jubilee College in 1887.[70] Started by Tej Narayan Singh, a local zamindar, it was maintained by subscriptions, donations and receipt from the fee. The college was made a first grade college in 1890.[71] Its progress was spectacular, the number of students going up from 17 in 1888 to 90 by 1892.[72]

The third college in Bihar, and the second in Patna, was the Bihar National College. It was established in 1889 by Bisheshwar Singh, the zamindar of Kulharia in the district of Shahabad,[73] who had himself received education at the Arrah Zila School, Patna Collegiate School and the Presidency College, Calcutta (though he left studies without graduating) and was practising at the Patna bar.[74]

The town of Monghyr in the Bhagalpur Division gave Bihar its fourth college in 1898. This was the Diamond Jubilee College. It was started with the expectation that it would afford facility for higher English education to the students passing from high English schools of Jamui, Begusarai, Jamalpur and Monghyr. Again both Hindu and Muslim elites contributed financially to the venture.[75] Thus by this time both Patna and Bhagalpur Divisions had got two colleges each. Chota Nagpur Division till that year lacked even one college.

In fact, areas north of the Ganges and the Chota Nagpur Division got a college each in 1899. In 1899 north Bihar got a college at Muzaffarpur. The Bhumihar Brahman Sabha in March 1899 passed a resolution to start a college with the objective of 'placing the benefits of higher education within the reach of the students of North Behar and of imparting physical and moral training to them'. The college named Bhumihar Brahman College was thus founded. This educational venture received help from non-Bhumihar Hindus and Muslim élites.[76] Thus a long-felt need of north Bihar students, who had to go to Patna, Bhagalpur or Calcutta for higher education till then, could be met.

The Dublin University Mission established a college at Hazaribagh (Chota Nagpur Division) in 1899. This was the St. Columba's College.[77]

Thus, at the end of the nineteenth century there were six colleges in Bihar. Of these, only Patna College was a government college. The college at Hazaribagh was run by missionaries. The rest of the colleges were established by the private efforts of the people.

As the above description makes it clear, there was a growing desire for English education in different parts of Bihar, which was manifested in the increase in the number of schools and colleges and students in them. However, not all castes or communities shared evenly in the benefits of the new education.

RESPONSE TO THE NEW EDUCATION

When viewed in terms of community participation, it becomes apparent that the Muslims showed greater response to the new education, a factor which was to prove crucial to the emergence of a joint Hindu-Muslim front in Bihar's search for a distinct identity.

From the very beginning of the expansion of English education they maintained a sizeable presence in schools. Thus, in 1869-70 in the higher schools, the Muslims formed 20.14 per cent of the pupils in the North-West Division[78] (of the Education Department, having Tirhut, Gaya, Shahabad, Patna, Saran, Bhagalpur, Monghyr, and Purnea districts).[79] Even in the Middle Vernacular schools they formed 26.57 per cent of the pupils.[80] Similarly, in 1872 out of 421 boys in Patna Collegiate School, 90 were Muslims[81] while in 1872-3 in Arrah High School out of 197, 45 boys were Muslims.[82]

They showed their eagerness for education throughout the period. In both divisions of the Bihar Circle (Patna and Bhagalpur Divisions) they did better than the Hindus in the competition for minor and vernacular scholarships.[83]

The percentage of Muslim pupils to the total number of pupils as compared to the percentage of their population to the total population remained much greater even in 1895-6 in the Patna Division as would be clear from Table 6.

Their eagerness for new education was also evident from their number in the professional institutions. In the Temple Medical School, Patna there were 141 Muslim students as against 51 Hindu students in 1876-7,[84] while in the Patna Survey School there were 22 Muslim students as compared to 23 Hindu students.[85]

This enthusiasm was manifested in other ways too. The Muslim elites had taken the lead in organizing the protest against the threatened removal of the B.A. classes from the Patna College as we have seen earlier. They also opened a Muhammadan Anglo-Arabic School at Patna.[86] It was also reported by a Hindi paper of

TABLE 6: PERCENTAGE OF MUSLIMS TO TOTAL POPULATION AND PERCENTAGE OF MUSLIM PUPILS TO TOTAL NUMBER OF PUPILS IN SCHOOLS IN THE PATNA DIVISION IN 1895-6

District	% of Muhammadans to total population	% of Muhammadan pupils to total no. of pupils in 1895-6
Patna	11.36	17.0
Gaya	10.60	17.9
Shahabad	7.10	15.9
Saran	11.80	11.4
Champaran	14.30	17.3
Muzaffarpur	12.20	17.1
Darbhanga	12.00	16.5

Source: Annual General Administration Report of the Patna Division, 1895-6, p. 67, in Bengal General (Miscellaneous) Progs. volume for (January-September) 1897.

Bihar in 1880 that every Sunday some Muslims gathered in the house of Shah Hifazat Hussain and read excerpts from English books.[87]

They also showed greater propensity for going abroad as they did not face any religious taboos. Syed Abdullah, a school teacher and later a Deputy Inspector of Schools at Muzaffarpur, taught oriental languages in the London University for some time. Maulvi Abdul Hasan Khan was called to the bar in the U.K. around 1880, returned and set-up practice at Patna.[88] This relatively advanced attitude of the Muslims had historical and sociological reasons. Their number in Bihar was comparatively small and they mostly belonged to the upper orders[89] and were plainly determined to maintain their strong presence in educational institutions.

We get an insight into the prevailing attitude of the progressive section of the Muslim population from a Hindi play written by Keshav Ram Bhatta. Even the two Muslim ladies in this play, Gulshan and Sumbul, have studied English.[90]

Among Bihari Hindus the lead in English education was taken by Kayasthas who were traditionally associated with administration and did not entirely depend on land for their livelihood. In 1869-70, in higher schools, Kayasthas formed 42.25 per cent of the pupils while in middle vernacular schools they formed 18.11 per cent of the pupils.[91]

Till early 1872 all the three Biharis to graduate from the Patna College were Kayasthas and out of 18 Bihari Licentiates in Arts which the Patna College had produced, nine were Kayasthas and they preponderated among the passed Bihari Entrance candidates from different schools in Bihar. In fact, the Kayastha boys were sent to schools as soon as they were fit for them.[92]

The Bhumihars and Rajputs who formed the bulk of the landed aristocracy also followed suit. By 1880 the demand for English education 'was beginning to extend into the interior of the districts among the Rajputs and Babhans'.[93] Even the Tirhooti (Maithil) Brahmins began to appreciate English education which was considered as an encouraging sign, 'because the tenets of their religion have hitherto led them to regard any attempt to educate the people in English with distrust and suspicion, in the ignorant belief that the teaching of English is indirectly intended to discourage the teaching of Sanskrit, their mother tongue'.[94] Thus the benefits of the new education were reaped by old literati classes and upper castes. The emergence of new social groups, consequent upon the expansion of education was to prove a major factor in the political mobilization of Bihar.

NEW SOCIAL GROUPS

A very important social group to come into existence as a result of the expansion of education was that of school teachers. The occupation had traditionally enjoyed high social prestige,[95] and the sharp increase in the number of schools in the last three decades of the nineteenth century (see earlier in the chapter) ensured that many of the newly-educated Biharis would go back to schools to teach. Though salaries offered were not often commensurate with qualifications,[96] schools turned out to be the largest employers of the newly-educated in certain years. For instance, in 1871-2, out of 108 pupils who found employment in Patna Division, 63 became school teachers.[97] No wonder, training schools for teaching became especially popular among the natives of Bihar, a situation which was immensely to the liking of the Education department officials.

Thus S.W. Fallon, the Inspector of Schools, could exult over the fact that whereas in Patna College and higher English schools Bengalis constituted sometimes a large proportion of the students, in the class in Patna Normal School in 1871-2 'all the 83 pupil-teachers are Hindustanis and Hindustani teachers are the crying want of Behar'.[98] However, Patna Normal School did not provide the solitary instance of this rush for training schools. All the pupil-teachers without a single exception at Muzaffarpur, Chapra and Purnea Normal Schools in 1871-2 totalling 53 altogether were Hindustanis.[99] The rush to get into them continued and for good reasons. A government report of 1882 while talking of Normal Schools noted, 'The fact is our normal schools cannot turn out teachers fast enough to meet the requirements of middle schools especially in Bihar. . . .'[100]

All in all, the circumstances clearly favoured increase in the number of native teachers. As early as 1872-3, out of 83 teachers in Government High Schools in Bihar, 48 were Biharis, 29 Hindus and 19 Muslims, while in Middle Schools out of 275 teachers, 247 were Biharis with a very fair proportion of Muslims in them (105 Hindus and 92 Muslims).[101] In later years, with the demand that Bengalis should not be appointed in schools gaining ground, the appointment of native teachers must have got a huge boost.

However, we should not merely look into the number of school teachers to assess their importance in the society at large. They were crucially placed in a position to mould the minds of their young students. Some of them like Keshav Ram Bhatta and Ambika Dutt Vyas were not only prominent literary figures of the period[102] but were also to act as members of the Bihar Text Book Committee[103] and were thus in a position to select study materials for the young impressionable minds.

Journalists were yet another influential group of people to emerge out of the new education system. Though their number was small as even as late as 1911-12, there were only 42 newspapers and periodicals in the whole province of Bihar and Orissa,[104] and there were not many full-time journalists on the scene, yet they became educators of the people on socio-economic and political affairs. The leading journalists of the period—Govind Charan, who edited *Mushire Bihar*, Mahesh Narayan who edited the *Behar Times*,

Anandi Prasad Mishra and Keshav Ram Bhatta, both of whom edited the *Bihar Bandhu* at different times—were products of this new education.[105] We shall discuss the role of the press in generating regional consciousness in Bihar in greater detail in the next chapter.

The third and by far the most important professional group—both in terms of wealth and influence on the larger civil society—that emerged was that of lawyers. In Bihar, as elsewhere in India, the most spectacular developments took place in the legal profession. The emergence of this profession had been made possible by the transformation the British effected in the Indian legal system by constituting new courts, enacting a large number of rules and regulations, which had to be strictly enforced and by granting rights both in criminal and civil cases to employ pleaders.[106] Because of this and a number of other reasons, law proved a very popular professional course and the profession became one of the most sought after.

First, among Hindus the dogmas of caste enjoined a strong code of purity and pollution, hence any kind of technical education was difficult to pursue as it involved manual work. Furthermore, lawyers did not need to come into physical contact with anyone.[107] Second, Bihar happened to be one of the permanently settled provinces and zamindari tenure, particularly in such provinces, gave rise to more litigation than happened in the areas under the ryotwari system.[108] The growing complexity of the agrarian system resulting from the growth of Patni, Dar-Patni system in the zamindari areas giving overlapping rights to different tenure holders gave rise to lots of legal disputes and recourse had to be taken to law courts. Lawyers were, thus, in great demand.[109] Third, the legal profession was regarded as one of the easiest and most effective way of acquiring 'social competence and wealth'.[110] Interestingly the old rule of regulating pleader's fee by law was superseded in 1864 and now they could settle their fee freely with the parties they represented.[111]

Law attracted a large number of those taking to new education. By way of proof we may cite the example of Patna College, where a law class had been added in 1864. In 1871-2 while there were 79 students, including 37 Biharis, in the general department; the number of students in the law classes was 89 including 57 Biharis.[112]

The addition of law classes to the first grade 'Arts' colleges like the Patna College, B.N. College, Patna, T.N.J. College, Bhagalpur[113] not only testified to the growing popularity of law education but more importantly ensured that those willing to study it would not have to travel very far for it. Many people also tried to enter the profession at the level of Mukhtearship.[114] Both Hindus and Muslims took to this profession with great enthusiasm from the very beginning. Of the two Bihari Bachelors of Law produced by the Patna College till 1872, one was a Muslim, the other a Kayastha.[115] In that year (1872), in the Pleadership and Mukhtearship examination, all the three candidates to pass the senior grade pleadership examination from Patna Division were Muslims, whereas in the lower grade examination Hindus passed in greater numbers.[116] The trend very similar to that witnessed in the United Provinces, where Hindus generally entered the profession at lower levels than Muslims[117] continued in later years. Thus while in 1891 Hindus formed a majority of lower grade practitioners in Monghyr,[118] a decade later (1901) at Patna out of the 17 barristers, 12 were Muslims.[119] We have already seen earlier in this chapter that the Muslim community had given Bihar its first barristers.

As elsewhere in India and precisely for similar reasons like being independent and having enough ability to enter into constitutional dialogue with the government, the lawyers in Bihar, too, came to play a central role in politics and became the chief spokesmen of the general interest of the region. As seen above, it was a lawyer, Khuda Baksh Khan, who played a key role in fighting against the contemplated measures of the government to remove B.A. and law classes from Patna College and out of the four leaders—Mahesh Narayan, S. Sinha, Shri Krishna Sahay, and Nand Kishore Lal[120]—who took the lead in launching Bihar's struggle for a separate politico-administrative identity, except Mahesh Narayan; all others were from the legal profession. In the early years of the twentieth century when this struggle and articulation of other regional interests was sought to be done on a more organized basis resulting in the birth of Bihar Provincial Association and organization of Bihar Provincial Conferences,[121] lawyers were again key players.

Even the Beharee Students' Conference after passing a resolution dissuading young men from joining the Bar yet chose a lawyer to preside over its deliberations. In fact, the first six sessions of this conference were presided over by members of this profession to the exclusion of educationists or distinguished men from other walks of life.[122] Bihar's struggle for identity was led, in the main, by lawyers.

The true significance of new education lay in the impact it had on the growth of social and political consciousness in the region. It created a very large number of literate people. By 1911, 4 per cent of the people were literate and their number approximated to about 15 lakh in the Province of Bihar and Orissa.[123] The increase in the number of literate people meant that a much larger number of people could now read newspapers and other printed materials. The establishment of printing presses in different parts made available books to people. By 1890 many district headquarters had printing presses.[124] Bookshops also had become a familiar sight in important places. The hero of *Sajjad Sumbul*, Sajjad goes out in search of a book and looks for them in bookshops (at Patna) when he is preparing for a speech, which he has to deliver against the vice of love.[125] Many libraries were also established.

The expansion of education thus created a large number of people among whom the consciousness of a common identity could be disseminated. It also created those groups who would take the lead in the fight for espousal of regional interests, who would assert the cultural-political personality of Bihar, who would act as the disseminators of regional identity. The growth of regional consciousness in Bihar was greatly facilitated by the fact of very good Muslim participation in the English education, and their strong presence both in the public service sector and professions.[126] They never felt threatened by the Bihari Hindus. This was a significant feature in the social and political life of Bihar.

We would end this chapter by noting the fact that the fourth session of the Bihar Provincial Conference held in 1911 (the last one before the creation of the Province of Bihar and Orissa) was to be presided over by a barrister, a Muslim, Mazhar-ul-Haque. The Conference also passed a resolution moved by a lawyer, a Muslim, Md. Fakhruddin, demanding the separation of Bihar.[127]

NOTES

1. See Bengal General (Education) A Progs, October 1881, nos. 1-3.
2. Sumit Sarkar, *Writing Social History,* New Delhi, 1997, p. 13.
3. J.S. Jha, *Education in Bihar (1813-1859)*, Patna, 1979, pp. 92-105.
4. Ibid., pp. 104-8.
5. J.S. Jha, 'Education in Bihar', in K.K. Datta (ed.), *The Comprehensive History of Bihar* (henceforth *CHB*), vol. III, pt. II, Patna, 1976, pp. 409-11.
6. Ibid. (Jha, *Education in Bihar*), pp. 409-11, and J.C. Jha and J.N. Sarkar, *A History of Patna College, 1863-1963* (henceforth *Patna College*), Patna, 1963, p. 15.
7. Jha, *Education in Bihar*, p. 410.
8. Ibid., pp. 412-13.
9. Ibid., p. 411.
10. Jha and Sarkar, *Patna College*, pp. 9-12; and Jha, *Education in Bihar*, pp. 178-9.
11. Ibid. (Jha, *Education in Bihar*), p. 183.
12. S.R. Mehrotra, *The Emergence of the Indian National Congress*, Delhi, 1971, p. 86.
13. S.N. Pandey, *Education and Social Changes in Bihar* (*1900-1921*), Varanasi, 1975, p. 4.
14. Jha and Sarkar, *Patna College*, p. 32.
15. *Report on Public Instruction in Bengal, 1869-70,* Calcutta, 1870 (henceforth *RPI Bengal*), Appendix A, pp. 143-4. North-West Division was a Division of the Education Department in Bihar. See Bengal General (Education) A Progs, April 1872, nos. 32-44.
16. *RPI Bengal, 1869-70*, Appendix A, pp. 143-4.
17. *RPI Bengal, 1871-72*, Calcutta, 1873, Appendix A, pp. 353-4.
18. *RPI Bengal, 1869-70*, Appendix A, pp.143-4.
19. Jha, 'Education in Bihar', p. 411.
20. Jha, *Education in Bihar*, pp. 176-7.
21. See *Report of the Regional Records Survey Committee, Bihar (1965-76)*, Patna, 1978, pp. 119-20. The report was by J.S. Jha.
22. See Jha and Sarkar, *Patna College*, p. 24.
23. Ibid.
24. *RPI Bengal, 1871-72*, p. 45.
25. See Anil Seal, *The Emergence of Indian Nationalism: Competition and Collaboration in the Later Nineteenth Century*, Cambridge, 1968, p. 302 fns.; and Jha, *Education in Bihar*, p. 425.
26. See Bengal General (Education) A Progs, October 1871, nos. 8-10.
27. *RPI Bengal, 1869-70*, Appendix A, pp. 153-4.

28. Ibid., Appendix A, p. 371.
29. See Bengal General (Education) A Progs, March 1872, no. 63.
30. Ibid., May 1872, nos. 91-4.
31. Ibid.
32. Ibid.
33. Ibid.
34. Ibid., September 1872, nos. 78-80.
35. See ibid., March 1875 nos. 9-10.
36. See *Report on Native Papers in Bengal*, no. 38, 1873 and no. 15, 1874.
37. *RPI Bengal, 1869-70,* p. 34.
38. See Chapter 3.
39. See Bengal General (Education) A Progs, October 1872, nos. 11-13. The orders were issued on 30 September 1872.
40. R.R. Diwakar (ed.), *Bihar Through the Ages* (henceforth *Bihar*), Calcutta, 1959, p. 714.
41. *RPI Bengal, 1881-82*, Calcutta, 1883, pp. 49-50.
42. See Bengal General (Education) A Progs, September 1899, nos. 73-86.
43. Ibid.
44. Ibid.
45. See Ramdeen Singh, *Bihar Darpan* (Hindi), 1st published in 1882, rpt., Darbhanga, 1996, under the editorship of Dhirendra Nath Singh under the Kameshwar Singh Heritage Series.
46. See Bengal General (Education) A Progs, September 1899, nos. 73-86.
47. Sudhir Chandra, *The Oppressive Present: Literature and Social Consciousness in Colonial India*, New Delhi, 1992, pp. 41-2.
48. See Bengal General (Education) A Progs, July 1872, nos. 1-2.
49. Shiv Prasad, *Bhugol Hastamalak* (Hindi), Calcutta, 1855, pp. 136-7.
50. Calculated from *RPI Bengal, 1871-72* and *1891-92*.
51. Ibid.
52. Jha and Sarkar, *Patna College*, pp. 1 and 48.
53. Jha, 'Education in Bihar', p. 415.
54. See Bengal General (Education) A Progs, January 1863, nos. 66-8.
55. Ibid., August 1863, nos. 26-7.
56. Ibid., March 1875, nos. 9-10.
57. Jha, 'Education in Bihar', p. 416.
58. *Report on the Administration of Bengal, 1870-71*, Calcutta, 1872, p. 287.
59. Ibid. *1871-72*, Calcutta, 1872, p. 226.
60. Figures compiled and calculated from *RPI Bengal, 1876-77*, Calcutta, 1877, p. 48.

61. Ibid., *1885-86*, Calcutta, 1886, p. 22.
62. Pandey, *Education and Social Changes in Bihar*, p. 24.
63. See *RPI Bengal, 1869-70*, pp. 19-23, *RPI Bengal, 1871-72*, p. 45, *RPI Bengal, 1885-86*, p. 22.
64. *RPI Bengal, 1871-72*, pp. 9-10 and Appendix A, p. 477.
65. Ibid., *1865-66*, Calcutta, 1866, p. 69.
66. Ibid., *1874-75*, Calcutta, no details, pp. 76-7.
67. Ibid.
68. Ibid., *1883-84*, Calcutta, 1884, p. 33.
69. Ibid., *1875-76*, Calcutta, 1876, p. 69.
70. Pandey, *Education and Social Changes in Bihar*, p. 6.
71. Ibid.
72. *RPI Bengal, 1891-92*, Calcutta, no details, p. 19.
73. Pandey, *Education and Social Changes in Bihar*, p. 6.
74. Ibid. fns.
75. India Home (Education) B Progs, November 1898, nos. 44-51.
76. Ibid., July 1899, nos. 34-45.
77. Pandey, *Education and Social Changes in Bihar*, p. 7.
78. *RPI Bengal, 1869-70*, Appendix A, pp. 178-9.
79. Ibid., *1870-71*, Calcutta, 1871, Appendix A, pp. 197.
80. Ibid., *1869-70*, Appendix A, pp. 178-9.
81. Bengal General (Education) A Progs, May 1872, nos. 91-4.
82. *RPI Bengal, 1872-73*, Appendix A, p. 583.
83. Ibid., *1874-75*, p. 100.
84. *Report on the Administration of Bengal, 1876-77*, Calcutta, 1878, p. 355.
85. Ibid., p. 359.
86. S. Gopal, *Patna in the Nineteenth Century*, Calcutta, 1982, p. 25.
87. Ibid.
88. See J.C. Jha, 'Political Consciousness in Bihar before the Formation of Indian National Congress', in P.N. Ojha (ed.), *History of Indian National Congress in Bihar, 1885-1985*, Patna, 1985, p. 10. It was in 1880 that Syed Sharfuddin and Syed Nurul Hudda passed the Bar-at-Law. See the *Bihar Bandhu*, 19 February 1880.
89. *Report on the Administration of Bengal, 1876-77*, p. 359.
90. Keshav Ram Bhatta, *Sajjad Sumbul* (Hindi), Calcutta, 1904 (rpt.).
91. *RPI Bengal, 1869-70*, Appendix A, pp. 178-9.
92. Bengal General (Education) A Progs, May 1872, nos. 91-4.
93. See *Report on the Administration of Bengal, 1879-80*, Calcutta, 1880, p. 52.
94. 'Annual Report of Anglo-Vernacular School, Madhubani, 1876-7', in J.S. Jha, *Beginnings of Modern Education in Mithila*, Patna, 1972, p. 39.

95. Jha, *Education in Bihar*, p. 5.
96. *RPI Bengal, 1869-70*, Appendix A, pp. 143-4.
97. Ibid., *1871-72*, Appendix A, p. 290.
98. Ibid., Appendix A, pp. 229-30. It is interesting to note that in 1871-2 in Patna College, the number of Bengali boys was 40 as compared to 37 Biharis. See ibid., Appendix A, p. 447. The people of Bihar were termed as Hindustanis at this time. The term 'Bihari' was not yet used on a large scale.
99. See ibid., Appendix A, pp. 325-56.
100. See *RPI Bengal, for 1881-82*, p. 106. In that year the school had 93 students coming from as many as nine districts.
101. Calculated from *RPI Bengal*, *1871-72*, Appendix A.
102. See Chapter 4 of this book.
103. Bengal General (Education) A Progs, August 1899, nos. 28-34.
104. See *Report on the Administration of the Territories now included in the Province of Bihar and Orissa, 1911-12*, Patna, 1913, p. IX.
105. I have discussed about them in later chapters.
106. Seal, *The Emergence of Indian Nationalism*, p. 123.
107. S. Gopal, 'Socio-Cultural Contours of Patna at the Turn of the Present Century', in Q. Ahmad (ed.), *Patna Through the Ages*, Delhi, 1988, pp. 127-8.
108. B.B. Misra, *The Indian Middle Classes: Their Growth in Modern Times*, London, 1961; Delhi, 1978, pp. 324-5.
109. Gopal, 'Socio-Cultural Contours of Patna at the Turn of the Present Century', pp. 127-9. Patni was a subordinate land tenure in Bengal, first formally recognized in 1819. See Seal, *The Emergence of Indian Nationalism*, p. 377.
110. *Report on the Census of the District of Monghyr*, *1891*, p. 17 (no other details).
111. Misra, *The Indian Middle Classes*, p. 173.
112. *RPI Bengal, 1871-72*, Appendix A, pp. 481-2.
113. Pandey, *Education and Social Changes in Bihar*, p. 33.
114. In the year 1870 while 41 and 219 candidates appeared for senior and junior pleadership examination respectively in the Bengal Presidency, the Mukhtearship examination witnessed a participation of 418 examinees. In all, 28 candidates passed from different districts of Bihar and going by their names, 26 appear to be Biharis. Two years later 87 passed this examination from Bihar districts. Again going by their names most appear to be Biharis. See Bengal Judicial A Progs, May 1870, nos. 51-3 and Bengal Judicial A Progs, April 1872, nos. 72-5.
115. Bengal General (Education) A Progs, May 1872, nos. 91-4.

116. Bengal Judicial A Progs, April 1872, nos. 72-5.
117. See Misra, *The Indian Middle Classes*, pp. 329-30.
118. *Report on the Census of the District of Monghyr*, 1891, p. 12.
119. Misra, *The Indian Middle Classes*, p. 330.
120. See Chapters 5 and 6.
121. See Chapter 6.
122. See the Compiled Volume of the *Presidential Addresses Delivered at the Beharee Students' Conference (1906-1923)*, compiled by B.N. Sinha, Patna, 1931, pt. I, pp. 35-7.
123. Pandey, *Education and Social Changes in Bihar*, p. 172.
124. See Annual Return of Presses worked and Newspapers published thereat in the Bengal Presidency in *Reports on the Administration of Bengal for 1887-88, 1888-89* and *1889-90*.
125. See Bhatta, *Sajjad Sumbul.*
126. A report by Patna Commissioner reveals the strong presence of Muslims in government employment in different districts of the division in the 1880s. In Patna district where the Muslims constituted only about one-sixth of the Hindu population they held one-third of the government jobs. In Gaya district with the population slightly greater than one-tenth of the total population they held half of the government posts. Similar situation existed in other districts, too. See Bengal General (Education) A Progs, October 1886, nos. 31-5.
127. See *The Beharee*, 17 November 1911.

CHAPTER 3

Colonial Construction

We opened this study by noting the crucial change, which took place in the last three decades of the nineteenth century and first decade of the twentieth century, in the way the people of Bihar were seen and categorized. The present chapter examines at length the role of the colonial government in the entire process, which made possible the transformation of the people of Bihar from being just 'Hindustanis', like millions of others spread across a large part of the country, into a distinct 'Bihari' community. It is argued that the evolving perceptions of and growing knowledge about Bihar and its people as also politico-administrative considerations led the colonial rulers to take a series of measures, which contributed to this making of 'Biharis'. Though there was no systematic or calculated process of social engineering at work in Bihar and many of the important decisions were taken, as would become clear later in the chapter, after much disputation and discussion within the bureaucracy with personal views and prejudices of officials playing no mean role in the decision-making process, the end result was both profound and permanent, for it not only influenced peoples' perception of their own selves but also served to define what constituted 'Bihar'.

The fact that colonial policies were so firmly anchored on the rulers' knowledge of Bihar was not surprising. India came under British control at a time when Britain and other European states were experimenting with new forms of exercise of power in which knowledge of and about the people played a critical role. The state became more and more interventionist and there was a great expansion of what Bernard Cohn has termed 'officializing procedures' which both established and added to their capacity to intervene, regulate and govern. Control was now established by counting and classifying people through census, by standardizing languages and scripts, by fostering certain beliefs and other devices. Investigations by Commissions, surveys and their reports, gazetteers, statistical reports and histories, all encapsulating knowledge of a particular kind, were meant to facilitate control over people, in other words, were projects of power. India, the largest colony of the British empire, witnessed the full play of these technologies of rule, for knowledge of the subject race was expected to make their management both easy and profitable.[1]

Though the process of acquisition of knowledge about India, Bihar included, acquired a new momentum in the post-Revolt (of 1857) period when there was a special emphasis on administration[2] and the government began carrying out census, feeling the urgent need, as the Government of India made clear in a letter to the Bengal government at the time of the first census of 'having in our possession full and complete statistics of the people in the most extensive province of British India in an administrative, political as well as scientific point of view',[3] the process had started much earlier, and Bihar's 'discovery' was an outcome of this. With this was initiated the process of colonial construction of Bihar.

THE 'DISCOVERY' OF BIHAR

It began in the very same year (1765) in which the British gained the Diwani of Bengal, Bihar and Orissa. James Rennel, a naval officer turned surveyor, was assigned the task of making a general survey of the newly-acquired territories.[4]

A hugely momentous step was taken in the same direction when Francis Buchanan was asked by the East India Company to enquire into the commercial and agricultural conditions of the province as also to report on aspects of society.[5] The survey was conducted in the second decade of the nineteenth century and yielded copious information not only on the commercial and economic conditions of the region but also on its history, legends and antiquities.[6] It was followed by different gazetteers prepared in the course of the nineteenth century.

The East India Gazetteer (1828) referred to Bahar (Bihar) as a large province situated between 22° and 27° of North latitude and clearly included Palamau, Ramgarh and Chota Nagpur in Bihar.

The major towns referred to were Patna, Chapra, Bhagalpur, Monghyr, Gaya and Muzaffarpur.[7] The *Gazetteer* went on to say, 'In a remote era of Hindu history as conveyed down by their mythological legends Bahar (Bihar) appears to have been the seat of two independent sovereignties, Magadha and Mithila.'[8]

A Gazetteer of the Territories under the Government of East India Company (1858) referred to Bihar as being a great suba of the Mughal Empire, talked about the great history of Magadha, which was treated as being identical with Bihar.[9]

Thus, while the geographical limits of Bihar were being defined, the history of Magadha and Mithila was being appropriated, too, in the name of Bihar. By 1870s Bihar was seen as consisting of Patna and Bhagalpur Divisions,[10] and peopled by Hindustanis.[11]

Interestingly, the areas of Chota Nagpur Division continued to move in and out of the colonial political geography of Bihar. In 1787, James Grant, chief sheristadar, writing about Ramgarh district mentioned that it formed part of the 'Suba Behar'.[12] Colonial authorities continued to hold the same view in the early nineteenth century as becomes evident from Hamilton's *Gazetteer* as we have seen above. Even in the beginning of the twentieth century, it was claimed that Chota Nagpur 'was included in Behar when the Diwani of that province, Bengal and Orissa were ceded by the Nawab'.[13] However, in the 1870s and later decades, Chota Nagpur was presented as a distinct entity[14] by the colonial authorities even though they maintained that it had many things in common with Bihar.[15]

One striking feature of the colonial construction of Bihar was an attempt to emphasize the similarities of the people of Bihar with those of the North-Western Provinces (present Uttar Pradesh) and their dissimilarities from the people of Bengal. These two themes were successively emphasized in official observations and reports.

While describing the population in the Lower Provinces of Bengal, one report recognized four distinct groups or races. While the Bengalis were seen as unwarlike and physically a feeble race,[16] about Hindustani races who were seen as inhabiting Bihar and adjacent plateaus, it was said: 'The races of Behar resemble people of Oudh and North-Western Provinces in many respects, many of them are physically fine men of the Aryan type, they are not unwarlike.'[17]

This view continued to find many articulations. The Lieutenant-Governor of Bengal, Sir George Campbell (1871-4) observed at one place, 'Behar is a country very different from Bengal, and inhabited by a people extremely different. All the official business and habitudes necessarily much differ.'[18]

As the government became more and more aware of Bihar's distinctiveness and its needs, the stage was set for a more interventionist role by it in its affairs. The signal that the days of old *laissez faire* policy were to be abandoned was given when the government chose George Campbell to be appointed as the Lieutenant-Governor of Bengal.[19]

His appointment was a departure from the tradition[20] in that he had not served much in Bengal, having spent most of the service career in the North-West Provinces and the Central Provinces.[21] Probably this fact also ensured that he would not be Bengal-centric in his approach[22] though it is difficult to accept the view that he had a natural antipathy for Bengal and Bengalis as a leading Bengali newspaper the *Amrita Bazar Patrika* claimed even before he had joined his post.[23] Under the administration of Campbell, a Benthamite and an 'enlightened paternalist aiming at the greatest happiness of the greatest number',[24] two important decisions were taken regarding Bihar. The first was regarding the introduction of Hindi as the vernacular language to be taught in schools in Patna and Bhagalpur Divisions and also to be used for certain official purposes. This decision contributed to the linguistic homogenization of Bihar through the medium of Hindi. The second decision was to reserve certain jobs in Bihar for the natives of that province, which significantly contributed to the making of a Bihari community.

INTRODUCTION OF HINDI: TOWARDS LINGUISTIC HOMOGENEITY

Hindi in Schools

Campbell's first decision regarding the introduction of Hindi as the vernacular language was basically motivated by a desire that a simple language, the 'real vernacular' as he termed it, should be taught in the schools in Bihar in place of the language then in use. The issue of language used in schools had cropped up in the very first year of his tenure (1871). It was in the course of a tour of Bihar districts that he discovered that Persian, although abolished as an official language long back, continued to flourish both in the public offices and schools in Bihar in the form of Urdu.[25] The teaching of this language in schools, which he found to be greatly 'artificial' and 'debased' one, meant its perpetuation and, hence, Campbell struck at the root itself, and decided to abolish it.

He, accordingly, ordered 'Urdu is absolutely abolished in all our schools and all our teaching'.[26] The Director of Public Instruction and the Inspector of Schools were held strictly responsible for ensuring that no book which was not in 'real and genuine vernacular' language was used in their schools.[27] However, it was not made immediately clear as to what this 'real vernacular' was. Hindi as the 'real vernacular' could be introduced in 1872 only, in the face of some opposition by the officials of the Education Department who believed that Campbell's decision to do away with the Urdu language was not proper. The opposition was first articulated by the Inspector of Schools in Bihar, S.W. Fallon, who pointed to the widespread use of Urdu. It was the language, he maintained, '*spoken in every town and village in Upper and Central India, Behar included*'[28] (emphasis in original). He argued that 'hybrid artificial' Urdu continued to flourish in Bihar and was taught in schools because of its use in official proceedings, which obliged people to learn it because their rights and interests were recorded and disposed of in this language. People also learnt it for the sake of lucrative appointments in the Amlah (class) and for the money to be made in the local bar. He, therefore, suggested the reform of the Urdu of the statute book and of courts as the prelude towards the reform of the Urdu (Hindustani) of the schools.[29] The Director of Public Instruction in Bengal, W.S. Atkinson, largely seconded the views of Fallon. While he too considered Urdu to be a hybrid language, yet he maintained, it was alike the language of books and newspapers, which were written, bought and read by the people and hence presumably had their approval. He felt that what was required, therefore, was its simplification rather than abolition.[30]

However, brushing aside all these arguments and suggestions Campbell decided to introduce Hindi in the government schools in Bihar. The decision taken in 1872 acknowledged and established Hindi as the 'real vernacular' of Bihar. The Bengal government orders maintained that there was a tendency to convert all upper and middle class schools in Bihar to the teaching of a high-flown Hindustani or Urdu language fitted to make the boys law agents and petition writers rather than useful members of society.[31] Teaching of Hindi was obviously aimed at remedying this state of affair.

The government orders which were to be applicable to the Patna and Bhagalpur Divisions made it clear that in every government school, Hindi was to be taught and 'efficiently taught'. The Headmasters were made responsible for due compliance with this order. It was unambiguously said that no Hindu boy was to be taught Hindustani in any government school till he had acquired facility in Hindi and no Hindu boy from aided or private school was to be admitted to any government scholarship, stipend, etc., unless he was similarly qualified.[32]

Further, in all primary schools, except in *maktabs*, no 'character' other than Hindi was to be taught on any pretext. Even in middle class and model schools, all instruction was to be given in general subjects up to the vernacular scholarship standard in Hindi and only those Muslim boys who had not learnt the Hindi character were allowed to use the Persian character.[33]

The orders were both comprehensive and of a forceful nature. By indirectly covering the private and aided schools in their ambit, they tried to ensure that Hindi would not face much challenge from Urdu. Campbell had taken the first critical step in establishing Hindi as the vernacular language of Bihar but its march to emerge as the undisputed language of standard speech and writing ran into difficulty very soon. Dismayed by the unpopularity of vernacular schools, the Inspector of Schools, Bihar, A.W. Croft, suggested the reintroduction of Hindustani (Urdu) in government schools for those who wanted to learn it. He attributed the unpopularity of these schools to the fact that they taught Hindi while for jobs in courts and offices, the language continued to be Urdu.[34] However; his efforts did not yield the desired result as his suggestion was opposed both by Bhagalpur and Patna Division Commissioners. The Commissioner of Bhagalpur Division commenting on Croft's suggestion favoured the continued teaching of Hindi in all schools below the highest level where he suggested that Persian alphabet should be taught.[35] The Patna Commissioner went further, took strong exception to the suggestion that schools were proving unpopular as their education did not fit people for court appointments, argued that education needed to have more legitimate goals like ending ignorance and enabling people for other occupations and ended up suggesting that the great mass of people needed to be instructed in Nagari, while in certain villages Persian could be taught.[36]

The Bengal government finally made it clear that it stood by the earlier decision that the use of Hindi character was to be encouraged though it was not to be made the exclusive language of either the schools or the courts in Bihar.[37]

However, as the years wore on and Hindi began to find more and more space in offices and courts, the opposition to it began to fade and its opponents, especially the Muslims, began coming to terms with the new situation. A government report of 1881 gleefully noted that the Muslim pupils of Bihar readily attended the Hindi classes in the Zila Schools, as in Bihar a knowledge of Hindi was of much more practical value than a knowledge of Urdu. In the *pathsalas*, too, Hindi was studied by the Muslims and Hindus to the exclusion of Urdu, the only difference being that the former showed a preference for the Kaithi and the latter for the Devanagari character. The report pointed out that of the 158 Muslim boys examined in the Patna district 109 were reading Hindi and not Urdu.[38]

By this time Hindi had also found a firm place in offices and courts in Bihar and to this story we must now turn.

Hindi in Courts and Offices

People have traditionally studied the languages which have helped them in gaining their livelihood. No wonder, the question of the language to be used in schools and that in the courts and offices got inextricably interlinked from the very beginning of Campbell's administration. In his drive towards the introduction of a simple language Campbell had also issued orders, at the time of the abolition of Urdu in schools, that public officials would allow nothing but real vernacular to be used in their offices except where English was used.[39] The cooperation of the High Court had also been sought in giving effect to the Lieutenant-Governor's view.[40] However, as we have seen above, what the real vernacular was, had been left undefined. It was only in 1872 that Campbell reached a definite conclusion on the subject.

That year the Government of India had asked for the introduction of Hindi language and character in those districts of the Central Provinces in which Persian character was used.[41] Campbell felt that so far as the language was concerned the position of the Bihar districts was similar to that of the Hindustani districts of the Central Provinces, Hindi being the universal language of the ordinary people while Hindustani was generally understood by the educated classes and used in courts and offices.[42]

In reaching this conclusion Campbell seems to have been guided by his experience in the Central Provinces where he had earlier served as the Chief Commissioner.[43] He decided that while the Persian script was to be retained for regular office work, the processes notifications and proclamations, etc., were to be issued in Hindi in the Nagari script. Thus, Nagari script found a place in the offices of the Patna and Bhagalpur Divisions. It was also made compulsory for all amla and superior officers of police to learn, within six months, to read with facility the Nagari printed character, failing which they were to be dismissed from service.[44] Such rigorous orders meant that all those who sought appointment in such offices were obliged to learn Hindi.

In a parallel, though far more smooth movement, Hindi was introduced in the Chota Nagpur Division, too, which contributed later to its inclusion in Bihar. Certain historical factors were at work, which ensured this smooth introduction of Hindi there. The Christian missionaries working there had chosen Hindi as the link language. They not only translated many religious texts into it but also taught it in their schools and even conducted church services in it in the Hazaribagh district.[45]

In the Singhbhum district all the rural documents were in Hindi and only a few mukhtears and dealers of tussar silk understood Bengali.[46] In 1837 in the Lohardagga and Hazaribagh districts it was decided that proceedings should be in Hindi and Nagari script but the courts relapsed to Urdu later. It was in the background of such wide prevalence of Hindi language that in 1862 itself, Colonel Dalton, the Commissioner of Chota Nagpur Division, had pleaded to the government that Urdu be discontinued and Hindi introduced in Chota Nagpur as people were accustomed to it. Though his request was not granted at that time but in 1867 Nagari script was introduced in place of the Arabic script in the Singhbhum district.[47] Hindi thus became the language of the courts and offices in Singhbhum much before it had attained this position elsewhere in Bihar.[48] However, finally in 1872, the Commissioner of Chota Nagpur Division was authorized to introduce Hindi in Nagari in the Hazaribagh and Lohardagga districts in the same way as was done in the case of Patna and Bhagalpur Divisions (for use in processes, notifications, proclamations, etc.) even though he was against the retention of Persian character for regular office writing, petitions, etc.[49]

Thus far the battle for or against Hindi had been fought only in the official circles, but once the decision to use it, though for limited purposes, had been taken, people began articulating their support or opposition to the decision. For some people the introduction of Hindi was the fulfilment of a long-felt need. No wonder, people in the Purnea district expressed the greatest satisfaction when informed about this decision. It was true that they had earlier shown preference for Urdu but it was done 'not only with the view to obtaining appointments in the police and other departments under government but also for their own protection'. Now of course, they were reluctant to learn it (Urdu).[50]

For the people in the Saran district it was a boon. In his annual report, the Magistrate wrote

> There is no doubt that the Persian character is as a sealed book to the mass of the people, and that its official use not only denies to all but a limited class the entry into the public service but also debars the people from the possibility of transacting their own business in our courts, even if so inclined.[51]

For the people of Chota Nagpur Division too, the decision was nothing less than a 'boon'.[52]

However, such an important measure was not likely to go unopposed. From the very beginning, the Patna Commissioner anticipated opposition. He felt 'It is accepted as a great boon by the rural classes but it cannot fail to be a thorn on the side of Mahomedans and of the old Amlah classes and these have still a good deal to do with the fashioning of European opinion.'[53] Soon a campaign was started to get it annulled. A number of petitions were submitted to the government in the name of the people of Bihar requesting revocation of the orders regarding the use of Hindi in Nagari script in the government offices and courts.[54] On the other hand, resurgent supporters of Hindi began to pray for the exclusive recognition of Hindi in Nagari script as the court and official language of Bihar. In a powerfully argued petition-cum- pamphlet, some residents of Patna and Bhagalpur tried to show the superiority of Hindi language and Nagari script over the Hindustani language and the Persian script and thus persuade the government to accept their demand.[55] The Patna Commissioner, S.C. Bayley, in a power-packed letter supported the petitioners' view that Nagari should be gradually introduced into the courts and offices, as it was the language of the people. He maintained that Nagari had been extensively introduced in the districts of Patna Division though the change was 'steadily opposed by this class of people who, as Kyests and Mussalmans, have almost a monopoly of the court language, and consequently of the court places'. He was emphatic 'Why the courts should continue to use an absolutely artificial language (Hindustani/Urdu), which has to counterbalance all its disadvantages, only one advantage of being more rapidly written, and more easily miswritten and misread, I cannot understand.' But A.W. Croft, the Inspector of Schools, opposed the proposal of the petitioners, drawing attention to the political danger in totally replacing Urdu by Hindi as it was likely to generate the disaffection of a class of men whose means of living were too scanty. He was emphatic that the Muslims would be ousted from public employment if Urdu was completely replaced. Eventually the Lieutenant-Governor of Bengal, Sir Richard Temple, in general concurring with the view of A.W. Croft, refused to accept the petitioners' demand.[56]

However, other steps were taken to give effect to the existing orders on the use of Hindi. In 1875 the Calcutta High Court was requested to issue orders for the issue of processes and acceptance of petitions in Nagari.[57] The most decisive step in creating linguistic unity at the level of official language was taken in 1880 by the Lieutenant-Governor, Sir Ashley Eden, when he made Nagari (or Kaithi) the character for exclusive use in official documents.[58] The provision was to come into effect from 1 January 1881 throughout Patna Division and some districts of Bhagalpur Division.[59] The orders were passed in the background of the Patna Commissioner F.M. Halliday's report to the Bengal government in March 1880 that Hindi was never made the exclusive court language and half-hearted measures were responsible for its unsatisfactory progress. This report proved crucial in bringing the government round to the view that drastic measures were required to introduce Hindi and the Nagari in the courts and offices.[60] Later the orders were extended to the Chota Nagpur Division,[61] where they were to apply to all the courts and offices in the districts of Lohardagga, Hazaribagh and Singhbhum with the exception of Dhalbhum Pargana. All assistants examined after 1 January 1881 were to be required to read documents in the Nagari character and not in Urdu.[62] By the orders issued in April 1880, the police officers and amlas were given warning that if they could not read and write the Nagari script by the above date they would have to make room for those who could.[63]

The Government of Bengal at the same time sought the co-operation of the High Court in enforcing orders of the exclusive use of Nagari script in all official documents in Bihar. The High Court lost no time in issuing a circular for the information and guidance of all District Judges and their subordinates regarding the introduction of Nagari.[64]

With this decision the process of establishing Hindi as the official language of Bihar came to an end. Ashley Eden finished what Campbell had begun. The decision was received with jubilation by a large section of the population and the Lieutenant-Governor, Ashley Eden, was showered with praise during his tour of Bihar.[65] Even more interesting is the fact that the government decision was so much appreciated in some localities that they became subjects of popular ballads.[66] Two songs popular in the Shahabad districts were:

I

Thanks to the English Government, which confers comforts on its subjects. It has put far away the Persian character, and introduced Nagari. Bhudeb Baboo called out to the Lord Sahib (saying) 'put far away the Persian character, and thereby put far away a grievance'. My Lord, many forgeries are committed through it, and the people will be happy when they obtain their own (peculiar) learning. O! brother praise the wisdom, learning and counsel which has done justice in Hindustani by introducing the character of its people.

II

Government gave the order, O! people learn Nagari. Put the Persian character far from your hearts, Learn Nagari, and when you are qualified do government work. Take books and read steadily, but sell your Persian ones to the druggists. Until you know Nagari well write Kaithi in your kachahris. Praise be to the counsellers who are well wishers of the people.[67]

The supporters of Urdu had not yet given up the fight and slowly voices of protest began to be heard. The National Muhammadan Association finally presented a memorial to the Government of India stating that nothing should be done to injure the professional prospects of Muslims by altering the court language in Bihar and pleading for the withdrawal of the orders of substituting Hindi for Urdu.[68]

The Bengal Lieutenant-Governor, however, refused to heed the plea. He held that the change had been effected without much difficulty and with much advantage to the public in general. It was pointed out that a new class of amla and legal practitioners acquainted with Hindi was emerging and all subordinate officials and law agents had some knowledge of Hindi. The Government of Bengal felt that:

There is a reason to believe that this outcry against the use of Hindi in Behar is rather a matter of factitious sentiment than of practical inconvenience. It is far louder among the Mahomedans of Calcutta who are not affected by the change than among the supposed sufferers.[69]

It was made clear that the change was the logical outcome of that excusive Hindi teaching which had prevailed for nearly ten years with such marked success in all the primary schools, *pathsalas* and vernacular schools of Bihar, the institutions from which the subordinate official class, on whose behalf this outcry was raised were recruited. Defending the government policy it was asserted that its aim has been 'to secure the greatest good of the greatest number, and to establish equal rights among all its subjects'.[70]

The decision of the government to introduce Hindi in schools and courts did not mean the setting or fixing of a literary standard language. It merely created the conditions and possibility for it. The task was to a great extent performed by the creation of a new series of textbooks. It was at this level that actual attempts were made at the creation of a copious, rich and harmonious language. The language of the books to be taught or used in schools had assumed importance since Campbell's Minute of 1871.[71] It had been made clear by the officials of the Bengal Education Department that Urdu books were highly Persianized, while the Hindi books were Sanskritized.[72] The problem, however, went deeper. Not only was there a paucity of suitable books but also in private schools no vernacular books were read. In fact, the very teaching of vernacular was a novelty especially abhorrent to maulvis and pandits.[73] To remedy the situation, S.W. Fallon, the Inspector of Schools, proposed the collection of materials for the compilation of suitable books in the mothertongue of natives of Bihar. He held that the Hindi literature of living speech, at once intelligible, popular and authoritative, could thus be created. He himself proposed to collect folk songs, proverbs, etc., from Magahi, Bhojpuri and Maithili.[74]

The government now took active steps for the preparation of textbooks in Hindi. The Lieutenant-Governor directed the Director of Public Instruction in March 1873 that Divisional Committees should be appointed in Bihar to consider and decide upon new books. One such committee was appointed by the Commissioner of Patna.[75] Finally in 1880-1 a Bihar Text-Book Committee was constituted for the examination and selection of textbooks for use in schools of Bihar.[76] It is important to note that even in the preparation of textbooks in Hindi, anti-Bengali sentiments were visible. In the 1880s the Education Commission noted while referring to the issue of textbook preparation that:

Although Hindi and Bengali are cognate languages, and translations from Bengali into Hindi are almost as easy as into Uriya, yet the Hindi-speaking people despise the less physically robust Bengali, and there is some reluctance on the part of the Behari to follow in the footsteps of his Bengali neighbour.[77]

Bhudev Mukherjee, a Bengali, who came as the Inspector of Schools in Bihar in 1875 encouraged a host of writers to prepare textbooks in Hindi. He also inspired Babu Ramdeen Singh to establish a press to bring out textbooks in Hindi. Ramdeen Singh not only established a press but also wrote *Bihar Darpan*, a biography of some great personalities of Bihar.[78] A number of textbooks were prepared which contributed to the evolution of Hindi as a standard language in Bihar.

The government also tried to promote the language through the publication of a Hindi Gazette. Again the idea was first mooted by George Campbell. He believed that the Government Urdu Gazette published from Allahabad did not meet the requirements of the majority of about 20 million people of Patna, Bhagalpur and Chota Nagpur Divisions as Hindi happened to be their mother tongue and they were not conversant with the character (Persian) in which it was written. He wanted the 'great province' of Bihar to have its own official organ, published at its capital (Patna) and under the orders of its own civil and educational officers.[79] The Patna Commissioner responded positively.[80] Though great hopes were generated,[81] the Gazette could not be started immediately due to certain difficulties, though its need continued to be felt. *The Bengal Administration Report, 1875-76* said, 'The establishment of a Gazette, composed in the Hindi language and printed in the Nagari character has long been a desideratum in Behar'.[82] The Bengal Lieutenant-Governor, Richard Temple, the successor of Campbell, too, believed that the publication of a Hindi Gazette would be greatly conducive to the spread of Hindi learning and would be a powerful educational engine. The report added, 'This is a patent consideration at the present time, when the government is trying to elevate the heretofore low condition of education in Behar.'[83] Finally with much rejoicing the *Behar Gazette* composed in Hindi and printed in Nagari was started from 1 January 1877,[84] from Patna[85] under the editorship of Rai Sohan Lal, Headmaster of the Patna Normal School.[86]

Hindi by the 1880s was finding a wide acceptance. The initial decisions regarding the use of Hindi in schools, courts and offices were taken under a belief that it was the vernacular of the large majority of people in Bihar[87] and people were obliged to learn Urdu only because it was the language in which official business was conducted. Later experiences largely confirmed the initial belief, and from 1881 it (Hindi) was made the exclusive language (so far as the vernaculars were concerned) to be used in courts and offices.

The decision of introducing Hindi helped in its evolution as a standard language in which to exchange ideas. Significantly the decision was taken at a time when education was making very good progress in Bihar and students could thus read similar texts, which helped them to become familiar with the standard language and attain proficiency in it.

The language policy of the government seemed to threaten the harmonious relation between the Hindus and Muslims, but since many Hindus also sided with the Muslims in demanding the retention of Urdu, the battle of the languages could not assume a communal colour. By the 1880s the Muslims were coming to terms with the changed situation. The growth of an over-arching regional identity was not threatened because the appeals for Urdu, too, were being made in the name of people of Bihar. And this was also the time when the people of Bihar (Biharis) as a group were working to fight the perceived domination of Bengalis in government service.

The policy of the government served to integrate even more firmly the Patna, Bhagalpur and Chota Nagpur Divisions linguistically. It was later to provide the leaders, demanding separation from Bengal, a very firm ground on which to demand separation of entire Bihar including Chota Nagpur and the government a very good reason to grant their wish. No wonder at the time of separation, Bihar was to include Chota Nagpur Division.

EMPLOYMENT POLICY: CREATION OF A 'BIHARI' CATEGORY

Simultaneously as Bihar was being constructed as a distinct linguistic zone, a host of considerations were obliging the colonial government to give a serious look at the principles and policies guiding recruitment to the government offices in Bihar. The resulting decisions greatly influenced the making of a Bihari political identity.

Though the system of recruitment followed by the British in India had seen a number of experiments but two dominant trends were visible most of the time. The first was the almost complete white monopoly of higher government posts, the principle being established as early as 1793 when it was officially laid down that all posts carrying a salary worth more than £500 a year were to be held by Englishmen.[88] The second feature was an increasing emphasis on the recruitment of properly qualified people and especially those having English education. The process began in 1844 with Lord Hardinge who introduced the regulation that all public services were to be filled up by an open competitive examination held by the Council of Education, preference being given to the knowledge of English.[89] The emphasis on high educational standards continued to gather strength in later years. In Bengal, from 1859, a quarter of the posts of deputy magistrates and deputy collectors were reserved for those who knew English and in 1863 it was ruled that half of the posts as munsifs, darogas and pleaders would be reserved for those who had passed the university entrance or higher examinations.[90] In 1864 the High Court ruled that all law examinations would henceforth be in English and in 1866 it was laid down that only Bachelors of Law would be eligible to become munsifs.[91]

However, despite all these measures, a very significant proportion of jobs at lower levels were still left open for people who did not always have high education. This was not to the liking of the Education Department officials, who felt that non-requirement of education for jobs made for the educational backwardness of the region. In 1861 W.S. Atkinson, the DPI of Bengal, made it clear to the Bengal government that 'As soon as a certain kind of education is known to be necessary for advancement in life, it cannot be doubted that the people of Behar will ask for it as eagerly as those of any other country.'[92] The Inspector of Schools in Bihar, S.W. Fallon, hammered the same point soon, arguing that in the province the public services continued to be the close monopoly of the uneducated. He pointed out that in the year 1861-2 out of 228 appointments to vernacular offices in the province all but four were conferred on uneducated natives.[93] It was apparent that the situation demanded remedial action. In 1869 the Lieutenant-Governor recorded a resolution which enjoined strict adherence to the rules circulated in 1865 for the selection of candidates for ministerial appointments. Through this the local officials were urged to counteract, as far as possible, the local influence which was likely to lead to the exclusion of better qualified and educated candidates in favour of those who had connections in the offices.[94]

Thus while the government was laying more and more emphasis on the selection of properly qualified candidates, preferably with English education, it was also being realized at the same time that the people who were in a disadvantaged position, so far as jobs went because of lack of proper qualifications, should be given special consideration.

The special disadvantage under which the people of Bihar suffered, was brought to the notice of the government by R.P. Jenkins, the Commissioner of Patna Division, in his annual report on the state of education in the division for 1870-1. Dwelling on the difficulties of promoting education he suggested that what was needed to encourage education among higher classes in Bihar was '*the certain prospect of employment under Government*' [95] (emphasis in original). In a state of society like that of Bihar, he observed, the advantages of education, if it was to be at all successful, must at first, and for some years, be shown to be both immediate and substantial. To supply the necessary encouragement 'I would strongly suggest that a certain number of appointments in the subordinate judicial and executive services be annually reserved for natives of Behar'. Going further he also suggested the modification of the rules under which, in filling up ministerial appointments, a preference was given to candidates possessing a knowledge of English. He noted with concern that of late it had become a practice in all the district offices to appoint Bengalis as much as possible and a similar partiality was observed in the employment of Bengalis as judges and deputy magistrates in the local courts. He felt that it was not difficult to conceive 'what effect this almost entire supersession of their own countrymen must have produced on the people of Behar'.[96] He admitted that though the more extensive employment of the people of Bihar might involve some sacrifice of administrative efficiency, 'I would still advocate such a measure'.[97]

The Commissioner thus recommended some reservation of jobs for the natives of Bihar both to encourage education among them and on grounds of political expediency. It needs to be seen that he had not yet suggested any policy of exclusion of Bengalis, though even in his presentation Bengalis were implicitly seen as not being natives of Bihar. However, the idea that the 'Bengalees, being looked upon as foreigners, should not ordinarily have Behar offices'[98] soon came to be explicitly articulated.

The Bengal government lost no time in responding to the suggestion of R.P. Jenkins and the Lieutenant-Governor of Bengal, George Campbell, was full of sympathy for the people of Bihar. While regretfully learning the state of affairs in Bihar he agreed to favourably consider the proposal of reserving a certain number of appointments. The Patna Commissioner was asked that he could with 'advantage direct that at least a certain number of probationary appointments, to ministerial posts, as they fall vacant, shall in each district of your division be given to persons who have received a good education in government or other schools.' He was also informed that 'excepting English clerks you might properly direct that no Bengalee should be employed without your special sanction on a report detailing the grounds of selection'.[99] The views of the Lieutenant-Governor were thus more in the nature of suggestions rather than firm orders but with this began the policy of exclusion of Bengalis, though it never became total and complete, as we shall see below.

Though the Bengal government expressed its difficulty to the Patna Commissioner in laying down a strict rule as regards the subordinate executive service since the service was treated as a whole, it was stated that the Lieutenant-Governor was prepared to give favourable consideration to the claims of qualified natives of Bihar and in their case the standard of qualification in English was to be relaxed. Simultaneously, with the acceptance of the view that Biharis did need special treatment in the matter of jobs, an attempt was also on to find further justification for this treatment. Now an opinion extolling the mental qualities of Biharis began to be articulated. The Lieutenant-Governor, it was made clear, while recognizing and appreciating the excellent mental qualities of the Bengalis, was not prepared to admit that the Hindustani races who inhabited Bihar fell behind in power of mind and practical efficiency, and since they succeeded in business there was no valid reason to think that they could not with advantage be largely employed in the service of government.[100]

This new and soon to be widely shared sympathy for the people of Bihar and respect for their mental qualities among the colonial officials became evident again immediately. The Government of Bengal requested the High Court of Calcutta, which controlled the appointment of munsifs to consider favourably the government proposal to reserve a certain number of appointments in the Subordinate Judicial and Executive Services for the natives of Bihar.[101]

Replying to the Bengal government letter, the Registrar of the High Court made it clear that the Court fully concurred with the Lieutenant-Governor 'as to the injustice and impolicy of systematically excluding natives of Behar from public employment in their own province'.[102] It was pointed out that owing to the nature of qualifications required in persons who were to fill judicial offices there was difficulty in

> laying down a rigid rule on the subject but that the Court would always prefer *cateris paribus* or even where qualifications are nearly balanced, to choose a Hindoostanee for service among Hindoostanees; and are not aware of any foundation for the belief which is apparently entertained in some quarters, that natives of Behar are inferior to the Bengalees in official aptitude or efficiency.[103]

Through these steps the government began the process of categorizing the 'natives of Bihar' as a distinct group of people who needed governmental support to secure jobs in an area seen as 'theirs'. These initiatives of the government began to strengthen the feeling among the people of Bihar that it was 'their' province. The ethnic solidarity of the Biharis was likely to get strengthened by some of the measures taken by the government. For instance the Lieutenant-Governor laid down rules for admission into the Subordinate Executive Service by which a candidate was required to produce a certificate as regarding his character, respectability and moral fitness. Interestingly, the certificate was to be signed by 'two gentlemen of his own nationality, resident in the district of which he is a native or where he usually resides'. Candidates who passed in Bengali only were not eligible for vacancies in Bihar.[104]

However, the colonial bureaucracy knew that despite putting some provisions in place for larger employment of Biharis they continued to be at a disadvantage under the existing system of appointment. George Campbell admitted with remarkable candour that in matters of employment the Muslims of Bihar did not have much to fear from the Bihari Hindus. The competition they had to fear

> . . . is rather that of the of the educated Bengalees, who come and get many good things. It is hardly possible that it should be otherwise, while Behar is attached to Bengal, and the administration is carried on by Bengal officers under a system under which English education and English-speaking natives have a very great advantage.[105]

No wonder, as the years wore on, with an increase in the number of educated people the clamour for protection in jobs was increasing in Bihar. During Lieutenant-Governor, Ashley Eden's tour of Bihar in 1880, the Bihari intelligentsia flooded him with requests to reserve the public employment in Bihar for the Biharis. Eden was quick to respond as he also found that the orders regarding preference being given to Bihari candidates for appointments in government offices in Bihar had been mostly disregarded in different offices. An order was issued in December 1880 directing that the orders of 1871 regarding the employment of qualified natives in Bihar in preference to Bengalis should be strictly enforced in all government and semi-government offices including those of the Commissioners', district offices, courts and police as also in the offices of different Municipalities and Road Cess Committees. Heads of many departments were requested to submit to the government a statement showing the number of vacancies which had occurred during the year, and whether they had been filled up by Bengalis or Biharis.[106]

These orders meant that Bengalis were not to be appointed in government and semi-government offices in Bihar except under special circumstances. However, the Bengalis permanently domiciled in Bihar were to be treated as natives of Bihar for the purpose of employment. The misuse of this provision was to be guarded against by excluding the sons of Bengalis who had merely accepted employment without making Bihar their homes.[107] These orders began to bear fruit soon.

In his report in 1883, the Patna Commissioner pointed out that out of 489 vacancies during the past year in the different offices of the division, 457 were filled by Biharis and 32 by Bengalis. Thus 93.4 per cent of vacancies were filled up by the natives of Bihar, while only 6.5 per cent of the appointments were given to Bengalis.[108]

This trend was to continue in later years. No wonder, the Government of Bengal was to express its satisfaction in the fact that while at one time almost all appointments in Bihar were filled up by Bengalis and were justified on the ground that suitable Bihari candidates did not come forward, it had now become possible to fill all vacancies locally, with great advantage to the efficiency of the public service as well as to the popularity of the administration. What further gladdened the hearts of colonial officials was the fact that a considerable and satisfactory proportion of those now employed were Muslims.[109]

Even later, the concern for the disadvantaged people was displayed explicitly whenever the question of recruitment to the Provincial Services cropped up. The Lieutenant-Governor of Bengal, Sir S.C. Bayley (1887-90) was emphatic while discussing this issue that it was desirable to treat Bengal, Bihar and Orissa as three separate provinces because in the existing state of education in Bihar and Orissa, the result of one competitive examination for the whole of Lieutenant-Governorship of Bengal, would be 'to exclude all Beharis and Ooriyas from the Provincial Service in their own Province'.[110]

It was repeatedly emphasized that recruitment in the Subordinate Executive Service should not only be through method of competition. In 1889 Bayley returned to the theme while discussing the issue. He felt that there was a need for introducing some comprehensive scheme of recruitment, which would take into account the essential and permanent requirements of these provinces and would provide for giving play to more than one method of selection. It was again made clear that at that time and for many coming years, the immediate effect of recruiting the Subordinate Executive Service on an exclusively competition basis

> would be to debar Muhammadans, natives of Behar and natives of Orissa from any reasonable chance of obtaining appointments. Not only this would be unfair in itself and contrary to established policy, but it would also tend to encourage feelings of race jealousy and antagonism which have already began to show themselves and which might at any time give rise to serious difficulties.[111]

The colonial employment policy immensely contributed to the making of a Bihari consciousness. The initial attempts to give preference to the natives of Bihar in jobs in the region were mainly motivated by a desire to promote education there. Very soon, however, the argument was reversed, education being promoted to make people capable of getting employment. That was the reason why higher classes in the Patna College were not abolished in 1872. By the 1880s, although it was articulated in 1870s also, the government had also become apprehensive that if disadvantaged sections of the society were not given special consideration in matters of employment especially in the areas of which they were the natives, it would cause trouble to the government in future. Thus to forestall any such eventuality from taking place it was necessary to placate them in advance.

Though the actions of the government could be seen as being a clever ploy to divide two regional communities (Bengalis and Biharis) but a sincere desire to give the Biharis a fair share of jobs in their region was the major guiding factor behind their actions. It was clearly understood by the officials that the people of Bihar suffered in matters of employment because they were unequal to the Bengalis in the English language and English education. This inequality was the creation of the colonial rule and it was they who could mitigate its negative consequences.

These actions and attitudes of the government encouraged the people to plead for the effective implementation of its decisions and at times forced the government to accede to their requests. In the process and because of this they came together to struggle. This was to contribute substantially to their growth as a distinct political community.

IMPROVEMENT IN THE MEANS OF COMMUNICATION

Simultaneously with these measures the colonial rule was also taking energetic measures in the second half of the nineteenth century to improve the communication system in Bihar which was to prove of great significance in the making of a Bihari political community. A number of scholars have drawn attention to the role played by the modern means of communication in the process of modernization and consolidation of people into nations and suggested that it was not a mere accident that the nineteenth century, the century of the invention of modern means of communication such as railways, steamships, post and telegraph, was also the century of emerging nationalism. These along with improved roads ensured that distances would shrink and localism would fade away.[112] The construction especially of railway lines, which offered both reliability and speed, and the roads to serve them

> resulted in a crash program(me) of national integration of unparalleled scope and effectiveness; a program(me) that could operate on this scale only because, for the first time, economic and technological conditions offered the possibility for radical cultural change. Before culture altered significantly, material circumstances had to alter; and the role of road and rail in this transformation was basic.[113]

It is not surprising then that the growth of regional consciousness in Bihar coincided with the coming of the railways.

During the medieval period and even till the first half of the nineteenth century, rivers which were the 'highroad in eastern India' and roads constituted the only means of communication in Bihar. In the dry season, carts laden with goods took 35 days to reach Agra from Patna and postal messages took a fortnight to reach the same place. In the entire eastern India there was heavy dependence on river transport especially for transport of goods.[114] Obviously in such a state of communication, growth of modern consciousness was extremely difficult. Even those roads that existed were in a poor state in the early nineteenth century as most probably from 1793 the maintenance of roads was badly neglected. It is no wonder that Francis Buchanan reporting in the early years of the nineteenth century deprecated the poor state of communication in the Patna district and was constrained to comment about roads 'I have seen no other country, where so little attention has been paid to this important subject.'[115] However, during the last quarter of the nineteenth century and early years of the twentieth-century communications received the attention of both the government and the District Boards in Bihar. The amount spent on road building and road repairing was considerable and many culverts and bridges were constructed.[116] However, it was the coming of the railway that was to revolutionize the whole scene.

The opening of the East Indian Railway, the main line of which passed through Bihar, was to prove very important for the purpose of transportation. In 1862, the main line of this Railway was extended to the Patna district[117] and Monghyr.[118] Seventeen years later (in 1879) Patna-Gaya Railway was also started.[119] By 1872 Bhagalpur district had been very well connected by this network with stations at Bhagalpur, Sultanganj and some other places.[120] An extensive railway network was created in northern Bihar too. In an extraordinary display of grit and determination 53 miles of temporary railway line was laid from Champa Ghat opposite the Barh Railway Station to Darbhanga in 53 days in 1874 as a measure of relief.[121] The Tirhut State Railway expanded rapidly. It had 46 miles open for traffic in 1876,[122] which went up to 227 miles by 1885 and 329 miles by 1891, a seven fold increase in a span of fifteen years. Lines extended from Muzaffarpur to Hajipur-Sonepur-Pahleza Ghat (opposite Patna), to Samastipur-Darbhanga-Jhanjharpur and also to Motihari and Bettiah. One line extended from Darbhanga to Sitamarhi.[123] The Tirhut State Railway thus extended in three directions throughout the most populous districts of north Bihar.[124]

By the middle of the 1890s the Commissioner of Patna Division was to note with satisfaction that 'Every district in the Division is penetrated by at least one line of railway, and the great rivers and innumerable roads admirably supplement the work of railways'.[125]

The British rule thus laid the foundation of establishing communication unity in Bihar. People could move faster and in greater numbers and they did. In 1882-3, the number of people who travelled on the Tirhut State Railway was 491,661 while on the Patna-Gaya Railway 624,238 people travelled.[126] In 1884-5, the number of people who travelled on the Tirhut State Railway was 881,889,[127] an increase of 100 per cent in a span of two years. Unfortunately in the *Report* for 1890-1 the figures of the number of passengers in the Tirhut State Railway and Bengal and North-Western Railway were merged and later *Reports* stopped giving any statistical figures altogether,[128] hence we do not know precisely how much increase in traffic took place in later years but it is safe to assume that the momentum of the early years must have continued. At the beginning of the twentieth century, north and south Bihar were linked by steamer services on the Ganges.[129] The number of post offices too rapidly increased. In 1884-5 while 490 post offices existed in Bihar their number went up to 514 the next year.[130] Without this improvement in communication, the social and political mobilization that took place in Bihar in the 1890s and thereafter would not have been possible.

NOTES

1. See Bernard S. Cohn, 'Introduction', in *Colonialism and Its Forms of Knowledge: The British in India*, New Delhi, 1997, pp. 2-5. Also see Nicholas B. Dirks' 'Foreword' in the same text.
2. S. Gopal, *British Policy in India, 1858-1905*, Cambridge, 1965; Madras, 1984, p. IX.
3. India Home (Public) A Progs, February 1871, no. 4.
4. Cohn, *Colonialism and Its Forms of Knowledge*, p. 7.
5. Francis Buchanan, *An Account of the Districts of Bihar and Patna in 1811-1812*, in 2 vols., 1st edn., Patna, 1934, rpt., New Delhi, 1986, vol. I, p. 2.
6. A study of accounts of different districts prepared by Buchanan at once makes clear the wide range of subjects covered by him.
7. W. Hamilton, *The East India Gazetteer* (1828), vol. 1, rpt., Delhi, 1984, pp. 102-5.
8. Ibid., p. 106.
9. E. Thornton, *A Gazetteer of the Territories under the Government of East India Company*, 1858, rpt., Delhi, 1984, pp. 83-4.
10. *Report on the Administration of Bengal, 1872-73*, Calcutta, 1873, p. 90. In the Education Department 'Behar Circle' included Patna and Bhagalpur Divisions. See India Home (Education) A Progs, June 1873, nos. 28-63. However, it needs to be pointed out that in 1818, Bhagalpur, Monghyr and Purnea were within the Murshidabad

Division. See B.B. Majumdar, *Indian Political Associations and Reform of Legislature (1818-1917)*, Calcutta, 1965, p. 1 fns.

11. *Reports on the Administration of Bengal* make this clear. See the *Report on the Administration of Bengal for 1871-72*, Calcutta, 1872, p. 31.
12. W.W. Hunter, *A Statistical Account of Bengal*, 20 vols., London, 1875-7; Indian rpt., Delhi, 1976, vol. XVI, p. 19.
13. F.B. Bradley-Birt, *Chota Nagpore: A Little Known Province of the Empire*, London, 1903, 2nd edn., 1910, pp. 16-17.
14. See *Report on the Administration of Bengal, 1872-73*, p. 90 where it was said, 'The Province of Behar contains the Patna and Bhagulpore Divisions. Each of the Province of Orissa, Chota Nagpore and Assam constitute a separate division'.
15. See ibid., where it said that the people of Bihar are Hindustanis and besides Bihar Proper, 'a good many are resident in the Sonthal Pergunnahs, throughout the largest districts of Chota Nagpore, they are numerous, and their language, manners and civilization, are those that prevail there as the aborigines succumb to external influences', p. 102. Hunter, too, referred to their presence in Chota Nagpur. See *SAB*, vol. XVI.
16. *Report on the Administration of Bengal, 1870-71*, Calcutta, 1872, p. 9.
17. Ibid., p. 10.
18. India Home (Public) A Progs, April, 1873, nos. 205-8.
19. See C.E. Buckland, *Bengal under the Lieutenant Governors*, vol. I, Calcutta, 1901; rpt., New Delhi, 1976, p. 484.
20. Ibid.
21. See Eric Stokes, *The English Utilitarians and India*, Oxford, 1959; Delhi, 1982, p. 331.
22. It was during Campbell's period that Assamese was introduced in local schools and law courts in Assam in place of Bengali. See Sudhir Chandra, *The Oppressive Present: Literature and Social Consciousness in Colonial India*, Delhi, 1992, p. 147. Similarly, Oriya was also recognized as the vernacular of Orissa. See *Report on Native Papers in Bengal* [henceforth *RNP(B)*], no. 38, 1873. Interestingly both the languages were fighting against the domination of the Bengali language.
23. See, *RNP(B)* unnumbered (for the week ending 26 November) 1870. The paper criticized him as a man very fond of his own opinion and strong words like 'hasty', 'dogmatic', 'crochety' and 'violent' were used to describe him.
24. See Stokes, *The English Utilitarians*, pp. 52 and 254.
25. See G. Campbell's 'Minute on the Teaching of Vernacular Languages', 4 December 1871, in Bengal General (Miscellaneous) A Progs, December 1871, nos. 17-19.

26. Ibid.
27. Ibid.
28. See the extract of a letter dated 19 January 1872 from S.W. Fallon, Inspector of Schools, N.W. Division to the DPI, Bengal in Bengal General (Education) A Progs, April 1872, nos. 32-44.
29. Ibid.
30. See letter dated 18 March 1872 from W.S. Atkinson, DPI, Bengal to the Secretary, General Deptt., Government of Bengal in ibid.
31. Bengal General (Education) A Progs, October 1872, nos. 11-13. See the letter dated 30 September 1872 from C. Bernard, Officiating Secretary, Government of Bengal to the DPI, Bengal.
32. Ibid.
33. Ibid.
34. See letter from A.W. Croft, Inspector of Schools, Bihar to the DPI, Bengal dated 10 August and Extract from Annual Report of Patna Division for 1874-5 in Bengal General (Education) A Progs, September 1875, File no. 155, Sl. nos. 1-7.
35. Extract from Commissioner's remarks on the Annual Education Report of the Bhagalpur Division for the year 1874-5 in ibid.
36. Letter from Officiating Commissioner of Patna to DPI, Bengal dated 27 August 1875, ibid.
37. See ibid.
38. *Report on the Administration of Bengal, 1880-81*, Calcutta, 1881, pp. 439-43.
39. See G. Campbell's 'Minute on the Teaching of Vernacular Languages', 4 December 1871, in Bengal General (Miscellaneous) A Progs, December 1871, nos. 17-19.
40. Ibid.
41. See in Bengal General (Education) A Progs, June 1872, no. 114. Extract from a letter from Secretary to the Government of India, Home Department, 13 May 1872.
42. Ibid.
43. See Stokes, *The English Utilitarians*, p. 331.
44. Bengal General (Education) A Progs, June 1872, no. 114 and November 1872, nos. 171-4.
45. See S. Mahto, 'Progress and Development of Language by the European Missionaries among the Tribals of Eastern India (Chota Nagpur, 1845-1918)', *Indian History Congress Proceedings Volume*, 41st Session, Bombay, 1980, pp. 740-7.
46. See L.S.S. O'Malley, *Bengal District Gazetteers, Singhbhum, Saraikela, Kharsawan,* Calcutta, 1901, p. 201.
47. See India Home (Judicial) B. Progs, June 1873, nos. 75-6.

48. *Report on Public Instruction in Bengal, 1871-72* (henceforth *RPI Bengal*), Calcutta, 1873, Appendix A, p. 396.
49. India Home (Judicial) B. Progs, June 1873, nos. 75-6, Bengal General (Education) A Progs, November 1872, nos. 171-4. and Bengal General (Education) A Progs, March 1873, File no. 39, Sl. nos. 1-2.
50. *RPI Bengal*, *1872-73,* Appendix A, p. 372.
51. See Annual General Report Patna Division 1872-73, Appendix III, p. 24 (it is the Annual Report of Saran District) in Bengal General (Miscellaneous) Progs volume for September-December 1873.
52. *Annual General Report Chota Nagpur Division for 1872-73*, p. 12 in Bengal General (Miscellaneous) Progs volume for September-December, 1873.
53. Ibid., p. 26. According to one Urdu paper, the *Akhbar-ul-Akhiar* (1 November 1873) the famine like conditions (in Bihar) were attributed by ignorant and half-educated Muslims to the introduction of Hindi. See *RNP (B)*, no. 48, 1873.
54. See A.P. Jha, 'Political History of Bihar (1859-1912)', in K.K. Datta (ed.), *The Compreheshive History of Bihar* (henceforth *CHB*), vol. III, pt. I, Patna, pp. 213-14. One petition from the Hindu and Muslim ryots of Bihar protested against the introduction of Nagari in courts and schools and prayed for the use of Urdu. See Bengal General (Education) B Progs, April 1874, File no. 104, Sl. nos. 31-9.
55. See India Home (Education) A Progs, November 1875, nos. 11-13. The petitioners argued that the allegation of the anti-Nagari party that Hindi was a rude language having neither a literature nor a grammar was not correct as Hindi was a branch of Sanskrit which according to principal English and German scholars (Colebrook, etc.) was the best language in the world hence it could not be unfit for the transaction of court business. They maintained that it could be learnt faster than Hindustani. They further pointed out that the Persian character could be altered with much greater facility than Nagari and hence it afforded greater temptation to fraudulent tampering with documents.
56. Ibid. Interestingly both the terms Urdu and Hindustani were used in the proceedingss.
57. Bengal General (Education) A Progs, September 1875, File no. 63, Sl. no. 8.
58. Bengal General (Miscellaneous) A Progs, April 1880, File no. 73, Sl. nos. 1-3.
59. Ibid.
60. Ibid.

61. Bengal Judicial B Progs, July 1881, no. 40. in Bengal Judicial Progs, volume for July-December 1881.
62. Letter no. 129 T from Government of Bengal to the Chota Nagpur Commissioner, 30 June 1880. No other details regarding prog. no. etc.
63. Bengal General (Miscellaneous) A Progs, April 1880, nos. 1-3.
64. Ibid., nos. 5-6.
65. *Report on the Administration of Bengal 1880-81*, summary, p. 1.
66. Resolution on the General Administration Report of the Patna Division for 1882-83 in *Calcutta Gazette*, Supplement no. 36 of 1883.
67. Ibid. The second song was written by Ambika Dutt Vyas, a distinguished Hindi poet of that period. See Shivpujan Sahay and B. Varma (eds.), *Hindi Sahitya Aur Bihar* (Hindi), vol. II, Patna, 1963, p. 272.
68. See Bengal General (Education) A Progs, January 1883, File no. 5, Sl. nos. 1-2.
69. Ibid.
70. Ibid.
71. See earlier in this chapter.
72. Bengal General (Education) A Progs, April 1872, nos. 32-44.
73. See ibid.
74. Bengal General (Education) A Progs, June 1873, File no. 75, Sl. nos. 1-5.
75. India Home (Education) A Progs, April 1877, nos. 53-61 and Bengal General (Education) B Progs, September 1873, File no. 54, Sl. nos. 12-16.
76. Bengal General (Education) A Progs, March 1881, File no. 24, Sl. nos. 4-6 and Bengal General (Education) A Progs, August 1899, nos. 28-34.
77. *Education Commission: Report by the Bengal Provincial Committee with Evidence Taken Before the Committee and Memorials Addressed to the Education Commission*, Calcutta, 1884, p. 37.
78. N. Kumar, *Image of Patna: A Supplement to Patna District Gazetteer*, Patna, 1971, pp. 88-9. Also see S. Gopal, *Patna in the Nineteenth Century*, Calcutta, 1982, pp. 67-8.
79. India Home (Public) A Progs, July 1873, nos. 241-5 and Bengal General (Miscellaneous) A Progs, February 1873, File no. 9, Sl. no. 1.
80. See ibid. [India Home (Public) A Progs, July 1873, nos. 241-5]. Upon enquiry from the Government of Bengal as to whether he could arrange for its publication the Patna Commissioner made it clear that he wanted to make the Gazette bilingual (Hindi and

Hindustani) because many officers did not understand Hindi, while the mass of the non-official population was ignorant of Hindustani. However, he also made it clear that if it was to be published in one language only, then it should be Hindi.

81. The Saran Magistrate hoped that the proposed *Behar Gazette* '. . . may do some real good in making the people acquainted with the various measures of Government and subjects of local interest.' See Annual Report of Saran District for 1872-3 in Annual General Report Patna Division 1872-73, Appendix III, p. 24 in Bengal General (Miscellaneous) Progs volume for September-December 1873.
82. *Report on the Administration of Bengal 1875-76*, Calcutta, 1876, pp. 431-2.
83. Ibid.
84. Bengal General (Miscellaneous) A Progs, February 1877, nos. 1-2. Both *Bihar Bandhu*, a Hindi paper and *Qasid*, an Urdu paper welcomed its publication. See *RNP (B)*, nos. 3 and 4, 1877.
85. India Home (Establishment) B Progs, August 1878, nos. 71-4.
86. Ibid.
87. This belief was further seen when the Government of Bengal decided to publish the *Behar Gazette* in Hindi. See earlier in the text.
88. See Bipan Chandra, *Modern India*, Delhi, 1971, pp. 108-9.
89. R.C. Majumdar, H.C. Raychaudhari and K.K. Datta, *An Advanced History of India*, rpt., Madras, 1985, p. 812.
90. See Anil Seal, *The Emergence of Indian Nationalism: Competition and Collaboration in the Later Nineteenth Century*, Cambridge, 1968, p. 302 fns.
91. Ibid., p. 302 fns.
92. See A.P. Jha, 'Political History of Bihar (1859-1912)', p. 218.
93. J.C. Jha and J.N. Sarkar, *A History of Patna College, 1863-1963*, Patna, 1963, p. 24.
94. J.S. Jha, 'Education in Bihar', in K.K. Datta (ed.), *CHB*, vol. III, pt. II, Patna, 1976, p. 425.
95. Bengal General (Education) A Progs, October 1871, nos. 8-10.
96. Ibid. The fact of this supersession is also borne out from another interesting source. In 1870 many public meetings were held in Bihar to protest against the government's education policy (regarding vernacular education). In one meeting at Muzaffarpur one Bengali officer illustrated the advantage of English education by showing the ascendancy of Bengalis over the Biharis in filling posts of honour and responsibility owing to their familiarity with the English language and their proficiency in it. He said that while scarcely a Bihari was appointed to any respectable post in the metropolis of Bengal several

Bengalis held most important situations in Bihar, snatching them away, as it were, from under the very nose of the Biharis. See *Report of a Monster Meeting, at the Town Hall on the Education Question held on 2nd July 1870*, Calcutta, 1870, pp. 151-ff.

97. Ibid. (Bengal General [Education] A Progs, October 1871, nos.8-10).
98. Ibid.
99. Ibid.
100. Ibid.
101. Ibid.
102. Bengal General (Education) A Progs, November 1871, no. 61.
103. Ibid.
104. India Home (Public) A Progs, October 1871, no. 38.
105. Bengal General (Education) A Progs, August 1872, nos. 71-98.
106. See Jha, 'Political History of Bihar', p. 224, and Bengal Appointment Department A Progs, January 1881, nos. 21-2.
107. Jha, 'Political History of Bihar', pp. 224-5.
108. Letter no. 254 G, 6 April 1883, from Commissioner, Patna Division to the Government of Bengal, in supplement to *Calcutta Gazette* no. 17, 1883.
109. India Home (Education) B Progs, November 1886, nos. 15-16.
110. India Home (Public) A Progs, October 1888, nos. 188-223.
111. Ibid., June 1892, nos. 46-9.
112. See Eugen Weber, *Peasants into Frenchmen: The Modernization of Rural France, 1870-1914*, London, 1977, pp. 195-206. A.R. Desai, *Social Background of Indian Nationalism*, rpt. Bombay, 1989, pp.126-34. David Thompson, *England in the Nineteenth Century, 1815-1914*, Harmondsworth, 1975, pp. 41-3. Bipan Chandra, *Modern India*, Delhi, 1971, p. 155. John R. McLane, *Indian Nationalism and the Early Congress*, Princeton, 1977, p. 4.
113. Ibid. (Weber, *Peasants into Frenchmen*), p. 206.
114. Jagdish N. Sarkar, 'Economic Life in Bihar', in S.H. Askari and Q. Ahmad (eds.), *CHB*, vol. II, pt. II, Patna, 1987, pp. 433-6, and S. Bhattacharya, 'Regional Economy (1757-1857)', in Dharma Kumar (ed.), *The Cambridge Economic History of India*, vol. II: *c. 1757-c. 1970*, Cambridge, 1982; Hyderabad, 1984, pp. 271-3.
115. N. Kumar, *Bihar District Gazetteers, Patna*, Patna, 1970, pp. 248-9
116. R.R. Diwakar (ed.), *Bihar Through the Ages* (henceforth *Bihar*), Calcutta, 1959, p. 776.
117. Kumar, *Bihar District Gazetteers, Patna*, pp. 248-9 and Diwakar (ed.), *Bihar*, p. 776.

118. L.S.S. O'Malley, *Bengal District Gazetteers, Monghyr*, Calcutta, 1909, p. 150.
119. Kumar, *Bihar District Gazetteers, Patna*, pp. 248-9.
120. W.W. Hunter, *A Statistical Account of Bengal*, vol. XIV, p. 185. It is interesting to point out that by 1874 the first Hindi newspaper of Bihar the *Bihar Bandhu* had correspondents both at Monghyr and Sultanganj (near Bhagalpur). See *RNP (B)*, nos. 33, 35, 38 of 1874. The presence of the railways must have facilitated the movement of news too.
121. Buckland, *Bengal under the Lieutenant Governors,* vol. II, Calcutta, 1901; rpt. New Delhi, pp. 594-604 and 701. See *Report on the Administration of Bengal 1873-74*, Calcutta, 1875, p. 13 (summary).
122. *Report on the Administration of Bengal*, *1882-3*, Calcutta, 1883, pp. 350-1.
123. *Report on the Administration of Bengal*, *1884-85*, Calcutta, 1886, pp. 199-221 and *Report on the Administration of Bengal*, *1890-91*, Calcutta, 1891, p. 25 (summary).
124. G.A Grierson, *The Administration of the Lower Provinces of Bengal from 1882-83 to 1886-87. Being a Supplement to Annual General Administration Report for 1885-86*, Calcutta, 1887, pp. 80-1.
125. Annual General Report Patna Division 1895-96, p. 10 in Bengal General (Miscellaneous) Progs, volume for January-September 1897.
126. *Report on the Administration of Bengal*, *1882-3*, Statistical Return, p. c.
127. Ibid., *1884-5*, Statistical Return, p. cx
128. See *Report on the Administration of Bengal 1890-91,* p. cxviii., *Report on the Administration of Bengal*, *1901-02*, Calcutta, 1903, and *Report on the Administration of Bengal*, *1904-05*, Calcutta, 1906.
129. Diwakar (ed.), *Bihar*, p. 776.
130. *Report on the Administration of Bengal*, *1884-85,* p. 222, and *Report on the Administration of Bengal, 1885-86*, p. 248.

CHAPTER 4

Regional Consciousness: Early Manifestations and Articulations

During roughly the same period when the measures of the colonial government were engendering and furthering the growth of a Bihari consciousness (discussed in the preceding chapter), its evolution also received a powerful impetus and accretion of strength through the activities and articulations of native elites and intellectuals, who began establishing voluntary associations and launching newspapers from around 1870, all seeking to work for Bihar and its people. What is especially noteworthy is the fact that these early leaders of Bihar chose, for the most part, the territorial-historical entity of Bihar as the symbol, as becomes evident from the names of these associations and newspapers, around which their socio-political activities revolved. 'Bihar' was thus given salience at a time when expanding educational network, fast improving communication system,[1] and increasing urbanization, discussed later in the chapter, was creating a new socially-mobilized population who could see or be made to see the interlinkage of their personal interests with the larger interests of the region. It is important to note that in Bihar, now much derided for its caste-based politics, purely caste-based associations or journals, which could have severely undermined the growth of an overarching regional identity in its nascent stage, made their appearance much later than purely secular organizations and journals or newspapers. In fact, it was only around 1890 that caste associations like the Bihar Kayastha Provincial Sabha and Pradhan Bhumihar Sabha[2] or journals like the *Kayastha Gazette* and *Dwiz Patrika* came into existence.[3] The present chapter takes a look at the activities and achievements of these voluntary associations, newspapers and other attempts to work for the region.

THE VOLUNTARY ASSOCIATIONS

Despite lying close to and in close proximity of Bengal Proper, being a part of the Bengal Presidency, the culture of associations made its first appearance in Bihar only towards the end of 1860s whereas it was in 1820s itself that the first association (Academic Association) had been established at Calcutta.[4] However, despite this late start, the next decade (1870s) witnessed a proliferation of these associations. A number of factors were at work behind this development. Some were common ones with other places, witnessing the same phenomenon. The most important of these factors was the spread of education. By the early 1870s new education had struck firm roots in Bihar and was beginning to produce new groups of people with new aspirations for their personal selves, the nation and the region. Richard Temple, the Lieutenant-Governor of Bengal, could see the importance of this factor clearly. He observed, 'Another result of education has been the formation of societies and associations, greater and lesser, in all parts of the country'.[5] The growth of urban centres in Bihar, too, contributed to the emergence of these associations by making it physically possible to create bonds at local levels. By the 1860s the district and divisional headquarter towns (Patna, Bhagalpur, Muzaffarpur, Monghyr, Gaya, etc.) not only housed government officials, clerks, lawyers and other professionals, but also teachers and young students, because all of these towns had at least one high school each. Many of their residents were Bengalis who were familiar with modern idioms of popular consciousness. As most of these towns had been administrative centres under the Mughals too, they also contained a sizeable number of landed and commercial elites,[6] who could be relied upon to give support, including financial ones, to any project aimed at the welfare and improvement of Bihar. However, this assemblage was not enough in itself to make the residents work together for any project. What impelled them in this direction was a newly-felt unease about the backwardness of Bihar and the resultant birth of an urge to do something concrete to remove this. Individual initiatives too played a major role.[7] Associations were born in many garbs—scientific or literary societies, societies for social and moral improvement, etc. The early associations did not generally have political objectives. Pertaining chiefly to educational and social matters as Richard Temple, the Lieutenant-Governor, observed accurately, they related to political affairs only in 'representing to the British authorities the wishes and interests of the people'.[8]

The city of Patna provides a fine example to see the assemblage of educated and socially conscious people at one place. Thacker's *Bengal Directory* for 1874 gives the names of 28 officers, ranging from that of the Divisional Commissioner to munsifs, who were working in the Revenue and Judicial Departments. Except a very few, who were posted in the subdivisional towns of Barh and Biharsharif, all others were stationed at Patna itself. Thirty-four people were serving the Education Department in the city, mostly working as teachers in Patna College, its school section or Normal School. Other government departments like the police, medical and public works, employed a fair number of people. As the smooth running of administration required the support of clerical staff their number too was significant. The names of 22 people are given as working in the clerical capacity in the Commissioner's office alone, and there were many other offices in the city, including those of the Postal Department and Railways. The legal profession had firmly established itself by now and the *Directory* gives the names of more than 50 pleaders who were practising in the local courts. The *Directory* is rounded up with the names of locally eminent people, landholders, bankers and the number is not inconsiderable.[9] It is important to remember that it neither was nor meant to be exhaustive.

As the city was the headquarters of the Patna Division, containing the districts of Patna, Gaya, Shahabad, Tirhut, Saran and Champaran,[10] many large-landed estates like that of Darbhanga, Hathua, Bettiah, Tekari and Dumraon came under its jurisdiction. Owners of many landed estates felt the need of a house in Patna where they could stay on their visits to deal with the government.[11] Following the establishment of Western educational institutions, it also attracted students, some of whom came from the family of zamindars. Thus, they also needed houses to keep their sons. The Maharaja of Darbhanga had, in fact, several houses in Patna. Similarly, the Raja of Bettiah and the zamindar of Tekari also had houses in Patna.[12] Though these landlords were not permanent residents of the city, they greatly influenced its social and cultural life. Lawyers, too, were gaining in importance so much so that many roads and lanes were named after them.[13] However, as we shall see below, the lack of individual initiative prevented Patna from getting the honour of establishing the first association in Bihar.

The assemblage of elites and members of intelligentsia produced its first tangible result at Muzaffarpur, the headquarter town of the sprawling Tirhut district. On 24 May 1868, a Muslim subordinate judge, Syed Imdad Ali, a long-time advocate of English education established the Behar Scientific Society[14] with the active aid and cooperation of both service and landed elites of the district belonging to both Hindu and Muslim communities. Extreme care was taken to associate such people in the organizational set-up of the society. Syed Muhammad Tuckee (Taqi) Khan, a respectable zamindar and banker of the district, also an Honorary Magistrate in later years, who had supported educational endeavours of the government in the past, was president of the Society, while Syed Imdad Ali himself acted as the secretary. Among the three vice-presidents two were Hindus. While Bhoopatty (Bhupati) Roy was the officiating Principal Sadar Ameen at Muzaffarpur, Sheo Prosunno (Shiv Prasan) Singh was the zamindar of Hardee, a man important enough to be appointed an Honorary Magistrate in later years. The third vice-president Munshee Muhammad Ameer, held the important post of Sheristadar. Moulvie Abdul Rahim, the Deputy Inspector of Schools, was one of the under secretaries.[15]

Though official encouragement in the shape of suggestion by S.W. Fallon, the then Inspector of Schools in Bihar, had played a role in the establishment of this association,[16] a far more important reason was the wish of Imdad Ali, as he informed the Commissioner of Patna Division, in August 1869, to 'make an effort to remove the opprobrium of ignorance which has so long rested on this province'.[17]

From the very beginning it attracted support from a large number of people, belonging to both Hindu and Muslim communities. In 1868, the year of its birth, it had a total membership of 318, according to the *Oudh Akhbar* of 10 November 1868, of whom 162 were Hindus and 128 Muslims.[18] Though the number remained the same in 1869, it went up to 511 by 1871,[19] an eloquent proof of its growing popularity and support base. There is a remarkable similarity in the objectives of this Society with the other famous Scientific Society established by Syed Ahmed Khan at Aligarh. These were to spread the science of the Western nations through the medium of vernaculars and with this view to translate scientific books from English into the vernaculars of the province.[20]

In, thus, emphasizing the cultivation of the vernacular languages as an important element in the regeneration of the province, Imdad Ali Khan was merely reflecting a continuous and progressively developing consciousness emerging all over India in the nineteenth century.[21] The Society also chose to publish a fortnightly paper the *Akhbar-ul-Akhiyar.*

As part of its programme to promote education it ran two aided vernacular schools in the Tirhut district, one at Muzaffarpur and the other at Paru. In spite of the fact that its chief promoter was a Muslim, the curriculum in the Muzaffarpur school provided for the teaching of Hindi too, apart from Persian and Hindustani. The Darbhanga Raj contributed Rs. 30 per mensem to pay the pandit.[22] The Society also opened a branch vernacular school at Chapra in 1870.[23] Later Syed Imdad All was transferred to Gaya,[24] where both a branch of the Society and a school were established in 1872.[25] Thus its influence came to extend to south Bihar, too.

The Society also sought assistance from the government in establishing its branch at Patna, with the objective of translating into the common vernacular of Bihar, whatever books in different branches of literature were needed for the education of the students up to the highest standard of the university.[26]

All these efforts suggest that the promoters and supporters of the Society basically linked Bihar's decline to the decline of education there. Imdad Ali, in a speech in 1873 at the Gaya branch of the Society, argued that the poor position of people was due to their lack of knowledge. In his opinion if they had acquired knowledge, the government would have given them advanced positions. He alluded to the openings made available to natives, since the Queen's Proclamation, like entry into the Civil Service, Bar, Governor-General's Council or a bench of the High Court.[27]

In this analysis of the existing condition of Bihar there was no understanding of the restricting conditions imposed by the colonial regime. However, this was to be expected. The Society never shied away from showing loyalty to the government. In fact, in 1869 the secretary made clear to the Commissioner of Patna that 'our sphere of operations is purely literary and we have been most careful in keeping ourselves clear of anything, which might look like interference in politics, in land questions or anything, which might prevent your showing any inclination to take a deep interest in the matter'.[28] This show of loyalty was obviously also aimed at securing the sympathy of the government for its objectives. It was believed that if the people of Bihar showed loyalty, the government would take care of their interests. No wonder, the Society always tried to prevent any ill-feeling emerging among the people against the government and always extended support to governmental measures. One such occasion arose in 1870,when the Government of India, in a major policy decision, declared that the motives which induced the people to seek English education were apparently sufficient for its development without any contribution from the government, whereas the desire for vernacular education needed stimulus and encouragement.[29] This declaration of the government led to widespread protests in parts of the Bengal Presidency, including Bihar, as it was interpreted by the educated class as a signal to withdraw government assistance from higher education.[30] The Behar Scientific Society, too, held a meeting at Muzaffarpur in July 1870 but to present an Address of thanks to the Governor-General for declaration of the vernacular policy. In this meeting Imdad Ali spoke on the merits of the policy in view of the benefits it would bring to the Bihar aristocracy. The Bengali speakers, on the other hand, considered the measure a reactionary one. The meeting finally decided to send the Address of thanks. Along with it, the secretary also sent the minutes of the proceedings of the meeting with a pointed reference to the difference of opinion expressed by the 'Bengali Baboos'.[31]

Not surprisingly it was never short of government patronage. The foundation stone of the new building of the school run by the Society was laid by the Lieutenant-Governor of Bengal, George Campbell.[32] Its effort to promote education and its role in translation of useful works were duly recognized in the government circles. The Commissioner of Patna felt:

I think the thanks of Government are due to Syed Imdad Ali, whose exertions organized and kept together the Behar Scientific Society and the Society's schools are doing a useful work throughout the division.[33]

Its activities were primarily undertaken keeping the province of Bihar in view. No wonder, in 1873, H.W. Gordon, the then secretary of the Society, requested the government to patronize its books. He regretted that none of the works, which were translated into Hindustani, had been made use of by the Education Department in Bihar. Gordon took care to point out that when the Society took up such a task it had expected that these books would be used as textbooks in the Vernacular and Normal Schools of Bihar. However, despite this show of neglect by the government the secretary offered to get rendered into Hindi the books already translated into Hindustani in view of the rising popularity of Hindi.[34]

The activities of the Society lessened after Imdad Ali went for Haj pilgrimage in 1875-6.[35] The membership also went down to 270 in 1875-6.[36] However, even then it was the largest public association in Bihar.

As the above description makes clear it did not concern itself with political issues. Its contribution basically lay in the fact that it brought on one platform a significant number of people and made them think in terms of Bihar. It was again significant that the secretary chose to give the Society a broader identity (regional) rather than a communal one.

The Behar Scientific Society represented an ambitious venture. However, the more localized associations,[37] also, through their activities, contributed to the growth of regional consciousness in Bihar. How they did so may be seen by the activities of the Chapra Association. It had come into existence by 1870 and its secretary was Keshub Lall Ghose, a Bengali lawyer. In 1870 a meeting was organized at Chapra with active involvement of the members of the association to protest against the government's new education policy, which emphasized the promotion of vernacular education. More significantly, a memorial, too, was presented to the government by the secretary of the association on behalf of the natives of 'Zila Sarun in the Province of Bihar'. It was also clarified that the province of Bihar was 'totally apart and distinct from Bengal'. However, even more significant was the fact that about 1,300 people, including zamindars, pleaders, officials, bankers, teachers, students (more than 200) and also common people put their signature on this memorial.[38] Thus through the efforts of one association more than 1,000 people asserted the distinct identity of Bihar and proclaimed their affinity to it.

While the towns outside Patna were witnessing the emergence of societies and associations, the chief city of Bihar as also the major educational centre was quiet. The Inspector of Schools in Bihar (North-West Division of the Education Department) S.W. Fallon reported ruefully: 'In Patna nearly everyone thinks himself entitled to a higher position than any other man. Societies or Associations for any literary or other useful purpose are impracticable and they do not exist.'[39]

However, the city soon stirred and a number of societies were born. The first such society was the Behar Literary Society, established in 1873.[40] It was the endeavour of the Muslim elites of Patna. Its secretary was Syed Mohamed Aboo Saeed, while the under secretary was Syed Mohamed Shamshul Huda. Syed Mazahar Imam was one of the members of the select committee. The objective of the Society was to invite men in a common effort to diffuse useful knowledge amongst the natives of Bihar and to improve and elevate their moral and intellectual powers.[41]

Both the secretary and under secretary were important members of the Patna society and were members of the District Education Committee as also members of Patna City municipality.[42] Its importance can further be gauged from the fact that the Lieutenant-Governor of Bengal agreed to become its patron.[43] In 1875-6 it had 200 members, which included 75 males and 125 juveniles.[44] It shows that it managed to mobilize a good number of people behind its objectives. In 1874 the Behar Association came into existence. Its objectives were literary, scientific, social and moral improvement of the inhabitants of Bihar. In 1876 it had 100 members.[45] We do not have, however, any knowledge about the activities of the above two societies. They do not appear to have been very active.

The Bihar Upkar Sabha, established in 1875, by Keshav Ram Bhatta,[46] a prominent intellectual of Bihar in the last quarter of the nineteenth century and early twentieth century, however, proved a very active organization.

This society of the Hindu notables of Patna had the aim of general improvement of Bihar. It wanted to establish schools and publish useful books.[47] Kunwar Sukhraj Bahadur was the president of this society,[48] while Ramkishen Pandey, a zamindar acted as the secretary.[49] That both the president and its secretary were important members of the Patna society may be seen from the fact that they were appointed as municipal commissioners.[50] Also associated with it was Babu Govind Charan,[51] the first Bihari postgraduate. The chief promoters of the Bihar Upkar Sabha were staunch supporters of Hindi and the Sabha actively worked for its progress. When the decision of the Bengal government to make Hindi the official language of Bihar was opposed by some Muslims, the members of the Bihar Upkar Sabha strongly came out in support of the government measure. At a Darbar held in the Patna College in August 1880, the leading members of the Sabha like Kunwar Sukhraj Bahadur, Babu Ramkishen Pandey, Babu Govind Charan and others not only presented a petition in reply to the petition of the Muslims but went further and thanked the Lieutenant-Governor, Ashley Eden, for introducing Hindi.[52]

An association with a greater spatial reach was established next. This was the Peoples' Association, established in 1879 at Patna.[53] Without specifying any particular objectives, it wanted to take up all such works which in its opinion were good for the common people. Membership rules were framed in such a way that even common people could join it. Thus, while the annual membership fee was Rs. 3 only (not a small amount then), a common person who could not afford this fee could yet become a member by simply writing to the secretary. The big zamindars and rich people, however, could become members only after paying donation. This association wanted to draw maximum support from every section of the society, and hence, no religious discussions were permitted in its meetings. Hindi was the language of its proceedings.[54] It succeeded in drawing membership from Patna, Chapra, Arrah, Gaya and other places,[55] and could justifiably claim to be a pan-Bihar organization. In 1880, Anandi Prasad Mishra was the secretary of this Association.[56]

The very general nature of the objectives that it set for itself would indicate that it was not a scientific or literary society, like the other associations we have referred to above. Rather it was more of a political body. Its political nature is corroborated by further evidences. This Patna-based association used to send delegates to the Congress sessions. In 1887 four prominent Biharis including Bisheshwar Singh, one of the founders of the B.N. College, Patna and Babu Govind Charan were its delegates.[57] In 1890 Mahesh Narayan and Moulvi Mahomed Ismail were the delegates.[58] The Association, thus, succeeded in enlisting the support of the most progressive sections of the Bihar society. It made an attempt to create a broad-based organization, which would work for the common people and in which common people could have a voice. It ensured this by deciding to give free membership and through its decision to remain secular and conduct the proceedings in Hindi.

The Bihar Landholders' Association, established in 1878,[59] proved the most durable of all the associations established in the 1870s. It was established in the aftermath of the great famine of 1874 in Bihar. The famine brought to the notice of the government the poor condition of the peasantry in Bihar and the official inquiry, conducted to find out the causes of the famine, held the rack-renting and oppressive conduct of the zamindars and indigo-planters largely responsible for the miserable condition of the peasants and fall in the output of grains.[60] The zamindars formed this association in order to protect their interests against the contemplated measures of land reforms by the Government of Bengal.[61] The president of the Association was Maharaja of Darbhanga, Lakshmeshwar Singh.[62] It was basically a class organization but it succeeded in bringing on one platform zamindars scattered over different districts of the region. We shall discuss more about its role in the public life of Bihar in a later chapter.

This Association, however, even in early years took stand on certain general issues concerning Bihar. For example, in the 1890s when pressure was mounted to reintroduce Urdu as the court language in Bihar as, it was argued that the Kaithi-Hindi was ill-suited to the requirements of the law courts, the Association opposed the proposal. It suggested that if Kaithi was less legible then Hindi (Devanagari) should be introduced in its place.[63] The fact that the Maharaja of Darbhanga chose to become its president was of some historical significance. It ensured that the emergence of a pan-Bihar identity would not face any challenge in the immediate future from the emergence of a Mithila and Maithil political identity.[64]

The emergence of societies and associations shows that the more conscious sections of the Bihar society were trying to grapple in their own way with the problems facing the region. The problems were too many. From the Behar Scientific Society's modest objective of translating European scientific works into the vernacular and making them available to students to the Behar Associations' objective of literary, scientific, social and moral improvement of the inhabitants of Bihar shows that a progressive realization was dawning that advancing education was not the only answer of Bihar's numerous problems. Peoples' Association's refusal to specify its aims is suggestive of this. However, the activities of these associations tended to make a large number of people conscious about the need of working for Bihar. The stir in the society was visible to all. Thus while the Patna Magistrate had reported in 1872, 'I have no belief in any strong political feeling in the city (Patna), on the contrary, I think the majority of the population may be described as indifferent and apathetic.'[65]

However, only four years later (in 1876), the Patna Commissioner had something very different to report:

> I may refer to another phase of public opinion, viz., that there is no longer the same apathy in the administration of the country which once marked the middle class. On the contrary, there is a very eager desire on the part of the educated and landed classes to take some active part in public business. . . . In the city of Patna there existed throughout the year several Societies, which have for their object the encouragement of learning. Very excellent addresses, both in English and vernacular languages, are delivered at their meetings on education and other social subjects. There is every disposition on the part of these Societies to develop into something practical and useful for the good of their province.[66]

He also expected the very best results from the encouragement of these societies. He could see that there was a feeling growing among the people that the government should interfere in social questions and play an active role in promoting public welfare, by improving habitation, erecting public libraries and museums, etc.[67]

Later some more societies were established in the Patna Division like the Bihar Young Men's Institute, the Bihari Institute, etc. Although these societies did not have a large membership and were not always very active,[68] yet their existence helped to concretize inchoate and hazy notions of a common identity.

The Patna Division, especially the town of Patna, showed the greatest activity of this kind. Bhagalpur Division also saw the emergence of two important associations, one of which was the Bhagalpur Landholders' Association,[69] a class organization of the zamindars, the other being the Bihar National Improvement Association. The establishment of the latter was considered a major step in the evolution of the idea of separation of Bihar from Bengal.[70]

The early associations and societies in Bihar played a crucial, although limited, role in the public life of Bihar. Limitations stemmed from the fact that their reach was very limited. It was only in the twentieth century that associations having a pan-Bihar network came into existence. They had often very short lives as the later reports on the administration of Bengal do not mention their names in their statistical returns. Their aims were also limited—limited to educational and social issues to a large extent. The presence of official elites in these organizations or the close ties of their promoters and members with the government also put fetters on their activities. Seemingly, early leaders and intellectuals placed greater faith in the efficacy of newspapers to propagate their ideas and to draw the attention of the government towards the problems of Bihar. Despite these limitations, however, these associations succeeded in forging bonds at local levels and in giving the people involved in them much needed political experience. Above all, they rescued 'Bihar' from passing into complete oblivion and set it up as a major symbol around which to engage in meaningful activities.

THE NEWSPAPERS AND THE 'BIHAR FOR BIHARIS' MOVEMENT

The newspapers launched in Bihar around the same time as the early associations and occasionally by the same set of people came to play a far more important role than the latter in reflecting, further engendering and disseminating, the consciousness of a common regional identity. This was on account of a number of reasons, some attributable in general to the crucial role newspapers play in nationality movements and in the very process of modernization in different parts of the world.

From the first half of the nineteenth-century newspapers were seen as performing the role of conducting social and, one may add, political electricity to different parts of a nation. They advanced the process of homogenization, by establishing a unanimity of readership in which local peculiarities lost their significance and thus facilitated the process of modernization.[71] However, while promoting homogenization among a people they also occasionally promoted a sense of differentiation from some other people, which was and continues to be a central factor in the genesis of identity movements.

A number of recent studies have argued that all communities are imaginary constructions in so far as these always exist through the imaging of the group of which one conceives oneself a member. These communities are imagined into existence by people by thinking that some people are like them while some others are unlike them. Newspapers play a conspicuous role in the process of identity formation as they enable the extension of the imagined community far beyond the bounds of face-to-face or knowable community. It occurs when the reader of the paper discovering a set of concerns which he recognizes as his own also imagines a multitude of other readers having the same concerns and is thereby carried out of the individual experience into collective phenomenon which the text articulates in national (or regional) terms. To put things more simply, this means essentially that triumphs and insults of an individual come to be seen as triumphs and insults of a whole community. Newspapers (whether daily or weekly) with their reach and regular output by bringing these stories to people hasten the process of identity formation. In addition, they also mobilize people politically and socially and make them ready for a more effective communication.[72]

Coming back to Bihar we can see the distinct ways in which they fostered a regional consciousness there. They asserted the personality of Bihar, showed the artificiality and unsoundness of its union with Bengal and finally highlighted the various harms resulting to Bihar as a result of this union. In this, special emphasis was placed on the issue of employment with Bihari papers demanding that employment in Bihar should be given to the natives of Bihar only. In this way they not only helped the people of Bihar to see themselves as a distinct community but also created the ground for demanding its separation from Bengal.

The role of the vernacular papers till the beginning of 1890s was much greater than those of English newspapers, both because of their larger number and greater reach. The vernacular papers could 'transmit ideas, plans and programmatic goals from the political elite in the local tongues, in a local idiom, to the people in the small towns and mofassal areas'.[73] The use of familiar symbols or allegories gained greater appreciation and empathy from an untutored audience.[74]

The two early newspapers in Bihar the *Akhbar-ul-Akhiyar* published by the Behar Scientific Society and *Chasm-e-Ilm* published by Munshi Suraj Mal of the Patna Normal School,[75] contained little news and little discussion and were actually vehicles for instructive essays which the Patna Commissioner felt, few would read and very few would pay for. According to him the influence exercised by them was imperceptible. The people of Bihar in his opinion were generally a long way 'even from the low level at which native papers circulate'.[76] Interestingly this was at a time when vernacular papers, as a rule, were not important even in the more advanced parts of the Bengal Presidency. A government report of the same year noted:

> The circulation in the Mofussil is small, the principal readers being the government servants and people who make their daily bread in government schools, or offices and public courts, who read the papers more for the scraps of news on social and local matters than for the purpose of imbibing opinions on political or other subjects. The vernacular papers, as a rule, are not important.[77]

However, contrary to officials' notions, an awareness was growing among the elites and intellectuals of Bihar that newspapers could be utilized to promote specific issues, to voice various grievances of the people and to shape public opinion at large. The result was that many of the newspapers, which emerged thereafter, had very pronounced stands on a number of issues, including political ones. *Bihar Bandhu*, the first Hindi newspaper to be started in Bihar, for instance, had the aim of disabusing the minds of all people of all error regarding political, educational and other important matters.[78]

One issue which figured very prominently in the discussion of Bihari newspapers was what they saw as neglect of Bihar or any hint of slight to its people. The government was immediately urged to take remedial measures. The *Bihar Bandhu* (1 September 1875) expressing indignation at the fact that the Prince of Wales was not coming to Patna, wanted to know if Bihar was the most interdicted of all of the provinces. Not ready to accept this non-recognition of Bihar lying down the paper asked the 'Bihar Friendly Association' and residents of Patna to strive to invite the Prince.[79] A similar sense of neglect was felt when the Lieutenant-Governor appointed members of the school committee as it consisted of three Bengalis and one Christian. The paper charged that the interests of Bihar had been left out of consideration.[80] Implied within such criticism was a belief that only Biharis were capable of looking after the interests of Bihar. Even a rumour that a higher-class school for Licentiate in Arts was to be established at Rungpur (Bengal) could make a Bihari paper the *Qasid* (12 February 1877) ask as to when would the government think of raising the Bhagalpur school. The paper itself answered the question also—perhaps not for many years, as Bihar did not seem to be much in favour of the authorities.[81] The newspapers also played a central role in launching and sustaining what was arguably the most explicit expression of emerging regional consciousness in Bihar—a campaign against the employment of immigrant Bengalis in the public offices and schools in Bihar, encapsulated in the pithy slogan 'Bihar for the Biharis'. They not only fostered the consciousness that indigenous people had the primary right over jobs in the region but also first drew attention of both the people and the government towards the economic and cultural aspects of the problem created by the immigration of Bengalis to Bihar and generally as a result of Bihar's union with Bengal.

The animus displayed against the Bengalis originated from a number of factors and got expressed in several ways including the particular demand for their exclusion from jobs in Bihar. However, this cannot be fully accounted for unless one keeps in mind the generally pathetic economic condition of Bihar, especially in the second half of the nineteenth century.

The post-1857 period was one of economic gloom for Bihar. The agriculturists were suffering in various ways. Heavy indebtedness kept them perpetually depressed while constant fragmentation of landholdings and low prices of agricultural products added to their woes.[82] Sir John Strachey observed aptly, 'There is hardly any part of British India possessing greater natural advantages of soil and climate, and no part where the condition of agricultural population is more precarious or the margin of subsistence smaller.'[83] Even the class of people believed to be fattening up at the expense of tenants[84] was not faring too well either. The permanently settled zamindaris got fragmented and partitioned in large numbers and by the late nineteenth century 88.5 per cent of 110,456 permanently settled estates of Bengal and Bihar were less than 500 acres in size, and had a mass of intermediate tenures below them. The petty zamindars and tenure holders were not always rich people[85] and needed to supplement their incomes from other sources. Richard Temple, the Lieutenant-Governor of Bengal, noted in 1876,

> most of the small zemindars, not only by hundreds, but by thousands, whose income from the land does not suffice for their support betake themselves to other profession. Let anyone count up the members of the professional classes in Bengal—solicitors, barristers, judicial and administrative officers, clerks and other ministerial officials, literary men, traders and merchants, who own some land, more or less, and he will perceive the intellectual activity and the spirit of self-help which pervade the land-owning community. . . .[86]

Adding to the difficult economic situation, and making it imperative to seek avenues of employment in public service sector, was the decline in the cottage industries of the region. Some recent studies have conclusively shown that Bihar suffered a major deindustrialization in the nineteenth century. A statistical comparison of Buchanan's survey of some Bihar districts in the early nineteenth century with the 1901 census data has shown that the percentage of population dependent on industries had declined from 18 to 8 per cent.[87] This decline must have impacted both those directly engaged in the process of manufacture and those engaged in the associated economic activities. Bihar also failed to gain from the innovations brought by the oceanic trade. Within the Bengal Presidency, it was Calcutta, the capital city, which gained. The docks, harbours, banks and insurance companies were all concentrated there.[88] It is easy to realize that for openings available to Indians in their offices, it would have been the English-educated Bengalis who would have got jobs.

It is apparent from the above discussion that with landholding not providing enough income and with industries in the decline not many opportunities existed for making a proper living and people were, in a way, forced to seek office employment under the government. And hence the anger was directed against the immigrant Bengalis.

We have seen in the first chapter how the process of immigration of Bengalis had taken place and how they had come to occupy posts in Bihar. However, this acquaintance had not actually led to stronger ties between the two neighbouring communities. The realization that Biharis and Bengalis differed in many ways was articulated even by some keen Bengali observers like Bankim Chandra Chatterjee. Writing in *Bangadarshan* in 1872 he said '. . . although Bengalis and Biharis are of the same race they are of different communities because of differences of language. . . .'[89]

Biharis felt the same. The Bengalis had generally displayed a kind of superior attitude towards the people of Bihar, as English education had not made much progress among them and they were seen as uncultured and uncivilized.[90] Articles published in magazines like the *Bengal Magazine* betrayed this sense of superiority, hidden behind a coating of sympathetic words. The magazine in 1880-1 published an article 'Photograph of a Bihar Village'. A photograph, as is known to all, is vastly different from a sketch. It is almost the 'real thing'. The next year the magazine returned to the same subject and published an article, 'A Bihar Village'.[91] Their excerpts are revealing

> . . . the children are found here to revel up to their 11th or 12th year in a state of Adamic nudity . . . the common people of Bihar are certainly like those tribes of the Himalayas, beyond the reach of our kind of storm, viz., the storm of expensive civilization which perhaps in no distant day will sweep over the whole of India.
>
> Pass a few weeks in Bihar and you will see bands of beggars issuing out of their indigent homes and actually surrounding the lodgings of the Bengali residents, with all the precision of a besieging force.[92]

The scorn shown by the Bengalis was returned in kind, interest added. The contemporary Hindi literature produced in Bihar gives a fascinating insight into how the Bengalis were viewed. A novel by Ambika Dutt Vyas, *Ashcharya Vritanta* (A Strange Narrative) has among its characters a Bengali gentleman. He is portrayed as a coward. In a typical manner he is also shown as having lost faith in the Hindu religion and Indian culture. He has become a Brahmo Samaji (a follower of Brahmo Samaj). He smokes a cheroot and has become subservient to his wife, who happens to be a doctor. He not only cooks food for her but also has to seek permission from her for going out. Lastly, he has a widowed daughter, who is to be married. The whole portrayal is calculated to show the Bengali character in a poor light. The novel was written at a time when female education in Bihar had not even taken firm roots, when the hold of the husband over wife was total and complete and when the question of marrying a widow could not have been even thought of.[93]

This anti-Bengali feeling was manifested in many ways. While the press in Bengal was universally criticizing George Campbell, the Lieutenant-Governor of Bengal, the Bihari newspapers came out in his defence. While the Hindi weekly *Bihar Bandhu*[94] (15 February 1874) spoke of the many benefits received from him, the Urdu weekly *Nadir-ul-Akhbar* praised him for establishing numerous *pathsalas* in cities and villages which induced both high and low, rich and poor to turn their attention to education.[95] In fact, this attitude was reflected in the dislike shown by Biharis for those papers which were seen as speaking for Bengalis' interests or were even run under Bengali influence. The non-influence of the *Behar Herald*, the first English paper to be started in Bihar, demonstrates this. This Patna-based weekly was started by the Bengali community in 1875. Though it received financial support from the Dumraon estate, for many years it was edited by Guru Prasad Sen, a Bengali lawyer and zamindar[96] and was seen essentially as an organ of the Bengali community. The Patna Commissioner noted in 1876 that the *Behar Herald*, conducted by the Bengali members of the Patna bar, had no influence as the more intelligent Biharis looked upon it rather as a Bengali organ than a faithful representation of wants and requirements of the inhabitants of Bihar.[97] This dislike was not confined only towards this Patna-based weekly but also even to papers published from Calcutta. In his annual report for 1876-7, the Collector of Muzaffarpur observed:

> . . . so long the writers in such newspapers as the *Hindoo Patriot*, *Amrita Bazar Patrika*, and the *Behar Herald* (which have some small circulation in the district) are, and are known to be only Bengalees, their violent attacks on public officers will never excite dissatisfaction among respectable and educated Beharees. Such writers by imputing to European officers the contemptible motives, which are wont to actuate the worst of their own countrymen, betray their nationality and insult the good sense of their Beharee readers.[98]

However, the key factor behind the animus was the large employment of Bengalis in Bihar. That the anger of the Biharis was not based on misconceptions but on very real grounds becomes evident when one notes the names of Indians occupying important posts in the two divisional headquarter districts of Bihar—Patna and Bhagalpur. In 1869 in the Patna Commissioner's office all the five clerical staff, whose names figure in Thacker's *Bengal Directory*, were Bengalis.[99] Things had not improved much even by 1874 even though by this time the government had already passed orders to exclude Bengalis from public offices in Bihar, for in that year, out of 22 clerical staff in the Patna Commissioner's office getting a salary of Rs. 35 or more per month, 17 were Bengalis. Interestingly it included the two key posts of PA to the Commissioner and Sheristadar.[100] Bhagalpur presented a similar picture. In 1869 in the offices of Divisional Commissioner, Collector and Judge out of 22 clerical staff whose names figure in the *Directory*, 17 were Bengalis. In the same year all the four teachers including the headmaster of the government school were Bengalis.[101] They also held complete sway in the higher legal profession. At Patna in 1874, all the pleaders having a Bachelor of Law degree were Bengalis.[102] The immigration of Bengalis continued apace in later years, as are indicated by immigration statistics. The total number of immigrants in the year 1881 was 49,321. While 37,282 persons were concentrated in those districts which had a contiguous territory with Bengal, more than 12,000 were dispersed over other districts. The number of Bengali immigrants went up to 1,26,318 in 1891. Most of these were white-collared people.[103] In the Patna district, the 1891 census report noted that there were 1,920 Bengali-speaking males of whom 1,536 resided in the city. They were 'chiefly clerks, lower officials and shopkeepers of the superior sort'. The more interesting observation was that, there used to be a great immigration of Bengalis into Patna, as 'There was a strong dislike to English education among the higher castes. This, however, seems to have broken down and the immigration of Bengalis is almost ceasing. This, however, is of very late years, as in 1881 only 614 Bengali males were returned for this district.'[104] It is interesting to note that in a period when immigration was supposedly ceasing, the number of Bengali males went up by 1,300 in a decade. The Arrah District report also said that immigrants from Bengal 'are almost all in government employment as clerks and school teachers'.[105]

The first salvos against the employment of Bengalis were fired by two Monghyr-based Urdu newspapers,[106] *Nadir-ul-Akhbar*[107] and *Murgh-i-Suliman*.[108] The Urdu-speaking elite of Bihar, belonging to both Hindu and Muslim communities, who had monopolized government offices in the region, were rising to protect their turf. Soon after its launch, *Nadir-ul-Akhbar*, started its anti-Bengali tirade. In 1874 the paper complained that the Bengalis had monopolized all the posts to the detriment of all other people. The paper charged that the government circular issued some time back to the effect that the educated natives of Bihar should be selected for posts in the courts of that province was acted upon only for a short time and was being disregarded as Bengalis were again selected. And

these take every opportunity to find fault with and expose the other employees to the officials, and have them discharged, and get their own relatives and friends installed; and no consideration is made as to those people of Bihar being but new hands, and just commencing education, who before they learn their drill, are called upon to venture at once into the battle-field.[109]

It wanted the government to strictly enforce the circular and appoint outsiders to high posts in Bihar only if a search ensured that a competent Bihari was not available for the post.[110]

The second round of fusillade was occasioned by the beating of two Muslim boys by the Bengali headmaster of the Bhagalpur school. The people of Bhagalpur presented a petition protesting the incident and demanding the removal of the Bengali headmaster. Using the occasion to good effect the editor not only wrote a lengthy dissertation upon the great dissimilarity of language and customs existing between the Bengalis and the people of Bihar, but went on to point out that if another Bengali headmaster was appointed things would remain as bad as they were. He urged upon the government the advisability of appointing competent educated Hindustanis in the first place to all such posts, and thereby to stimulate the cause of education, which had just begun to make some progress in the province. The dislike for the Bengalis was so great that he even suggested the appointment of Hindus of North-West Provinces in schools of Bihar if competent native men were not found. The reason advanced by him was that their language was in some ways similar to that of Bihar. It was argued that a Bengali found it extremely difficult to make himself intelligible to Hindustani pupils of higher classes while in the case of the lower classes, where explanations of the simplest kind were required, matters were likely to be even worse (if a Bengali teacher was employed).[111]

It is interesting to see how the linguistic and cultural differences were highlighted to differentiate the people of Bihar and Bengal from the 1870s. The Bengalis were portrayed as manipulative and as favouring their kin.

The *Murgh-i-Suliman* picked up the theme of unemployment of the people of Bihar in Bihar. In its issue of the 7 February 1876 it impressed upon the government the necessity of employing Biharis instead of Bengalis.[112] However, these papers had not yet grasped the fact that the employment of Bengalis was one of the consequences of Bihar's inclusion in the Bengal Presidency. This fact was to be grasped soon, however, by a Patna-based Urdu weekly the *Qasid* (Messenger). It for the first time pointed out the incongruity of the union of Bengal and Bihar and the evils emerging out of it. In its issue of the 22 January 1877[113] it was argued that such a union was no more suitable than for a crow and *bulbul* or an Englishman and Frenchman to live together. It drew attention to the fact that though coinciding to a great extent in matters of religion, the manner and customs of Biharis and Bengalis were quite distinct and they were of different nationalities. They neither intermarried nor their families associated. How, the paper asked, could any friendship spring between them? On the contrary, they used the harshest possible expression against each other and the greatest indifference, contempt and scorn existed between them.[114]

The paper further said that when new people came from England, they landed first at Calcutta and were in constant intercourse with Bengalis. When these Englishmen were posted in Bihar, Bengalis followed them and were given high posts by them and these, in turn, started serving the cause of fellow Bengalis with the result that the Biharis suffered. As a consequence of this, Biharis neglected education as they took to it only to improve their worldly prospects. It was argued that the languages of these two provinces were distinct and the appointment of Bengalis as headmasters in the schools of Bihar contributed to the deterioration of its dialect. It was pointed out that because of their superior English education the Bengalis had learned to despise their own religion and become infidels and they carried with them this bad example into Bihar with all its attendant evils. The *Qasid* asserted that the Bengalis in their manners were far inferior to the Hindustanis and association with them tended to deprave the latter. Alluding to the temporary nature of their stay it was pointed out that with the construction of railway links the Bengalis were no longer coming to Bihar to settle down. When they made it their home (in the past) no injury resulted. The paper concluded by saying that although the people of Bihar were the subjects of only one nation but in reality they were subordinate to two races. It said that while the people of North-West Provinces were highly favoured, the people of Bihar were neglected and made an appeal to the government to relieve the people of the double burden imposed on them.[115]

Here was an exposition and analysis of the cultural differences between the Bengalis and Biharis, which could find an instant response in Bihari minds. The use of symbols of crow and *bulbul* to differentiate them, the proof that they did not intermarry, were to be easily grasped even by ordinary people. The exposition gives an insight into how the educated classes in Bihar perceived cultural differences. Language was considered a very important marker of group identity. Religious differences were not important but the cultural differences were. How a gradually negative perception was being built-up of the immigrant Bengalis also becomes clear.

They were seen as not only of the manipulating sort, as even the *Nadir-ul-Akhbar* had pointed out, but also culturally inferior to Biharis. The Bengal connection, in this analysis, was harmful not only economically but also culturally. There was also a veiled suggestion to separate Bihar. The British, it was taken for granted, were there to stay. It was the presence of the Bengalis that was unbearable.

This exposition may be seen as a major statement of the emerging regional consciousness in Bihar. Like in 1870s, in 1880s too, the papers continued to attack the Bengali immigrants.[116] They were portrayed as being inimical to the interests of Bihar and the Biharis. The newspapers, while denoting a general perception prevailing among the people of Bihar that they were natives to the soil and the Bengalis were outsiders, through their columns, further contributed to the spread and strengthening of such perceptions. A favourite strategy of the newspapers was to publish letters supporting their point of view. The vituperation could, on occasions, take extreme forms. A telling example was provided in 1880 when the *Bihar Bandhu* in its issue of 11 February 1880, gave space to a letter from a 'well-wisher' of Bihar who had questioned the right of Bengalis of getting employment there even though they did not know either Hindi or Urdu, the language of the people of Bihar. The letter-writer maintained that all big posts in Bihar were occupied by the Bengalis and they had swamped the collectorate, police offices, the Commissioner's office and the schools like locusts. He argued that just as the farmers lost crops to the swarm of locusts, similarly the Biharis lost jobs to the Bengalis. It was maintained that many good families had been ruined because menfolk could not find employment. The letter-writer was implicitly not surprised that there was no love between the Bengalis and the Biharis because from every point of view the Bengalis encroached upon the rights of Biharis.[117]

The same paper of 16 February 1882 wanted removal of a Bengali Sub-Divisional Officer accusing him of acting with high-handedness and said, 'It is men like him who have made Bengalis unpopular in Bihar'.[118] While one Bengali paper the *Sahachar* condemned Ashley Eden for reserving jobs in Bihar for the Biharis and argued that the plea advanced by the British officers that the Biharis were opposed to the appointment of Bengalis was a specious one, as in its opinion none but an idiot could believe that the Biharis preferred Europeans who were aliens, both in race and creed, to the Bengalis who were their fellow countrymen,[119] one Calcutta paper, the *Urdu Guide* almost refuting *Sahachar's* argument demanded that the headmastership of Muzaffarpur school, which was to fall vacant should be given to a European or a Eurasian, but never to a Bengali, who belonged to a people who were so much opposed to the advancement of Biharis.[120]

The theme of Bengali domination of the government jobs was a regular feature not only of the vernacular papers but also of the English-language ones. For example, the *Indian Chronicle*, an English newspaper, which was started at Patna by Babu Bisheshwar Singh in 1881,[121] devoted its columns to the airing of the supposed grievances of the educated Biharis in the race for employment under government.[122]

Though the newspapers, in a large measure, reflected and contributed to the development of a reactive, negative anti-Bengali Bihari consciousness, the concern for the interests of Bihar was manifested in other ways, too, by them.

Some journals were explicitly started to promote education in Bihar. From Patna, Munshi Hasan Ali started the *Motichoor* for *pathsalas* and schoolboys. This Hindi monthly had come into existence by 1876. Interestingly, in its publication, help was rendered by the people of Darbhanga and Purnea.[123]

In a similar vein, a Hindi weekly journal, the *Shiksha* (Education), was started from Patna. The editor expressed the feeling that prompted him to start the journal in a touching Hindi poem,

अभिलाखा उर माहिं, बहुत दिनन ते मुहि रही
पै पूरिहि कै नाहिं, दुविधा संसय द्यो रह्यों
बालन शिक्षा हेत, "शिक्षा" नामक पत्र इक
जनम काहु विधि लेत, मिटत अभाव बिहार को[124]

[There was a desire in my heart, Since a long time,
But whether it would be fulfilled, Was always doubtful,
(The desire was that)
For the education of children,
A journal named *Shiksha*,
Could ever be started,
So that the need of Bihar
Could be met.] (Translation mine)

These were some very concrete ways in which those who started these newspapers sought to work for Bihar. However, there were other ways too, in which newspapers fostered a Bihari consciousness. This critique of the government policy by the *Bihar Bandhu* (6 September 1876) would illustrate the point. The newspaper while accusing the Englishmen of not trusting the Indians said,

When will god show us the day in which the people of Bihar will be eligible as Captains of the regiments, Colonels and Generals. We wish not to rebel and take by force the above appointments, for us possess neither the nature nor the ability now so to do. If anytime our Biharis have rebelled and shown that they were heroes and had still a spark of independence left in them, of what avail is it? Since we have not the same Koer Singh nor the same independent Santals.[125]

Within this critique one may see an earnest appeal to the government to appoint Biharis to high posts in the army. At the same time one can see that it is reminding the government and the people that once they possessed the ability to take these posts by force. It was thus trying to keep alive the memory of Kunwar Singh and the brave Santhals. The most interesting thing to note about this outburst is that it included the Santhals, too, among the category of Biharis.

In their construction of a Bihari identity the newspapers deliberately ignored the inconvenient facts of social existence within the region. Thus the linguistic or cultural differences, for example, between Mithila and Magadha were never referred to. In fact, both the people of Bihar and those of Bengal were treated as two blocks of undifferentiated, homogeneous communities. However, it has to be admitted that newspapers in Bihar did succeed in drawing the attention of the people to the symbol of 'Bihar'. Their appeal and reach extended to a large part of Bihar.[126]

Through their writings the newspapers translated into the consciousness of the people[127] the fact—partly real, partly perceived—that under the existing administrative arrangements Bihar's interests were largely neglected, that the union of Bihar and Bengal was not based on any sound principles, that the interests of people of Bihar were being hurt as a result of this union and, above all the feeling that Bihar belonged to the natives of Bihar. By the time the *Behar Times* appeared, in 1894, spadework had already been done for demanding the separation of Bihar.

MEMORIALS AND PETITIONS

Specific campaigns on issues of regional interest made a great contribution to the growth of regional consciousness in Bihar. Agitations were conducted through memorials and petitions. There were three main issues over which the politically conscious section of the Bihar society expressed its opinion. The first issue was one of language. We have in the earlier chapter seen how groups of Bihari people struggled for or against the introduction of Hindi. The second issue on which the elites of Bihar made representation was what they saw as government's negligence towards the promotion of education in Bihar, as we have seen in the second chapter. The third issue over which they agitated was that of public employment, as it vitally affected the interests of the educated people.

A general feeling had come to prevail that the Bengalis had got a monopoly of good jobs in Bihar. The government had in 1871 decided to give preference to the Biharis for employment in Bihar. However, it seems that the orders were not fully carried out as one finds that in 1878 a number of petitions were presented to the government, in which prayer was made that the orders already issued to the local authorities in different districts regarding the employment of Biharis (that they were to be appointed in preference to other countrymen in all available posts) be carried to its full extent.[128]

However, the orders passed in 1871 had not been extended to the Bhagalpur Division. It was in early 1880s that the Biharis started agitation for the recognition of their right for employment in the Hindi-speaking districts of the Division. They conducted agitation through the columns of papers, by anonymous petitions and by direct petitions to the government. In fact, they demanded that the Bengalis be excluded from employment in the Bhagalpur Divison.[129] It was only after such protests that the Government of Bengal extended the orders to the Monghyr and Bhagalpur districts of the Division.[130] This may be seen as an early example of a successful constitutional agitation in Bihar.

By the mid-1890s largely through the combined efforts of the voluntary associations and newspapers and also occasional groupings (to fight for specific issues concerning Bihar), Bihar had awakened as a distinct region. The emerging regional consciousness had reached a point where a demand was imminent for its separation from Bengal and its constitution as a separate province.

NOTES

1. See Chapters 2 and 3.
2. See F.R. Frankel, 'Caste, Land and Dominance Order', in Francine R. Frankel and M.S.A. Rao (eds.), *Dominance and State Power in Modern India*, vol. I: *Decline of a Social Order*, Delhi, 1989, p. 63.
3. N. Kumar, *Journalism in Bihar: A Supplement to Bihar State Gazetteer*, Patna, 1971, Preface, pp. vi-vii.
4. Anil Seal, *The Emergence of Indian Nationalism: Competition and Collaboration in the Later Nineteenth Century*, Cambridge, 1968, p. 196.
5. Minute by Richard Temple, 14 January 1876, p. 93 in *Report on the Administration of Bengal, 1874-5*, Calcutta, 1876.
6. See Chapter 1 of the study. Also see *Thacker's Bengal Directory* for these years especially those of 1869, 1874 and 1879 for information on this assemblage of people.
7. For example, it was not Patna, the chief city in Bihar, to get the earliest association but Muzaffarpur. Similarly, Uttar Pradesh got its most famous association, Scientific Society at Ghazipur. All this happened because some strong personality took the lead in establishing them.

8. Minute by Richard Temple, 14 January 1876, p. 93 in *Report on the Administration of Bengal, 1874-75.*
9. *Thacker's, Bengal Directory for 1874*, Calcutta, 1874, pp. 1070-5.
10. *Report on the Administration of Bengal, 1872-73*, Calcutta, 1873, p. 91.
11. Surendra Gopal, *Patna in the Nineteenth Century*, Calcutta, 1982, p. 10.
12. Ibid., pp. 7-10.
13. Ibid., p. 10.
14. See Return of Scientific and Literary Societies in Bengal, in *Report on the Administration of Bengal, 1875-76*, Calcutta, 1877, p. CLXXIX and Resolution, General Department (Education), May 1873, in *General Report on Public Instruction in Bengal* (henceforth *RPI Bengal*), *1871-72*, Calcutta, 1873, pp. 21-2.
15. The information on the organizational set-up has been pieced together from Patna Commissioner, Basta No. 231 (Important Bundle, Judicial Department) file no. not available. See *Thacker's Bengal Directory for 1869*, pp. 264-7, 1874, pp. 1157-60, *RPI Bengal, 1869-70*, p. 149 and J.S. Jha, *Education in Bihar*, Patna, 1979, p. 204.
16. *RPI Bengal, 1872-73*, Calcutta, 1874, Appendix A, pp. 622-3.
17. Patna Commissioner, Basta No. 231 (Important Bundle, Judicial Department), file no. not available.
18. This information was given to me in 1996 by Mohamad Rizwan, then a research scholar at Centre of Indian Languages, School of Languages, Jawaharlal Nehru University, New Delhi.
19. W.W. Hunter, *A Statistical Account of Bengal* (henceforth *SAB*), London, 1877, rpt., Delhi, 1976, vol. XII, p. 164.
20. Return of Scientific and Literary Societies in Bengal in *Report on the Administration of Bengal, 1875-76*, p. CLXXIX.
21. See K.N. Panikkar for a discussion of the evolution of this consciousness, 'Historiographical and Conceptual Questions', in K.N. Panikkar, *Culture, Ideology and Hegemony: Intellectuals and Social Consciousness in Colonial India*, New Delhi, 1995, pp. 80-2.
22. *RPI Bengal, 1872-73*, Appendix A, p. 618.
23. *RPI Bengal, 1871-72*, Appendix A, p. 337.
24. Ibid., Appendix A, p. 329.
25. Return of Scientific and Literary Societies in Bengal in *Report on the Administration of Bengal, 1875-76*, p. CLXXIX.
26. Bengal General (Education) B Progs, April 1878, File no. 58, Sl. nos. 1-3.
27. *Report on Native Papers in Bengal* [henceforth *RNP(B)*], no. 41, 1873.
28. Patna Commissioner, Basta No. 231 (Important Bundle, Judicial Department), File no. 345.

29. S.R. Mehrotra, *The Emergence of the Indian National Congress*, Delhi, 1971, pp. 247-8.
30. *Report of a Monster Meeting at the Town Hall on the Education Question held on 2nd July 1870*, Calcutta, 1870, pp. 151 ff.
31. A.P. Jha, 'Political History of Bihar (1859-1912)', in K.K. Datta (ed.), *The Comprehensive History of Bihar* (henceforth *CHB*), vol. III in two parts, Patna, 1976, pt. I, p. 229.
32. *RPI Bengal, 1871-72*, Appendix A, pp. 327-8.
33. Resolution General (Education) Deptt., Calcutta, 19 May 1873, in *RPI Bengal, 1871-72*, pp. 21-2.
34. India Home (Education) A Progs, April 1877, nos. 53-61.
35. Q. Ahmad, 'Islam', in K.K. Datta (ed.), *CHB*, vol. III, pt. II, Patna, 1976, p. 101.
36. 'Return of Scientific and Literary Societies in Bengal', in *Report on the Administration of Bengal, 1875-76*, p. CLXXIX.
37. A number of such societies and associations were established around 1870. Thus in Muzaffarpur itself a society named Anjum Tahzib (Society for General Culture) was established with the objectives of promotion of liberal education and good conduct, the reading of essays, etc. See *RPI Bengal, 1869-70*, Appendix A, p. 151. The Monghyr Public Association was similarly established for social and intellectual improvement. See Return of Scientific and Literary Societies in Bengal in *Report on the Administration of Bengal, 1873-74*, Calcutta, 1874, p. CXVII.
38. India Home (Education) A Progs, January 1871, nos. 1-4.
39. *RPI Bengal, 1871-72,* Appendix A, p. 320.
40. 'Return of Scientific and Literary Societies in Bengal' in *Report on the Administration of Bengal, 1875-76,* p. CLXXIX. This is interesting. While in Calcutta a Muhammadan Literary Society was established, in Ghazipur a Scientific Society was set-up. However, in Bihar 'Behar' was used as the symbol and the reference point in both Behar Scientific Society and Behar Literary Society, although Muslims were instrumental in establishing both the societies.
41. Bengal General (Education) B Progs, May 1875, File no. 107, Sl. nos. 1-7.
42. See Patna Commissioner, Basta Nos. 230 and 236 (Important Bundle, Judicial Department).
43. Bengal General (Education) B Progs, May 1875, File no. 107, Sl. nos. 1-7.
44. Return of Scientific and Literary Societies in Bengal, in *Report on the Administration of Bengal, 1875-76*, p. CLXXIX.
45. Ibid.

46. Keshav Ram Bhatta (1854-1905) studied Hindu, Urdu, Persian and English. After doing entrance he got admitted to the F.A. classes. However, he later gave up studies and started the Bihar Bandhu Press. He edited the *Bihar Bandhu* for many years. He also worked as a school teacher. He was a prominent Hindi writer and wrote plays like *Sajjad Sumbul*, *Shamshad Sausan*. He actively worked for the adoption of Hindi as the vernacular language of Bihar. See B. Varma and K. Sharma 'Nayan' (eds.), *Hindi Sahitya Aur Bihar* (Hindi), vol. IV, Patna, 1984, pp. 36-7; Banshidhar Lal, *Bhatenduugin Hindi Patrakarita* (Hindi), Kanpur, 1986, pp. 144-5.
47. Return of Scientific and Literary Societies in Bengal, in *Report on the Administration of Bengal, 1875-76*, p. CLXXIX.
48. Ramji Mishra 'Manohar', *Dastanne Patliputra* (Hindi), New Delhi, 1989, pp. 136-7.
49. See *Calcutta Gazette*, no. 48 (29 November) 1876.
50. Ibid.
51. *Bihar Bandhu*, 19 August 1880.
52. Ibid.
53. Ibid., 18 April 1880. J.S. Jha says that it was known as Bihar Peoples' Association. See his 'Emergence of the Indian National Congress: Responses and Reactions in Bihar (1885-1908)', in J.S. Jha, *Aspects of the History of Modern Bihar*, Patna, 1988, p. 21 and fns.
54. *Bihar Bandhu*, 18 April 1880.
55. Ibid.
56. Ibid. From it, it becomes apparent that Anandi Prasad Mishra was a physician by profession. One Hindi source refers to one Anandi Prasad Mishra who was born in 1852, and was the son of Pandit Ayodhya Prasad Mishra of Gaya. According to this source, Mishra after early Sanskrit education joined the Patna High School where he studied till entrance. On the basis of self-study he acquired knowledge of Hindi, English, Gujarati, Marathi, Latin and German. He was the correspondent of many English papers and edited the *Bihar Bandhu* from 1890 to 1895. He was also a physician. See Varma and Sharma 'Nayan' (eds.), *Hindi Sahitya*, vol. IV, p. 19. This last fact and the trend of his career suggest that he must have been the secretary of the Peoples' Association, though the above Hindi source does not mention this.
57. See Jha, 'Emergence of the Indian National Congress', p. 21.
58. B.B. Majumdar, *Indian Political Associations and Reform of Legislature (1818-1917)*, Calcutta, 1965, Appendix I, p. 403.
59. Jha, 'Political History of Modern Bihar', p. 242.
60. Jha, 'Emergence of Congress in Bihar', p. 2.

61. Jha, 'Political History of Modern Bihar', p. 242.
62. Ibid. The Association first elected him as vice-president. Later and for long he remained the president. See Stephen Hennigham, *A Great Indian Estate and its Landlords in Colonial India: Darbhanga, 1860-1942,* Delhi, 1990, p. 71.
63. Jha, 'Political History of Bihar', pp. 216-17.
64. See Paul R. Brass, *Language, Religion and Politics in North India*, Cambridge, 1974, for a discussion of the Maithili movement.
65. Annual General Report of the Patna Division 1871-72, p. 22, in Bengal General (Miscellaneous) A Progs, October 1872, nos. 31-2.
66. Annual General Report of the Patna Division, 1875-76, pp. 26-7, in Bengal General (Miscellaneous) A Progs, August 1876, nos. 1-16.
67. Ibid.
68. Miscellaneous Annual General Report of the Patna Division, 1902-3, p. 9, in Bengal General (Miscellaneous) A Progs, November 1903, nos. 25-6.
69. General Administration Report of Bhagalpur Division, 1888-89, p. 13, in Bengal General (Miscellaneous) A Progs, volume for September-December 1889.
70. V.C.P. Chaudhary, *The Creation of Modern Bihar*, Patna and Darbhanga, 1964, p. 63.
71. See Eugen Weber, *Peasants into Frenchmen: The Modernization of Rural France, 1870-1914*, London, 1977, pp. 467-9.
72. See Benedict Anderson, *Imagined Communities: Reflections on the Origin and Spread of Nationalism,* London, 1983, pp. 37-40 and Glenn Bowman, '"A Country of Words": Conceiving the Palestinian Nation from the Position of Exile', in E. Laclau (ed.), *The Making of Political Identities*, London, 1994, pp. 138-70.
73. R.I. Crane, 'The Development of Nationalism in India in the Late Nineteenth Century: The Bengal Press and Associations in the Diffusion of Nationalism', in Paul Wallace (ed.), *Region and Nation in India*, New Delhi, 1985, pp. 95-6.
74. Ibid.
75. See N. Kumar, *Journalism in Bihar*, pp. 49-50, *RNP (B)*, no. 1, 1873 and Bengal General (Miscellaneous) A Progs, May 1871, no. 36.
76. Annual General Report of the Patna Division 1872-73, September 1873, p. 25, in Bengal General (Miscellaneous) A Progs, October 1873, File no. 1, Sl. nos. 100-13.
77. *Report on the Administration of Bengal, 1872-73*, p. 458.
78. *RNP (B)*, no. 35, 1873.

79. *RNP (B)*, no. 37, 1875. The report uses this term. It almost certainly was referring to the Bihar Upkar Sabha.
80. Ibid.
81. *RNP (B)*, no. 8, 1877.
82. J.C. Jha, 'Political Consciousness in Bihar before the formation of Indian National Congress', in P.N. Ojha (ed.), *History of Indian National Congress in Bihar, 1885-1985*, Patna, 1985, pp. 6-7.
83. See Chaudhary, *The Creation of Modern Bihar*, p. 26.
84. Ibid., pp. 26-9.
85. S. Sarkar, *Modern India: 1885-1947*, Madras, 1983, p. 33.
86. See Seal, *The Emergence of Indian Nationalism*, p. 57.
87. See Sarkar, *Modern India,* p. 30.
88. Seal, *The Emergence of Indian Nationalism*, p. 32.
89. Rachel R. Van Meter, 'Bankimchandra's View of the Role of Bengal in Indian Civilization', in David Kopf (ed.), *Bengal Regional Identity*, Michigan, 1969, pp. 67-8.
90. It is true that this superior attitude was not manifested only towards the Biharis. Madhusudan Das, the noted Oriya leader, has described poignantly how he had to suffer scorn and humiliation at the hands of fellow Bengali students at school. See John R. McLane, *Indian Nationalism and the Early Congress*, Princeton, 1977, p. 101.
91. See Chaudhary, *The Creation of Modern Bihar*, p. 34.
92. The excerpts have been taken from ibid., pp. 34-5.
93. Ambika Dutt Vyas, *Ashcharya Vritanta* (Hindi), Bhagalpur, Samvat 1950.
94. *RNP (B)*, no. 9, 1874.
95. *RNP (B)*, no. 18, 1874.
96. See Jha, 'Political History of Bihar', pp. 233-4 and MacLane, *Indian Nationalism and the Early Congress*, p. 207.
97. Annual General Report of the Patna Division, 1875-76, p. 29, in Bengal General (Miscll) Progs, Vol for January-August 1876.
98. See 'Annual General Report, District of Muzaffarpur, 1876-77', June 1877, in Annual General Report of the Patna Division, 1876-77, Appendix A, p. 16, in Bengal General (Miscellaneous) Progs, Volume for January-December 1877.
99. *Thacker's Bengal Directory*, Calcutta, 1869, pp. 201-4.
100. Ibid., Calcutta, 1874, pp. 1070-5.
101. Ibid., Calcutta, 1869, pp. 42-4.
102. Ibid., Calcutta, 1874, pp. 1070-5.
103. See H. Chattopadhyaya, *Internal Migration in India: A Case Study of Bengal*, Calcutta, 1987, pp. 262-5 and 475.

104. See *District Census Reports 1891, Patna Division, Patna District*, no other details, p. 6.
105. See *Arrah District Report* in ibid., p. 4.
106. Till 1873 there was no public press in the Division and scarcely any correspondent of newspapers published elsewhere. See Annual General Report of Bhagalpur Division, 1872-73, July 1873, p. 16, in Bengal General (Miscellaneous) A Progs, September 1873, File no. 1, Sl. nos. 42-52.
107. The fortnightly, later a weekly newspaper was started by some Hindus including Babu Ram Pershad (Prasad), who owned the paper in February 1874. The editor promised to advocate the interests of the fellow countrymen as well as supply them with all the current news and topics of the day and also invited the public in general to make known their respective opinions through the columns of the journal. The information has been pieced together from *RNP (B)*, no. 10, 1874, *RNP (B)*, no. 17, 1874 and Bengal General (Education) B Progs, June 1874, File no. 29, Sl. nos. 23-5.
108. The paper, a weekly, came out in 1874 and had as its aim bringing of local and other news within the reach of the underprivileged. It had circulation among the respectable Muslims of Monghyr. See *RNP (B)*, no. 30, 1874 and Annual General Report of Bhagalpur Division, 1875-76, July 1876, p. 16, in Bengal General (Miscellaneous) A Progs, August 1876, File no. 85, Sl. nos. 5-19.
109. *RNP (B)*, no. 24, 1874.
110. Ibid.
111. Ibid., no. 9, 1875.
112. Ibid., no. 8, 1876.
113. Ibid., no. 4, 1877.
114. Ibid.
115. Ibid.
116. It is interesting to note that at this time some Hindi and Urdu newspapers published from Calcutta but obviously having circulation in Bihar, consistently supported the cause of the Biharis, as we shall see later in this chapter.
117. *Bihar Bandhu*, 11 February 1880.
118. *RNP (B)*, no. 8, 1882.
119. Ibid., no. 5, 1881.
120. Ibid., no. 9, 1884.
121. *The Beharee*, 12 August 1910. In 1881 an Anglo-Indian A.N. Chick acted as the editor and later Mr. Money and still later Mahesh

Narayan was entrusted with the editorship of the paper (*Indian Chronicle*), see ibid.

122. Annual General Report of the Patna Division, 1881-82, p. 19, in Bengal General (Miscellaneous) Progs, vol. I for 1882.
123. *Motichoor*, 15 June 1876.
124. *Shiksha*, vol. II, no. 1 (6 April 1899), Patna, Bankipore, pp. 1-3.
125. *RNP (B)*, no. 38, 1876.
126. In this, one may give the example of the *Bihar Bandhu*. The publication of this newspaper was received with great enthusiasm by the elites of Patna, people in some districts and even in 'Chotanagpur and Ranchi', as it was something new in Hindi. See *Bihar Bandhu*, 20 July 1901. The paper by 1874 had correspondents at Monghyr, Sultanganj (near Bhagalpur) and Gaya. See *RNP (B)*, nos. 33, 35, 38 of 1874. That newspapers had become important in Bihar may be seen from an episode in Keshav Ram Bhatt's play *Sajjad Sumbul*, where an advertisement about a lost young lady is placed in a number of newspapers. See Keshav Ram Bhatta, *Sajjad Sumbul* (Hindi), Calcutta, 1904 (rpt.).
127. What the newspapers wrote was of significance as they started wielding influence in society by the mid-1870s. We have seen earlier in this chapter that in 1873 the Patna Commissioner had felt the influence of newspapers to be imperceptible but by 1876 he was obliged to change his opinion. In the annual report that year he wrote, 'The effects of English education, the circulation of newspapers and the increase of general intelligence are beginning to show themselves, and as far as this province is concerned, the first symptom is for a gasp of fresher air, purer water, better habitations'. See Annual General Report Patna Division, 1875-76 (21 July 1876), p. 27, in Bengal General (Miscellaneous) Progs, volume for January-August 1876. A telling proof of the newspapers' contribution to the making of Bihar is the title, 'Maker of Modern Bihar' given to Mahesh Narayan, the first editor of the *Behar Times*. See *The Beharee*, 5 August 1910.
128. Bengal General (Education) B Progs, October 1878, File no. 116, Sl. no. 1 and Bengal General (Education) B Progs, November 1878, File no. 116, Sl. nos. 2 and 3.
129. Bengal General (Education) B Progs, September 1882, File no.15, Sl. nos. 6-8.
130. Ibid.

CHAPTER 5

Bihar's Quest for Identity: The Beginning

The two decades of the 1870s and 1880s had seen a marked growth of regional consciousness in Bihar. Its most striking expression had been the 'Bihar for Biharis' slogan, which, in essence, signified and articulated a deeply felt resentment against what was seen as excessive employment of Bengalis in Bihar, who were seen and projected as not being natives of the soil but mere outsiders. But the growing consciousness continued to gather strength and manifested itself not only in the field of politics but also culture. The *Census Report* of 1901 took note of a new cultural development in Bihar and adduced factors, which had led to this:

> The Province of Bihar was for centuries much more connected politically with the United Provinces of Agra and Oudh than with Bengal. . . . The face of the Bihari is ever turned towards the North-West; from Bengal he has only experienced hostile invasions. For these reasons, the language of Bihar has often been considered to be a form of the 'Hindi' said to be spoken in the United Provinces, but really nothing can be further from the fact. In spite of the hostile feeling with which Biharis regard every thing connected with Bengal their language is a sister of Bengali, and only a distant cousin of the tongue spoken to its west. Like Bengali and Oriya, it is a direct descendant of the old Magadha Apabhramsa . . . and still retains nearly all its characteristic features. In one particular of pronunciation alone does it depart from its parent, viz. in the pronunciation of the sibilants. This is accounted for by the political influence of the North-West. The pronunciation of these letters is a literal shibboleth between Bengal and Central Hindustan. *A man who pronounces his s's as if it were sh would at once be known as a Bengali, and treated as such. The Biharis, therefore, in their desire, which has existed for centuries, to sever all connection with the people of their east, have striven after the pronunciation of the s's of the west, and have now acquired it, but it is a modern innovation*.[1] (emphasis added)

But regional nationalism, like other nationalisms, is primarily a political phenomenon and it is the political agenda and associated activities that needs to be examined. Here the most important development was the birth of the idea in the 1890s that Bihar needed to be separated from Bengal for the full flowering of her personality and the protection of native people's interests. In other words, it was believed, as C.J. Bishop notes, that meaningful political and social changes could take place only after provincial autonomy had been attained.[2] As we have seen in the preceding chapter the view that the union of Bihar with Bengal was not based on any sound principle and that it was proving detrimental to the various interests of the region had been occasionally propounded through the columns of newspapers and at least one paper, the *Qasid*, in 1877, had clearly urged the government to relieve the people of Bihar of the double subordination—that of the English and the Bengalis—that had been imposed on it, yet no clear-cut demand for provincial autonomy had been made. In fact, the desire did not largely exist then. A number of reasons had made for this condition. The most important reason was that the idea that a region and its people could not flourish properly without having a separate political identity of its own had not yet struck roots in the minds of the people. Secondly, prominent Bihari leaders of the time like Bisheshwar Singh, Saligram Singh, Gajadhar Prasad, Syed Sharfuddin and others were men who had passed many years of their life living under the existing system and very often because of their intimate contact with Calcutta and friendship with Bengalis had reconciled themselves to the existing situation. Even when realizing the desirability of a separate administration for Bihar they were convinced that any effort to secure the same was useless as such a demand was not likely to be conceded by the government. It was 'beyond the range of practical politics'.[3]

What finally changed the situation was the emergence of new leaders, men with passion and perspective, a number of whom were educated in England. They felt more keenly the absence of this identity than the older leaders, considered its achievement to be materially significant for the region and judged any struggle to achieve it morally just. Determined, persistent collective effort, in their opinion, was the key to achieve this goal. Before going into the circumstances under which the demand for separation was made it would be prudent to look into the formative influences on the two most important leaders of the movement, Mahesh Narayan and Sachchidananda Sinha, who were later to be known as the 'Makers of Modern Bihar'.

THE NEW LEADERS

Mahesh Narayan (1859-1907) occupies a pre-eminent position among the list of leaders who led the Biharis' struggle for a distinct identity. This 'Maker of Modern Bihar' was born in the Babhangama village of the Santhal Pargana district and was educated at Bhagalpur, Patna and Calcutta.[4] While in Patna he studied at the Patna College and after doing Entrance went to Calcutta where he gave up studies while still a student of B.A.[5] He was brought up in the company of his distinguished and public-spirited elder brother, Babu Govind Charan, who had the unique distinction of being the first Bihari to have obtained the M.A. degree and who had been a pioneer of many progressive movements in the region. Govind Charan had not only been associated with the Bihar Upkar Sabha which had worked for the introduction of Hindi in Bihar[6] but it was at his suggestion that the *Bihar Bandhu,* the first Hindi newspaper in Bihar, was brought to Patna from Biharsharif.[7] Again it was at his and some like-minded peoples' suggestion that Babu Bisheshwar Singh started an English newspaper, the *Indian Chronicle*, at Patna.[8] When the Indian National Congress came into being, Govind Charan was among its early participants from Bihar and attended both its sessions in 1886 and 1887, on the second occasion as the delegate of the Bihar Peoples' Association.[9]

The elder brother's company rubbed off on Mahesh Narayan's personality in many ways and his career reveals many striking parallels with the career of his sibling. An ardent lover of Hindi he wrote with great ability in that language, most of his writings being published in the *Bihar Bandhu.*[10] His journalistic career began as an apprentice to his elder brother whom he helped in editing the *Mushire Bihar*, a weekly. When the *Indian Chronicle* was established he began by writing in it and later became both its sub-editor and editor.[11] The paper devoted its columns to the airing of the supposed grievances of educated Biharis in their claim for employment.[12] This vantage point gave an unique opportunity to him to get fully conversant with the problems of Biharis. However, by 1888 the *Indian Chronicle* got merged with the *Behar Herald*, which had been a mouthpiece of the Bengali community in Bihar.[13] Mahesh Narayan now launched the *Kayastha Gazette*[14] (1888) and began rendering service to the cause of social reform of the community. However, after this paper ceased publication in 1891[15] he started editing the *Shahabad Gazette* and his reforming spirit was in full evidence when he defended Sachchidananda Sinha, the first upper caste Bihari to have gone to England,[16] who was facing hostile reception when he returned home in 1893. Mahesh Narayan, too, like his elder brother participated in the Indian National Congress sessions. In 1890 he participated as a delegate of the Bihar Peoples' Association.[17]

With such a varied experience of working as a journalist, it is no wonder that Mahesh Narayan emerged as the leading publicist of Bihar in the 1890s and early years of the twentieth century.

Unlike Mahesh Narayan, the information on the intellectual evolution of Sachchidananda Sinha is far more copious. S. Sinha (1871-1950) came from a very respectable family of the Shahabad district. An only child of Ramyad Sinha, who had been in the Executive Service in the North-West Provinces and later a lawyer at Benares and Arrah, Sinha did his school education from Arrah and Patna. Though he joined the Patna College, foreign shores beckoned him and breaking from the caste taboos he went to England to study law and thus became the first upper caste Bihari to do so. He joined the Hon'ble Society of Middle Temple and the University College, London, where he lived with Hasan Imam, whom he had befriended in school days itself and who, like Sinha, was to emerge later as one of the most important leaders of Bihar. In London, Sinha attended regularly lectures of eminent professors in Law, History, Politics, Logic and Economics and fully utilized his time in improving his mind with 'study, observation and reflection'.[18] His speeches and writings reveal his great mastery over Western political thought as they are replete with references of Spencer, Acton and other Western intellectuals[19] and thus clearly point to his studious habits. It would be interesting to speculate on what he could have been observing and speculating upon. But before doing that we need to point out that he was no armchair intellectual and, in fact, was an active worker on behalf of the National Indian Association of the British Committee of the Indian National Congress. Sinha was called to the bar in 1893, returned to India the same year and started practice at Patna.[20]

The three-plus year stay in England proved crucial in the intellectual development of S. Sinha. These were the years when the Victorian era was coming to its end and the United Kingdom was witnessing a great surge of nationalist and separatist movements. It was not only Ireland, the least homogeneous national element in the Kingdom which erupted in a demand for Home Rule but similar forces of separatism began to emerge forth in Wales and Scotland too. The 1880s not only saw a movement to introduce bilingual teaching into Welsh schools[21] but also the passing of the Welsh Sunday Closing Act of 1881, an overt recognition of Welsh national interest. Simultaneously, Scotland witnessed the growth of the Home Rule movement, got a Scottish office in government and was assured a guaranteed share of public expenditure of the United Kingdom.[22] Gladstone's 'Newcastle Programme' of 1891 included Irish Home Rule and church disestablishment in Wales and Scotland.[23] Questions of identity had assumed a great importance in the contemporary political discourse. It is no wonder that in such an atmosphere the discovery that his own province Bihar was largely a *terra incognita* hurt him greatly. This personal experience proved as crucial in the formation of Sinha's personality and shaping of his outlook as his studies and observations in England. This discovery was made by Sinha and his friends while studying in London. It is best to quote him:

> This was forced on my attention during my stay in London, as a student, during the early nineties of the last century (19th century), when I made the painful and humiliating discovery that not only was Bihar a *terra incognita* to the average Britisher, and to even the retired Anglo-Indians, but also to the majority of the Indians there. Some of my Indian friends, in Britain, even challenged me to a literary combat, and dared me to point out any such province as 'Bihar' in a recognized textbook of geography! It would be difficult for me to convey to the Biharees of today the sense of shame and humiliation which I, and some other equally

sensitive Biharee friends, felt while prosecuting our studies in Britain, on realizing that we were a people without any individuality, without any province to claim as ours; in fact, without any local habitation with a name.[24]

Later experiences only confirmed this discovery. While on the way back from London, he met a person from Punjab on the ship who, too, was returning after doing Bar-at-Law. When replying to a question from him S. Sinha said that he belonged to Bihar, the fellow from Punjab kept silent for a few moments and then told Sinha that he had not heard the name before.[25]

The painful discoveries that he had made thus far were once again repeated. When on return to India at the very first railway station in Bihar, 'I noticed a tall, robust and stalwart Biharee constable wearing the badge with the inscription "Bengal Police". It almost embittered my feelings of joy and gratification on my return home after an absence of more than three years abroad.'[26] This was the moment when he decided to do 'all that lay in my power to secure for Bihar a distinct and honorable status as an administrative unit, with an individuality on the same footing as that of the more important provinces in the country'.[27]

He was to recall later with some exaggeration that 'this was to be thereafter the mission of my life, and its realization the greatest source of inspiration permeating my public activities'.[28]

However, it was not only Sinha and Mahesh Narayan who were bitter about the condition of Bihar. As Sinha himself says, many of his Bihari friends (obviously people like Ali Imam and Hasan Imam, with whom he lived in London and who both did Bar-at-Law from the Middle Temple as Sinha did) felt equally bad about the absence of Bihar's distinct political identity.[29]

THE BIRTH OF *BEHAR TIMES*

It was left to Sinha, however, to lead the way though the journey promised to be difficult. His suggestion to start propaganda work for the separation of Bihar was initially received with indifference by the senior leaders, who sincerely believed that the effort would be useless. He, however, got crucial support from Mahesh Narayan, Krishna Sahay and Nand Kishore Lal (of Gaya).[30] In order to work for this objective it was felt desirable to start a journal in English as without such a journal of their own the Bihari politicians were in a helpless plight because their opinion did neither gain any publicity nor carry any weight with the 'Local Government'. Finally a weekly journal named the *Behar Times* was launched. Interestingly the first name suggested for the journal was *Beharee* but it was regarded by some of the leaders who had contributed financially to the venture, to be betraying an 'undue and undesirable spirit of provincial assertiveness'.[31] The *Behar Times* made its appearance in January 1894 with Mahesh Narayan as its editor.[32]

Thus far the venture had been a concern of the English-educated elites. Not unexpectedly, the decision was to start a paper in English. The targeted group of readers was obviously an English-educated one. It thus limited the reach to which the idea propagated through the paper could have spread. Any movement for the creation of Bihar was thus destined from the very beginning to be elite-dominated as also largely dependent on their support.

It seems that at this stage no attempt was made to enlist the support of the Muslim elites, which apparently is rather strange as S. Sinha had very good relationship with Ali Imam and Hasan Imam, having lived in London, in fact, with Hasan Imam. One possible reason appears to have been the fact that Hindu-Muslim relations had suffered a temporary set-back around that period as a result of a renewed Hindi-Urdu controversy and cow protection riots.[33] Also presently there was absolutely no talk of establishing any political organization for the purpose.

It is no wonder then that the Patna Commissioner reported about the paper as representing the educated Hindu party in Bihar.[34] Soon, however, the popularity of the paper increased and perceptions regarding it changed. By 1895 it had 600 subscribers,[35] undoubtedly a very good figure for that time. By 1896 it was seen as the organ of Biharis[36] and in 1897 the Patna Commissioner saw it as representing the patriotic Bihari elements.[37] Obviously it was no longer seen as representing only the Hindu section in Bihar.

The appearance of the *Behar Times* with its pro-Bihari policy[38] introduced a qualitative change in the political scene of Bihar. There had been vernacular papers in Bihar like the *Bihar Bandhu*, the

Qasid, *Murgh-i-Suliman* and others which had championed the interests of the region as we have seen earlier in the study but the *Behar Times* was launched by its English-educated elites and spoke in the language and idiom of rulers, and thereby was more graspable for them.[39] Unlike the previous newspapers it had set a specific mission for itself—to work for the separation of Bihar. Though its launch did not mark the beginning of a renaissance in Bihar, as S. Sinha claimed, it certainly marked the beginning of a new phase in the growth of regional consciousness there. However, the demand for separation was not on the immediate agenda. Rather the initial efforts were directed towards convincing the government that Bihar formed a distinct region with distinct needs which needed to be recognized and addressed to. In the course of an address presented to the Lieutenant-Governor of Bengal, Charles Elliott, at Gaya in 1894, the point was explicitly made:

> We crave leave to submit that it is the fate of Behar that it forms, for administrative purposes, a mere appendage of the larger province of Bengal. Perhaps, by reason of the very position which that province occupies as the most advanced in India, the interests of Behar and its people are liable to be lost sight of; but we earnestly hope that its importance as a separate province, containing a separate people, will be always consistently recognized in matters of legislation and administration.[40]

Charles Elliott was sympathetic to the core. The claims of Bihari leaders for treating Bihar as a separate unit in certain matters of importance, he said, had found a response in his heart. No wonder, the *Behar Times* jubilantly wrote that the declaration of Charles Elliott 'may be taken as a great advance made in the direction of the establishment of Behar as a separate provincial administration. The event may be distant, but it is inevitable'.[41] Even in January, 1896 while pleading the case of Bihar for separation, the paper felt that the creation of Bihar as a separate provincial administration 'is a distant event', but asserted 'the mission of this paper is life-long'.[42]

However, what appeared a distant event soon began to look like an immediate possibility due to a certain turn of events, which had been maturing for some time past. These had to do with the transfer of some territory to the province of Assam.

TOWARDS THE MOVEMENT OF 1896

The Government of India had been concerned about the large and unwieldy size of the Bengal Presidency since the 1860s. The Orissa famine of 1866 and the inadequate measures to deal with it had exposed the unwisdom of keeping such a large area under one person's charge.[43] In the period thereafter a number of solutions to deal with the problem were contemplated in the official circles. Not surprisingly, the proposal to separate Bihar used to emerge forth as a solution with remarkable regularity. In 1868, the Governor-General, John Lawrence, while pressing for the separation of Assam to afford relief to the Bengal government suggested the separation of Bihar, if additional relief was sought, 'which has no real affinity to Bengal Proper and which together with some parts of Benares, might be formed into a separate Lieutenant-Governorship, as was done temporarily by Lord Canning in 1857-58'.[44]

It was only in 1874 that Assam was separated and made into a Chief Commissioner's Province. Even at that time the Bengal Lieutenant-Governor, George Campbell, in a minute (27th January, 1873) pleaded for special administration in Bihar.

> Behar is a country very different from Bengal, and inhabited by a people extremely different. All the official business and habitudes necessarily much differ. I think that in Behar also there should be a special administration. The whole of the Patna Division, and at any rate, the District of Bhagulpore and Monghyr of the Bhagulpore Division, are purely Hindustani Districts and would eventually go into the Behar Division.[45]

However, nothing concrete happened as regards Bihar. Rather over the years the colonial government developed a new interest in the development of Assam. But as the years passed it came to be realized that the separation of Assam had not fully solved the problems caused by the unwieldy size of the Bengal Presidency.

It was in this background that the question of transfer of Chittagong Division to Assam emerged in the last decade of the nineteenth century. In July, 1892 the question was first started in a Resolution of the Foreign Department in connection with the administration of the country of the Lushai and Chin tribes. In the Resolution it was said that Chittagong district should be transferred from Bengal to Assam, as soon as the settlement operations then in progress had come to an end, and that the Government of Bengal and the Chief Commissioner of Assam should be consulted on the expediency of transferring to Assam the whole of Chittagong Division, including the political charge of Hill Tipperah. Later the Government of India informed the Assam administration that the transfer of the plain districts of the Chittagong Division from Bengal to Assam need not be carried out until the settlement operations were completed and the Chittagong-Assam Railway had at least progressed so far towards completion that the people and letters could go by that route. Later it was ascertained that Railway from Chittagong to Silchar would be ready for traffic by 1 April 1896 and the entire settlement operations would be completed by March 1897.[46] The proposal to transfer the entire Chittagong Division was made by Sir Alexander Mackenzie, who was a member of the Viceroy's Council.[47] In reply to a member's question in the Bengal Legislative Council in 1896 the government made it clear that it was of the view that it was desirable to relieve the Lieutenant-Governor of Bengal of some portion of a charge which owing to the development of the country and the growth of the population threatened to become too large to be administered by one government. 'Assam, on the other hand', it was said 'is the smallest Province in British India for which there is a separate administration, and the addition to it of the Chittagong Division would not have the effect of throwing too great a burden on the Chief Commissioner.' The prospect of material benefits to the province were also advanced as a purpose.[48]

The news of the proposed territorial redistribution gave the Bihari leaders the chance to mount a campaign for its separation and the year 1896 witnessed a major constitutional agitation in the region.

THE MOVEMENT OF 1896 AND ITS AFTERMATH

The movement started rather modestly in the month of March. The first phase consisted, in the main, of press campaign, which was followed by a period of more direct political activity, mainly public meetings. It came to a sudden end in the month of July.

As the year opened, the news of the proposed changes began to trickle down and the people in Bengal rose in protest. Protest meetings began to be held at Comilla and other places in East Bengal in the month of January itself.[49] While a Bengali daily *Dainik-o-Samachar* advanced reasons why Chittagong should be retained with Bengal,[50] Surendra Nath Banerjee's *Bengalee* carried a protest memorial against the proposed separation.[51]

After lying quiescent for the first two months Bihar began to stir in the month of March when an article was published in the influential Anglo-Indian newspaper, the *Pioneer.* As the article played the role of a catalyst in giving rise to the movement of 1896, as admitted by the leading members of the movement, a close look into it is in order. To begin with, it did not outright support the separation of Bihar as selective quotes, both in some primary sources and secondary works, have sought to suggest.[52] The paper while discussing the question of territorial redistribution in the eastern part of India began by admitting that if Assam continued to have separate existence some such enlargement was necessary as it was obliged to borrow all the civilian and police officers from Bengal and was facing difficulties in running the administration. It pointed out, however, that even the proposed change would increase the anomalies in which the province already abounded and would also be an expensive proposition. The paper while pointing out that the partition of Bengal was not an easy matter went on to say,

> If the question had arisen for the first time it might easily be argued that the inevitable partition need not necessarily be in the East; that it would be better to lop off such homogeneous tracts as the Orissa Division or the Chota Nagpore Division, or both. Again, Behar would be a separate and entirely homogeneous charge which would afford tempting opportunities to an administrator. It is a difficult charge; and in at least one Behar Commissioner we have an ideal Chief Commissioner ready made. If we English were a logical people and impatient of anomalies, the relief of the overworked Government of Bengal would lie irresistibly in the separation of Behar. But our genius lies in the direction of the acceptance of accomplished facts, and the separation of Assam was accepted twenty years ago. Hence we do not stop to ask whether that separation has been altogether a success, and yet it is clear that the history of the Chief Commissionership has been chequered. . . . Assam cannot be, will never be, a charge so popular, so likely to attract the best men, as for instance, a Chief Commissionership of Behar.[53]

The paper went on to conclude that if Assam was to be enlarged it should be done on a large scale.[54] At this stage the *Pioneer* was hinting at a solution which should have been resorted to earlier to reduce the burden on the Lieutenant-Governor of Bengal.

The appearance of this article emboldened the Bihari leaders and through the columns of the *Behar Times* the government was sought to be convinced that from every point of view the separation of Bihar offered better prospects of giving relief to the overworked Lieutenant-Governor of the Lower Provinces than the transfer of Chittagong or even a larger slice of Bengal to Assam.[55] According to it, it would be an act of administrative justice. Making out a powerful case for the separation of Bihar it pointed out that the region was in possession of all the elements for the successful creation of a local administration. It said:

> Geographically it may be said to be complete and compact for this purpose, it is inhabited by a homogeneous people, who are differentiated from the people of Bengal in manners and customs, language and literature, in the degree of their educational and political progress, in the measure of their requirements, in the character of their aims and ambitions, and in the quality of the treatment they require at the hands of the Government.[56]

It was further pointed out that growing administrative needs of Bihar had led to the creation of special arrangements in the administration like the posting of DIG of Police and a Deputy Post Master General. It was also argued that the difficulty of governing Bihar from Calcutta was bound to increase and before long the establishment of a local government in Bihar would cease to be a matter of choice and become one of urgent administrative necessity. Therefore, the Government of India was asked to think, before finally sanctioning the separation of Chittagong from Bengal, whether the separation of Bihar would not be a matter of greater administrative convenience and political wisdom. It also drew attention to the fact that Chittagong was opposed to the separation whereas there would be no opposition in Bihar.[57]

However, the case made out by the *Pioneer* and the *Behar Times* did not go unchallenged, not even in Bihar. The Bengali settlers and their principal mouthpiece the *Behar Herald* as also some Calcutta-based newspapers like the *Bengalee* and the *Amrita Bazar*

Patrika vehemently opposed the proposal,[58] while the *Al Punch* of Patna as also some Calcutta-based Hindi and Urdu newspapers stoutly supported the demand of Bihari leaders.[59] What resulted was a furious war of words.

In this war of words the principal argument advanced by the anti-separation group, as exemplified in a series of articles written by Guru Prasad Sen in the *Behar Herald*, was that if Bihar was separated bankruptcy would follow. He tried to show that Bihar was too poor and contributed too little to be able to pay for the expenses of a separate administration and if the province was separated, additional taxation would be the price, which the Biharis would have to pay for the privilege of getting rid of the yoke of Bengal,[60] On the other hand, the papers supporting the separation demand sought to convince the government that it was a better option than any other scheme of territorial distribution to ease the burden on the Bengal government.

By April, the *Pioneer* openly began supporting Bihar's demand. On 8 April it reiterated its views that the transfer of the Chittagong Division to Assam would not satisfactorily solve the two problems which it was intended to do. It would not appreciably reduce the unwieldy hugeness of Bengal and the impossibility of working a small province satisfactorily would also remain. It was also argued that the measure would divide a homogeneous population between two governments. The paper offered an alternative solution-restoration of Assam to Bengal and creation of new Bihar Chief Commissionership. It argued and showed through facts and figures that the solution offered by it was better in all respects. It went on to say,

> There is the great advantage that the change instead of being resisted would be hailed with delight by that part of the population concerned which has advanced far enough to have any ideas at all on the subject; nor it is probable that any difficulty would be forthcoming from the public services.

The paper believed that the separation of Bihar would be opposed by the large and growing company of Bengalis who served as clerks in Bihar. 'A separate Government of Behar would assuredly encourage local talent in this direction and favour the quilldriving of Beharis.' It also expected a Council for Bihar and 'a High Court might follow in time'. It pointed out, there have been advantages in the past to rulers and ruled from the association of Behar and Bengal under one rule. . . . But Behar has always been Behar, Bengal Bengal; and it will be just as easy to lop off the districts of Behar from Bengal as to add Orissa to Ganjam. . . . The people and nobles of Behar are justly proud of their country, and will doubtless rejoice to see it severed from a common rule with a province with which in climate, in crops, in men, manners or morals, they have little in common.[61]

The *Bengalee* took little time in responding. It sarcastically took note of the *Pioneer* write-up. 'As might be expected, our contemporary shows considerable warmth in the discussion of the question. *His love for Bengal and the Bengalees is apparent in each line of the article.*'[62] (emphasis added) It is important to point out that both the *Pioneer* and the *Bengalee* had circulation in Bihar and they enjoyed a certain influence.

However, soon the *Al Punch* (an Urdu weekly from Patna) also threw its weight behind the demand for separation and put forward what had become by now the stock argument that without such a separation the Biharis being backward in education would never be able to secure a fair share of posts under government.[63] The press campaign succeeded in mobilizing the educated people in Bihar and soon the movement entered a more popular phase. Meetings began to be organized in different parts of Bihar in the months of May and June.

The town of Bhagalpur was the first to give the wake up call. The 'true-born Beharis' of the town appreciating the suggestion given by the *Pioneer* began taking practical steps to accomplish the separation of Bihar. A meeting was held at Bhagalpur on 26 May at the premises of an influential local zamindar and promoter of education Rai Tej Narayan Singh Bahadur to discuss the subject and resolutions were finally adopted in the meeting to send petitions to the government.[64]

A similar large and enthusiastic meeting held at Purnea on 7 June not only gave its approval to the suggestions put forward by the *Behar Times* and *Pioneer* for the separation of Bihar but also proposed a course of action. First, it wanted a committee to be appointed to watch the events and take appropriate actions. Second, it proposed to request the Maharaja of Darbhanga, the president of Bihar Landholders' Association, to move that association to take up this issue.[65] The meetings at district headquarters within the Bhagalpur Division suggest that the movement was having enthusiastic support of the educated classes there.

Meanwhile Patna, the chief city of Bihar, was also stirring in a big but organized way. The leading Hindu and Muslim elites of the city met in a meeting in the first week of June at the B.N. College. Prominent among those present were S. Sinha, Chhote Nawab (son of Nawab Lutf Ali Khan Bahadur), Narayan Prasad, Sarfaraz Hussain and Pandit Jai Narayan Vajpayee. This meeting not only decided to hold a more general meeting later but also appointed Krishna Sahay and Sarfaraz Hussain to collect opinion from the leading men in other districts.[66] In the meeting, that was held later in the month, all the speakers except Gajadhar Prasad supported the demand for the separation of Bihar.[67]

The month of June not only witnessed great political activity, rarely seen in Bihar before, but also a ferocious war of words, rich in sarcasm. The *Bharat Mitra* (a Hindi weekly from Calcutta) reported on 11 June that both the Hindu and Muslim leaders of the Bihar community would petition the Government of India asking for a separate administration for Bihar. It pointed out that the public meetings being held by the Biharis in different districts were of the firm opinion that under the Bengal government the community, because of its educational backwardness, would not attain to material prosperity because while filling up vacancies in government offices even in Bihar, heads of the departments gave preference to better-qualified Bengali candidates.[68]

Positions were gradually hardening. The papers controlled by the Bengalis consistently questioned the wisdom of those wanting the separation of Bihar and accused the Anglo-Indian community and especially the *Pioneer* of engineering the whole movement. The *Hitvadi*, a Bengali weekly from Calcutta, in its issue of 19 June, found it difficult to praise the wisdom of those wanting the separation of Bihar from Bengal. According to it, the *Pioneer* and certain selfish and narrow-minded civilians, whose policy was to divide and rule, were at the bottom of the agitation for the separation of Bihar. It accused them of inciting the ignorant Biharis who were incapable of seeing to their own interests and were only too anxious to please Englishmen and finally expressed the hope that Biharis would desist from their mischievous course of action.[69] The *Bengalee*, another Calcutta paper, dated 20 June 1896 also attacked the whole separatist movement and felt that it was engineered by the Anglo-Indian Community. It termed as 'curious' the separatist movement which 'has been thoughtlessly set on foot for the complete severance of Bihar from the Administration of the Bengal Government'. It observed that the proposal, altogether novel in its character, 'seems to have been first broached in the columns of the *Pioneer*, in connection with the scheme for the transfer of Chittagong Division to Assam'. The paper felt that the proposal at that time was not given much credence but there was always a fear that 'a few at least, of the Biharis would play into the hands of an Anglo-Indian newspaper whose counsels we should always be disposed to receive with extreme caution'. Displaying traces of the Brown Man's burden (the self-imposed duty taken by the more advanced Indians to ensure the progress of less educated people, similar in nature to the White Man's burden) it condescendingly wrote, 'We firmly believe that a close association with an advanced province not only tends to keep up the standard of administration in the less favoured districts but also levels up their (less favoured districts') inhabitants'.[70]

However, and for obvious reasons, Bihari leaders were not prepared to drop the idea and meetings continued to be held. In July, the Patna Commissioner writing about the state of public feeling noted:

> Some interest has been excited among the upper classes and the educated men of the Division, and class feelings have been aroused by the academic suggestion that Behar should be separated from Bengal and placed under a separate Administration. The strongest supporters of separation are the *Muhammadans of Patna* with a contingent of Behari Hindus, while the unionists are chiefly composed of the Bengali colonists reinforced by a few of the older and wiser men who recognize how much the Division would lose by the separation.[71] (emphasis added)

He went on, 'Meetings have been held at Patna and elsewhere, and a society has been projected, the object of which is to bring about, by every means in its power, the separation of Bengal from Behar'. Interestingly, he noted that the presidency of this Association was offered to the Maharaja of Darbhanga, but he, 'with characteristic prudence declined the proffered honour'.[72] This report too, thus shows that the movement was fairly widespread. Attempts made, however, to get the support of the Maharaja of Darbhanga, did not succeed. It also seems that no attempt was made to spread the movement to the Chota Nagpur Division or get the support of the common people there or elsewhere.

However, after four months of flexing of intellectual muscles in the verbal exchanges with Bengali leaders and their press as also the organization of public meetings, the Bihari leaders finally got a chance, in the month of July, to directly confront the government with their demand (to separate Bihar) but their nerves failed at the last moment.

They shied away from making an explicit demand, resting content with only making a qualified reference to it. Even this mild reference brought a strong reprimand from the Lieutenant-Governor, Sir Alexander Mackenzie, and the whole movement suddenly collapsed. The denouement was both tragic and anti-climactic. The received version on the events of those days would have us believe that the unsympathetic attitude of the Lieutenant-Governor was the sole factor which caused the collapse of the movement. However, our examination of the events of that period and of the critical omissions that inform some important sources as also the availability of some crucial information have led us to conclude that a complex matrix of factors like the political culture of the day[73] and absence of an experienced leadership well-versed in the art and science of political agitation as also, of course, the unsympathetic attitude of not only the Lieutenant-Governor but other officials too were responsible for the sudden ceasing of the movement.

All this needs a detailed narration of events as they unfolded. While the Bihari leaders were engaged in press campaign and public meetings, came the news that the Lieutenant-Governor of Bengal would be making a visit to Bihar and the first place in his itinerary would be the town of Gaya, where Nand Kishore Lal, an active supporter of the separation demand, happened to be the vice-chairman of the municipality. It was decided by the Bihari leaders that in the joint address to be presented to the Lieutenant-Governor, Sir Alexander Mackenzie, by the local municipality and the District Board, the question of separation should find a prominent place.

Nand Kishore Lal did succeed in bringing around to this view not only the European members of these local bodies but even two Bengali members of the Municipality, Upendra Chandra Mitra and Durga Shankar Bhattacharya.[74] However, the reference to the separation question was quite nullified by what was said next in the text. We produce in extenso the part of the Address dealing with the question as also the whole part of the Lieutenant-Governor's reply to the above question. This is done with a view to present the complete picture, as selective references and selective quotes in the major primary sources for the study of this period tend to create an impression that the Lieutenant-Governor was unusually harsh or he refused to concede a demand actually made. This is not to say that he was really sympathetic toward Bihar. The Address presented by the local bodies and read out by Nand Kishore Lal (Nund Kishore Lall) said on the separation issue:

> . . . . The representatives of the district of Gaya, when addressing your predecessor in office on his visit to this town in 1894, respectfully represented that the Government may be pleased 'to recognize the importance of Behar as a separate province containing a separate people in matters of legislation and administration'. *Since then certain events have led thoughtful men in the province to advocate the separation of Behar from Bengal for administrative purposes. This is no doubt a very wide question which, we feel certain, will receive the attention of Government at the proper time; but so long as separation of the two provinces is not deemed practicable, we venture to express the earnest hope that the reasonable claim of the Beharis, that their interest as a separate people is liable to separate treatment in several matters of legislation and administration, be not lost sight of.*[75] (emphasis added)

The Lieutenant-Governor's reply makes an equally interesting reading. He made clear that he did not have time to prepare a formal reply to the address presented to him and that he would 'deal with it paragraph by paragraph in a conversational way'. But in spite of this it was not 'thoroughly demoralizing' as a selective quote would make us believe, though it was certainly a discouraging one. In reference to the separation issue the Lieutenant-Governor said:

> In your next point you refer to the fact that thoughtful men in the province are advocating the separation of Behar from Bengal for administrative purposes. Now 'thoughtful' is not precisely the term that I should apply

to the gentlemen who are working this agitation, which is a mere balloon without any substance whatever in it. It is undoubtedly purely a newspaper agitation of the kind, at present in vogue. It appears to me very much like the newspaper agitation at home in what is called the 'silly season', when Parliament is not sitting and newspapers have to exercise their ingenuity on something sensational for their readers and they start some such discussion. 'Is Marriage a Failure?' or describe the proportions of some portentous goose-berry. I have observed that this discussion about the separation of Behar started while the Provincial Council was not sitting. It must have been a silly season for the Behar and other papers to have taken up this question. They had apparently nothing more useful to discuss. It is the last thing likely to happen within our time. Neither the Government of India nor the Secretary of State is likely to propose the creation of another Local Government in Upper India. *To a certain extent I sympathize with the feelings of Beharis in the matter and those who are bona fide agitating this question. There is no doubt that the Beharis have been left rather behind in the race for office and employment. There is no doubt my Bengali friends have proved too many for the Beharis, as they have proved too many for the Englishmen, Eurasians, Punjabis and North-West men; but I don't despair myself of Beharis being able to turn the tables.* I asked Sir Alfred Croft, Director of Public Instruction, the evening before coming away, if my impression was correct, and whether Beharis were not gradually improving and coming to the front. Sir A. Croft tells me that for a long time schools in Behar were staffed mainly by Bengalis, because Beharis of the proper qualifications were difficult to find, and a large number of teachers of this class still remain; but with the gratifying spread of higher education in Behar which has taken place of late years the difficulty is rapidly disappearing, and *Behar graduates are securing their full share of the higher education appointments. . . . I was very happy to find, when making the last appointments for the Subordinate Executive Service that the Beharis had done so well that I was able to confer upon them a full share of the appointments; and it appears to me, if things go on in that way, that the question of separation will soon cease to be urged.*[76] (emphasis added)

It is apparent from the Lieutenant-Governor's reply that he did not consider the demand powerful enough to respond to it positively, even though it had not been openly made. It was also perfectly in tune with the opinion of the Patna Commissioner who in his annual report had termed as 'academic suggestion' the demand for the separation of Bihar, and pointedly said that 'older' and 'wiser' men were opposed to the demand and who also found the decline of the offer by the Maharaja of Darbhanga of presidency of an association, which was to work for the separation, as a sign of his 'characteristic prudence'. The bias among officials against the movement was very apparent.[77]

It came to an end immediately after the Gaya fiasco. Nowhere after there during the course of Lieutenant-Governor's tour in Bihar in the different Addresses presented to him at places like Muzaffarpur,[78] Darbhanga,[79] Monghyr,[80] or even Patna[81] and Bhagalpur[82] (the two chief cities of the region) was even a mild reference made to the separation issue. The *Behar Times* contented itself by saying that the last word on the subject had not been spoken and that as soon as the contemplated separation of Chittagong would be taken up for discussion again, the question of the separation of Bihar, as an ideally perfect and final administrative measure, would naturally arrest the attention of the public and the Government of India.[83]

A pall of gloom enveloped those who had so enthusiastically launched the movement and supported it. While S. Sinha, a major moving spirit behind the movement fell ill and left the province for some years, many of the people who had supported the movement, now feeling that it was an unwise course of action left it altogether.[84] A contemporary Urdu poem by a 'Bihari' best captured the despondency of the times. Contained within it was also a sense of anger against those British officials who were perceived to be pro-Bengali. A government report produced in extenso its translated version:

1. The days of impartial justice have gone away with Sir Charles Elliot. May God save the Biharis. The Babu-loving policy of Bayley has again been introduced. We can only look up to Her Gracious Majesty.
2. Everything will be quite all right with you babus under Sir Alexander Mackenzie who loves you and likes you. Your sharp writings will make an impression on the government and your newspaper articles will terrify the ruler.
3. You are contented because you enjoy his protection. And you have ample opportunity to oppose us. It has fallen to our lot to see an evil day. There is neither Mr. Cotton nor Sir Charles Elliott to take care of us.

4. The Chief Justice has, with the sanction of the Lieutenant-Governor required the Bihari candidates to pass an examination in Bengali.
5. Sir Alexander Mackenzie must bear it in mind that the Biharis have a language of their own. How can he require us, Biharis, to learn Bengali? He must withdraw his order.
6. He gave a rude reply to our address. He said what should not have fallen from a ruler. One has only to ask the people of Gaya to know what he said. We would not say anything.[85]

The Patna Commissioner, in his annual report could thus write in 1897:

> At the beginning of the year there was a good deal of feeling among the educated classes in favour of a movement to petition for the separation of Behar from Bengal, but this was crushed for the time at any rate by the Lieutenant-Governor's speech at Gaya.[86]

By 1897 the plan of transfer of Chittagong to Assam too stood abandoned. In a blunt note J.P. Hewitt, the Secretary to the Government of India, pointed out that though every one admitted that the Lieutenant-Governor of Bengal required relief but

> in order to relieve him effectively, it would be necessary to remove a much larger portion of the territory under his charge. The proposal made in the *Pioneer* to remove Behar from his control would not meet with the support of any of the people affected, and I doubt whether any territorial re-arrangement of his duties could be devised which would at the same time really give him effective relief and be free from very grave objections.[87]

The abandonment of transfer plan also removed the context in which the Bihari leaders had demanded its separation. Now with this question out of the way the newspapers in Bihar once again fell back to the two familiar tasks of criticizing the discriminatory attitude of the government towards Bihar and the disproportionate employment of Bengalis in the region.

In 1898 the disproportionate number of Bengali officials in the Education Departments came in for severe criticism by the *Behar Times*.[88] In 1899 the affairs of the Calcutta University and non-appointment of Biharis as officers in the different Estates of the region were discussed. The absence of any role for the Biharis in the administration of Calcutta University, the poor number of Bihari Fellows in it and the non-inclusion of Hindi in its curriculum came in for censure. The paper in its different issues also detailed the process through which Bengalis had come to monopolize all important posts in the Hathwa raj. This fact and the fact that an overwhelming share of ministerial posts was also held by them was heavily criticized and justice was demanded for the people of Bihar.[89] Demands for a better representation of the Biharis in different branches of administration were made. In the case of judicial appointments, it was submitted that all the posts that existed in Bihar should go to the Biharis, 'the children of the soil'. It went to the extent that even in matters like the conferment of titles people of Bihar were seen to be neglected.[90]

COMING OF THE PARTITION: DIFFERING OPINIONS AND EARLY REACTIONS

The proposal to transfer Chittagong was again to be revived and in a larger form. At the time when proposals had been mooted earlier in the 1890s, William Ward, the Chief Commissioner of Assam, had also favoured the transfer of Dacca and Mymensingh districts of the Dacca Division and the creation of a new 'North-Eastern Provinces'.[91] However, Ward's successor Sir Henry Cotton had strongly opposed the proposal[92] and the whole plan, as seen above, was shelved. The transfer proposal was again revived by Sir Andrew Fraser who had been appointed as the Lieutenant-Governor of Bengal in November 1902, but who took over the charge only in November 1903, in a note on 28 March 1903. In the note he not only urged the transfer of Chittagong Division but also of Dacca and Mymensingh. At the same time, he also, for the first time, highlighted the political benefits of the scheme.[93] Fraser's note had been a part of a larger discussion on the question of territorial changes in India which were taking place then as Berar had been recently acquired and inevitably the question of giving relief to the Lieutenant-Governor of Bengal had emerged as an important issue. No wonder, the 'Bihar solution' figured prominently in the discussion. Denzil Ibbetson, a member of the

Governor-General's Council, in his note of 23 April 1903, while discussing the question of relief of Bengal felt that the ideal method would be to create a new Chief Commissionership out of Bihar and the permanently-settled portion of the United Provinces. He, however, opined, 'But for various reasons I look upon this as outside the region of practical politics. But the transfer of Chittagong area is very much within that region.' Ibbetson pointed out that Fraser had discussed the matter with him and his (Fraser's) feeling was that the influence of Eastern Bengal in the politics of the province was great and 'out of all proportions to its real political importance in so much that the Bengali altogether overshadows the Behari, who is in everything save the use (or abuse) of language immeasurably his superior'.[94] However, this solution remained a matter of academic interest only. Curzon accepted the proposals put forward by Fraser, in a famous 'Minute on Territorial Redistribution in India', where he planned to 'fix the administrative boundaries of India for a generation'.[95] The final proposals were announced in Home Secretary, Risley's letter of 3 December 1903. The proposals included the transfer of Chittagong Division, Dacca and Mymensingh districts and the Tippera Hills to Assam and Chota Nagpur to the Central Provinces, while certain areas from Central Provinces and Madras were to be added to Bengal.[96]

Relief of Bengal and the improvement of Assam were the two grounds on which the transfer plan was supported by Risley.[97] However, the government plan came in for sharp and immediate opposition from both serving and ex-officials who while discussing the issue suggested the separation of Bihar for giving relief to Bengal. J.B. Fuller, the Chief Commissioner of Assam, in a note of 5 April 1904, felt that the most convenient method of relieving the Government of Bengal would be by cutting off Bihar and 'constituting this province—for province it is—a Chief Commissionership'. He suggested that Hazaribagh and Palamau districts might conveniently be added so as to give the province a sanatorium. The total population of the province, he said, would be 17 million 'all Hindi-speaking, and most of them (I believe) disliking the Bengal connection'. If a larger area was required Monghyr and Bhagalpur could be added to the province. Fuller believed that 'the people of Behar would rather welcome separation than object to it'.[98]

C.C. Stevens, a former official, opposing the proposal suggested a better scheme of division of Bengal whereby it was to be divided into an Eastern and Western Administration. In the Western Administration, Patna Division, Chota Nagpur Division (British Districts and Tributary States), Bhagalpur Division (minus Malda) and the Raniganj sub-division of the Burdwan district were to be included. The rest of the areas were to be under the Eastern Administration. The capital of Western Bengal (Western Administration) was to be 'the great city of Patna, or some place close to it'.[99] This proposal too, in essence, meant a distinct identity for Bihar.

While Fuller and Stevens were pleading for the separation of Bihar, Sir Andrew Fraser, the Lieutenant-Governor of Bengal, got busy in opposing the proposal to transfer the Chota Nagpur Division or part of it to the Central Provinces.

While the threatened transfer of Chota Nagpur was waking up the elites of that division from a slumber and provincial governments were busy giving their opinion on the proposals, the Bihari leaders and papers were taking note of the swift-moving developments. Though the leaders, still licking the wounds of 1896, chose to tread the path of caution and no meetings of the kind which had been a conspicuous feature of the previous movement took place, the newspapers were not so circumspect. They immediately got into the act of demanding Bihar's separation from Bengal and building a foolproof case for the same. Two newspapers, the *Behar Times* of Patna, which had played an important role in the abortive movement of 1896, and the *Behar News* of Bhagalpur led the press campaign on this occasion.[100] Popular enthusiasm was also not lacking. The *Behar Times* was deluged with letters asking it to agitate for the separation of Bihar. One letter-writer urged the people and the Bihar Landholders' Association to start an agitation and many letters were directly addressed to the above Association.[101] People waited and wanted to be led in a movement but the leadership was not forthcoming.

Early in 1904 though some support did come the Bihari newspapers' way. In February, Maulvi Dilawar Hussain Ahmed, the late Inspector-General of Registration of Bengal, after a powerful critique of the government proposals, which sought to divide

Bengali-speaking people in two parts, suggested the merger of Assam into Bengal and detachment of Bihar and its elevation to the rank of an independent province with Chota Nagpur and the eastern and permanently-settled districts of the United Provinces. Drawing attention to the differences in matters of language and script he sarcastically sought to know, 'Does the Government believe the people of Behar will ever become fused with the people of Bengal. If it does not, why does it persist in keeping under a single administration two peoples so essentially different?'[102]

The *Behar Times* lost no time in making use of this suggestion to back up and legitimize its own demand.[103] However, the Bihari leaders, as said above, continued to be cautious and shunned open agitation. Instead in a change of tactics, they tried to convince the Bengali leaders to accept the separation of Bihar as the preferred alternative to their own proposal which was to convert the Lieutenant-Governorship of Bengal into a Governorship with an Executive Council like that of Bombay and Madras to ease the workload both on the Lieutenant-Governor and administration of Bengal.[104]

FERMENT IN CHOTA NAGPUR

The situation was vastly different in Chota Nagpur. The threat of its transfer to the Central Provinces had jolted its landed elites and educated people out of slumber. However, once awakened they showed great courage and with some support of the Christian missionaries rose in strong protest against the government proposals and ended up proclaiming their Bihari identity. A detailed look at this protest movement is worth looking, for in no distant future was it to witness the birth of the Jharkhand movement, which only goes to prove the dynamic and fluid nature of identity formation.

Though home to a number of powerful tribal movements, the region had largely stayed aloof from the more modern forms of political movements. While the Patna and Bhagalpur Divisions, the 'Bihar' of the official discourse, had seen since about 1870 many articulations of modern political consciousness and especially of a Bihari identity, Chota Nagpur, despite having a sizeable Hindi-speaking population mostly of Bihari origin, had chosen not to nor was called upon to proclaim this identity. The government, on its part, had not specified even one district in that division to the natives of which the preferential treatment given to Biharis in employment under the government were to be given.[105] However, now in the first decade of the twentieth century the numerically dominant population in the division was to announce that it was a Bihari population.

Protest started immediately after the government went public with its proposals. It came in many forms like public meetings, memorials and personal communication to the officials. In fact, no instrument of constitutional protest was left unused by the opponents of the transfer plan. The protest had a broad sweep as well, with all the threatened districts—Hazaribagh, Ranchi and Palamau participating in it. Without getting into the confrontational mode, the major emphasis of the protestors was on making light of the arguments on which the transfer proposals were sought to be justified. The similarity of the language in some memorials is indicative of some coordination among the protestors.

The first argument of the government that in character and state of development these areas corresponded more closely to those in the Central Provinces than the population of Bengal was easily disposed off both in the Ranchi and Hazaribagh memorial.[106]

The Ranchi memorial, adopted after a meeting on 29 December 1903, held under the chairmanship of Maharaja Pratap Uday Nath Sahi Deo, the Maharaja of Chota Nagpur and with active participation of the Christian missionaries, speaking for the British districts said:

> The inhabitants of these (leaving Manbhum and Singhbum out of account) are closely akin to the people of Bihar, and as a matter of fact too, they have always been looked upon as Bihar districts. The Hindu population of Chota Nagpur, so far as their spoken language, habits of life and social and religious customs are concerned, have no difference whatever with the people of the neighbouring districts of Bihar, such as Gaya, Monghyr and Shahabad.[107]

The memorial submitted by the people of Hazaribagh was more specific. 'Hazaribagh has been looked upon as a part of Bihar. Sherghatty in Gaya was the headquarters station of the district now called Hazaribagh, and Patna was the Executive, Revenue, and Judicial centre.' It was asserted that the population of

Hazaribagh, 'so far as their spoken language, habits of life and social and religious customs are concerned, have no difference whatever with the people of the neighbouring districts of Bihar, such as Gaya and Monghyr'.[108]

The memorialists, thus, after proclaiming their affinity with the people of Bihar went on to demolish the government's major argument that the Bengal form of administration was too highly developed, too legalized, and too impersonal for backward tracts and primitive hill tribes. The Hazaribagh memorial pointed out that it was simply not applicable to Hazaribagh district where only one-twelfth part of the whole population were from the hill tribes and they were scattered all over the district, '*as would appear from the last census report*' (emphasis added). It was further pointed out that they (the tribal people) had adopted the language, custom and manners of the people among whom they lived. Attention was also drawn to the fact that the Bengal system had been in existence for more than a century and no grievance had been felt.[109]

During this period the government officials had been busy both gauging public opinion and seeking concrete opinion of influential people in different districts. The opinions, everywhere, were unanimously against the government proposals.

While the Maharaja of Ramgarh Estate (in the Hazaribagh district) Shri Ram Narayan Singh took recourse to the most impeccable of government sources, W.W. Hunter's *Statistical Account of Bengal* to show that Hazaribagh (formerly Ramgarh district) was part of 'Suba Behar',[110] the landed elites of Palamau were not so circumspect.

Raja Bhagawat Dayal of Chainpur in a powerful letter to the Deputy Commissioner of Palamau asserted that the district had little in common with the Central Provinces and that the population of the district 'including both the zamindars and the common people, consists almost wholly of emigrants, or the descendants of emigrants, from Bihar . . . and differ widely from the backward people of the Central Provinces'. Even the few hill tribes, he argued, had come to correspond very closely with the Biharis as regards religion, customs and language as a result of the civilizing influence of the Bihari emigrants and with the exception of aborigines in a part of the district, the population was entirely 'a Bihari one'.[111]

But these emotional arguments clearly did not exhaust his arsenal. It was pointed out that a community of interests and tradition had grown up between them and the provinces of Bengal and Bihar by their having been associated with them (Bengal and Bihar) for more than a century and if they were to be cut-off from their brethren and joined to the 'alien and backward people' of the Central Provinces it would not be only a shock to them but would also 'tell heavily upon our present interests and future prospects'.[112]

While the Raja of Chainpur had refrained from including all the aborigines in the category of Biharis, the zamindar of Bisrampur felt no hesitation in doing so. In this letter to the Deputy Commissioner he asserted that even the aboriginal tribes 'have become Bihari in every respect'.[113]

The opposition to the government proposals was not voiced only by the landed elites. In his communication to the Deputy Commissioner, the Secretary of Bar Library, Daltonganj made it clear that the opinion of the local bar was fully stated in the representation of the zamindars.

By the end of January 1904 district officials were ready with their reports as also their personal views on the government proposals. Their views, too, ran contrary to what the government might have been hoping for.

While the Deputy Commissioner of Hazaribagh contented himself merely by stating that he shared the views expressed in the Hazaribagh memorial, which we have referred to and discussed earlier, it was the Deputy Commissioner of Palamau, who put a huge question mark on the rationale of the government scheme, going as far as refusing to accept these as being far-sighted. He not only refused to accept the argument that in character and state of development the people of Chota Nagpur corresponded much more closely with those in the Central Provinces but also laid bare the whole composition of the district to support his contention.

Thus, out of the four parganas, of which Palamau was made of, Japla was, in every respect, similar with Gaya, both in natural physical condition and in its population. Belonja, till 1872 a part of Gaya, was inhabited practically exclusively by Biharis. The third pargana, the Deputy Commissioner noted, was Palamau where 'all the leading zamindars and tenants are Rajputs and Brahmins' and which was 'intimately connected in marriage with the residents of Shahabad, Mirzapur, Benaras and Gaya'. The fourth pargana was Tari, where the chief inhabitants were 'Kherwars, Mundas and (a hill race)'. He noted, 'In all these parganas except Palamau Hindi is the language *exclusively* spoken' (emphasis in original). In Palamau only one area consisting of 88 villages had a predominant Kol Population. There were two other tribes in the district having a language of their own which was fast dying out and being replaced by Hindi. He also argued that Cheros and Kherwars forming a large portion of the population 'have become practically Bihari Hindus with a higher grade in the caste system'.[114] As the government proposals were to still leave Bengal with a very large population, he suggested the formation of a separate administration for Bihar, Chota Nagpur, the Santhal Parganas and Bhagalpur, Monghyr and possibly Purnea.[115]

By early February the Divisional Commissioner, F.A. Slacke, was ready with his report, which yet again turned out to be a strong indictment of the government proposals. He was emphatic that the proposed amalgamation of the Hindi-speaking districts of the Division with the Central Provinces would be detrimental 'to the interests of the people as well as of the districts themselves'. As for the popular feeling on the subject he was again under no illusion and summarily expressed 'it is one of unqualified dislike'.[116] Such a determined and strong opposition from both the educated and landed elites as also the bureaucracy was not to go in vain.

When Andrew Fraser visited Chota Nagpur in early 1904, in reply to the addresses presented to him at Hazaribagh by the District Board and Municipality, he assured that the argument against the proposed transfer of portion of the Hazaribagh district would be carefully considered by the government.[117] He was as good as his word and when finally the Bengal government sent its own opinion on the proposals to the Government of India, it clearly expressed itself against the transfer of Chota Nagpur Division to the Central Provinces.

SITUATION IN 'BIHAR'

The two divisions of Patna and Bhagalpur had merely seen press campaigns conducted by the *Behar Times* from Patna and the *Behar*

News from Bhagalpur. Here there was no display of the raw courage as seen in the case of Chota Nagpur Division.

The Bihar Landholders' Association despite requests from some quarters did not involve itself in any movement for the separation of Bihar. Nor even the leaders who had played an important role in organizing the movement in 1896 took any direct measures to apprise the government of the desire and the demand for this separation. This absence of any direct articulation of any such demand was pointedly referred to by the Government of India, both in 1905 and 1911, the second time with some approval.

One reason for this apparent silence could be that at first the plans of the government did appear too fantastic. Secondly, very little was said publicly about the behind the scene activities leading to the partition decision by officials between February 1904 and July 1905.[118] When the Maharaja of Darbhanga asked a question in the Governor-General's Legislative Council as to whether any plans had been made regarding partition issue and as to what was the nature of such decision, both as regard to districts to be severed and the administration to be given to the new province, it was replied that no decision had been arrived at on the subject.[119]

Meanwhile the leaders of Bihar continued chasing a chimera—persuading the Bengali leaders to accept the separation of Bihar and forge a joint Bengali-Bihari front to force the government to undo the partition of Bengal. However, Bihari leaders refused to bet everything on one horse, for simultaneously, they also made an attempt to use the platform of the Indian National Congress to put forward their demand. The Bombay Congress of 1904 provided such an opportunity. Sir Henry Cotton, who was the president of the Congress, set the ball rolling. While referring to the partition proposal he said:

> I admit that it is desirable to relieve the Lieutenant-Governor of the Lower Provinces of some of the responsibilities which rest upon his shoulders. But this end may easily be attained by other means, either by the appointment of an Executive Council, or preferably I think, by the separation of Behar and Chota Nagpore which are not peopled by Bengalis, and the constitution of that province, with a population of 30 millions in round numbers, as a separate administration.[120]

He not only suggested the separation of Bihar in his speech but also planned to move a resolution on these lines. However, the attempt failed as his proposal to push such a resolution in the Subjects Committee, despite being seconded by S. Sinha, the only Bihari delegate present and supported by Ganga Prasad Varma of Lucknow, editor of the *Advocate*, met with strong Bengali opposition. The Bengali delegates simply laughed down the idea and with their preponderance in the deliberations of the Congress shot it down. The Bihari leaders still made an attempt to get the backing of Bengali leaders. Immediately after the Bombay Congress, a conference was held in Calcutta where Cotton put forward the idea that it would be wise to put an alternative proposal to that of the scheme formulated by the government. He suggested that if dismemberment must be made (of Bengal), then 'separate Behar and Chota Nagpore from Bengal and establish them under a separate administration. It would be immeasurably preferable to any proposal of dismembering Bengal. There is a large section of the Behar population which would welcome it.' However, the suggestion was not embodied in the resolution adopted at the conference.[121]

The attempts thus made to persuade the Bengali leaders to propose the separation of Bihar as an alternative to that of the splitting of Bengal failed. As seen above, even the Indian National Congress had failed to extend a helping hand to the Bihari leaders. The papers in Bihar, however, did not give up hope nor abandoned their efforts. The *Behar News* in January repeated its suggestion that if the real object of the government in partitioning Bengal was to relieve the Lieutenant-Governor of some of his burden, the most rational course was to sever Bihar from Bengal Proper and to form a Lieutenant-Governorship with Chota Nagpur and the permanently-settled districts of Banaras Division. The paper argued that if the Biharis were anxious to have an administration of their own and the Bengalis were equally anxious that their province should remain intact, then wisdom and common sense pointed to the desirability of carrying out the project of territorial distribution in such a way as to give the minimum of pain to the Bengalis and the maximum of pleasure to the Biharis. It also gave a call of action to the people of Bihar asking them to place their views before the government in clear and moderate language.[122] However, this appeal to both the government and the people went unheeded.

An exasperated *Behar News* (15 March 1905) compared the Indians to Russian peasants, especially with regard to the political condition. It felt that the Indians preferred an atmosphere of oppression to liberty. The anger of the paper was actually directed against the people of Bihar. It wanted to know as to why did the people of Bihar not organize irresistible constitutional agitation to get the scheme of territorial redistribution so altered as to lead to the separation of Bihar from Bengal and its creation as an independent administrative unit. The Biharis, the paper felt, apparently preferred to serve as the footstools of every exploiting race, European or Indian.[123] The question of the paper remained unanswered, the accusation unchallenged.

In the meantime the original transfer proposals were being enlarged, and now a partition proposal was maturing. Under it, a new province of Eastern Bengal and Assam incorporating Chittagong, Dacca and Rajshahi Divisions, Hill Tippera and Malda apart from Assam was to be constituted.[124] Curzon also repeatedly dismissed both the proposals of setting up an Executive Council or separation of linguistically-different Bihar and Orissa to relieve the burden on the Bengal administration on political grounds. The Secretary of State had been toying with the idea of separating Bihar and Orissa, but Curzon pointed out to him that it would tend to 'consolidate the Bengali element by detaching it from outside factors and would produce the very effect that we desire to avoid'.[125]

PARTITION IS ACCOMPLISHED AND THE BIHARIS ARE NOT SAD

The final proposals were communicated to the Home Government in February 1905. Even at this stage the question of separation of Bihar did find a mention there. The dispatch referred to 'an alternative plan, which had attracted some attention and may possibly be put forward for your serious consideration by the opponents of our own proposals'.

The leading features of the alternative plan were:

1. The transfer of the Chittagong Division from Bengal to Assam.

2. The formation of a Chief Commissionership of Behar which would include the Patna Division, the Hindi-speaking districts of Chutia Nagpur (namely, Hazaribagh, Palamau and Ranchi), the Benares Division of the United Provinces, and possibly, the districts of Monghyr and Bhagalpur.
3. The transfer of Orissa to the Central provinces, and the conversion of that province into a Lieutenant-Governorship.[126]

Interestingly, it was stated, 'It may be admitted that such a scheme would be popular with the Bengali opponents of re-construction, as involving a practical surrender to their agitation against any division of Bengali-speaking territory'. The dispatch went on '*It may be thought by some that it would also appeal to local sentiment in Behar*' (emphasis added). The government perhaps did not think so. However, there was an awareness as to why such a separation could appeal to local sentiments as it was immediately said next 'the cry of Behar for the Beharis has frequently been raised in Bengal in connection with appointments, and it is possible that a large number of the people would be disposed to welcome administrative union with their brethren in the United Provinces'. Before, however, giving its reasons for opposing such proposals it took care to point out that, '. . . during the year throughout which the question of redistribution has been the subject of public and newspaper controversy, not a single representation of any kind has reached us from a single individual or body in Behar.'[127]

That this was merely an excuse was to become evident from the Government of India letter of 1911, wherein it was clearly stated 'the Beharis are a sturdy, loyal people, and it is a matter of common knowledge that although they have long desired separation from Bengal, they refrained at the time of the Partition from asking for it, because they did not wish to join the Bengalis in opposition to Government'.[128] Even otherwise the government could not have been unaware of the press campaign demanding the separation of Bihar. (Even the government compiled and edited Reports on Newspapers wrote extensively on the subject as we have seen earlier in this chapter.) However, in an attempt to present an even better and foolproof case for not accepting the proposal, the government enumerated the objections 'which greatly outweigh any supposed advantages that may be claimed for it'. It was a classic case of defence marching across the enemy territory even before the attack had come.

It was said that the proposed Commission (Chief Commissionership) would not be large enough to recruit for itself, and would have to borrow officers in the fashion of Assam. A possible solution was hinted at. It was that it could be attached for recruiting purposes to the United Provinces, as considerations of language would seem to suggest, but it was felt, 'it is probable that officers of those provinces would be nearly as unwilling to serve in the new provinces as Bengal officers are to go to Assam'.[129] Another reason for opposing the proposal was that it would take from Bengal all of its best districts and make the province universally unpopular. A third reason was that it would establish a final obstacle to the territorial expansion and administrative development of Assam.[130] The last and possibly the most important reason against the above proposal was that

> It would tend still further to consolidate the influence of Calcutta over the Bengali-speaking population. This would be an unhealthy rather than a healthy symptom. The true ideal, in our view, is to create wholesome centres of provincial opinion, rather than to strengthen the predominance of those political organizations in the capital which . . . use their power in a manner that can only be described as tyrannical.[131]

A solution to ease the burden on the Bengal administration had thus been proposed and dismissed. The government went on with the partition proposals and the Secretary of State's approval was obtained. The Resolution was passed in July and the Proclamation was made on 1 September 1905.[132] The partition came into effect on 16 October.[133]

During this period there seems to have been no serious effort by the leaders of Bihar to get the region separated. It seems that once they were unable to get the support of Bengal leaders for their proposal, they decided to wait and watch events. They expected that the Bengal leaders would be ultimately forced to give up the demand for organic change in the Government of Bengal and demand the merger of two left-out Bengali divisions into the new province, which would then mean an automatic separation of Bihar.

As events began to unfold, these expectations of the Bihari leaders proved entirely right. By the month of July 1905, it had become clear that the Bengali leaders and people had failed to bend the government to their will and with the dawning of this realization a sense of extreme discomfort began to envelop them. Having in a large measure dominated the affairs of the Bengal Presidency till then, on account of their superior education and numerical strength, they were now to become a minority in the parent province and they knew very well that being in a minority was not a happy proposition.

They were afraid of many things but essentially they feared for the loss of job opportunities and reduction of political influence. The *Sanjivani* (27 July) articulated these fears most explicitly. The Bengalis, it believed, would be trampled under foot as in the parent province the Bengali-speaking population would be 17 million only, while the Hindi-speaking population of Patna and Bhagalpur Divisions alone would be 24 million. Drawing attention to the fact that they were already refused admission into schools and public services in Bihar, it accused the Englishmen of not wanting that Bengalis should live in Bihar. It feared that with the Bihari race in numerical preponderance over the Bengali, the government would show greater regard for the interests of the Biharis than for those of the Bengalis. The Bengal Council would also have more Hindi-speaking members than Bengali-speaking ones. Bengalis would not be admitted into the public service anywhere in the province except the Presidency and Burdwan Divisions.[134] The fear of being in a minority was acute. The Maharaja of Cossimbazar in presiding over the mass meeting of 7 August 1905, held at Calcutta spoke in a similar vein:

> Among the six divisions of the old province, there will be left only a division and a half containing a Bengali-speaking population. We shall be in a hopeless minority and the prospect of public employment of our people will dwindle in the proportion of our numerical insignificance. We shall be strangers in our own land.[135]

The Bengali leaders and their press were finally coming round to the view of the Bihari leaders. After the publication of July Resolution a large meeting was held in Calcutta where a resolution was adopted asking the Secretary of State-in-Council to reconsider and withdraw the orders that had been passed. The resolution also asked the government that if partition was unavoidable, to modify the orders in such a way that the Bengali-speaking race may form part and parcel of the same administration by incorporating the Presidency and Burdwan Divisions into the newly formed province.[136] The *Sanjivani* (27 July) voiced the same feelings. The paper wanted to know as to why 43 million Bengali-speaking people were being placed under two administrations. The paper felt that if the Lieutenant-Governor of Bengal did require relief it could have been given without placing Bengali-speaking people under two governments. Assam and Bengal Proper could have formed one charge while Bihar, Chota Nagpur and Orissa could have formed another charge with a population of 33 million. Interestingly, it felt that the scheme would have met with no opposition and would not have been very expensive.[137] The Bihari leaders drew their own conclusions from these complaints, laments and other developments. Even if they were not going to get the status of a separate political unit they would at least be in a position to assert both their regional identity and regional interests. The desire for separation, however, still existed. In August 1905 Mahesh Narayan presented an alternative scheme of partition in the pages of *Hindustan Review*. The Congress session of that year (1905) finally saw the merits of that view. The president of the Banaras Congress, G.K. Gokhale, in his presidential speech made it clear that in his opinion even if a reduction in the charge of the Lieutenant-Governor had really become inevitable, 'one would have thought that the most natural course to take was to separate Behar, Chota Nagpur and Orissa from Bengal and form them into a separate province'.[138]

The Congress also passed a resolution appealing to the Government of India and the Secretary of State to reverse or modify the arrangements already made in such a manner so as to conciliate public opinion and recommended 'the adoption of some arrangement which would be consistent with the administrative efficiency and would place the entire Bengali community under one undivided administration'.[139] The resolution certainly implied the separation of Bihar and other non-Bengali tracts but it was not explicitly demanded. However, this Congress session dropped the suggestion for the appointment of Governor-in-Council (for Bengal) and pinned its faith on territorial separation. This was of some significance. The leaders in Bihar had sensed a smell of victory. If Bihar could not get *de jure* recognition, they could still always assert its *de facto* individuality. They gave an indication of their new mood.

The Bihar Landholders' Association in a meeting held under the presidency of Maharaja of Darbhanga, Sir Rameshwar Singh, decided that in view of the fact that by the partition of Bengal, which had already been accomplished,

> Behar becomes the predominant partner both in point of area and population in the Presidency of Fort William as now constituted, this Association (as soon as the validity of the partition is placed beyond doubt) should memorialize the Local Government and if need be the Imperial Government that the said province be now designated as the Province of Behar, West Bengal and Orissa, and the Lieutenant-Governor be further addressed as the Lieutenant-Governor of Behar, West Bengal and Orissa.[140]

The process of appropriation of Chota Nagpur, as the suggested nomenclature would show, had already thus begun.

What had been seen as a huge calamity by the leaders of Bengal was evidently seen as a positive development for Bihar. They (the Bihari leaders) would press the point of predominance of Bihar and Biharis in future. They, however, had a problem to solve. They still wanted a government of their own. They still wanted a Province of Bihar. What could be the strategy to achieve the objective? The Congress had not extended much support. The leaders in Bengal had refused to grasp their extended hands. The Bengal government under Andrew Fraser appeared sympathetic. They decided to lean on to his shoulders. Loyalty to government would be their watchword in future. It was a feeling not only shared by the elites but even by the common people. Thus, while following the partition, Bengal was rocked by the Swadeshi movement, Bihar remained quiet in 1905 and it was to remain so in future.

Thus, the *Behar Herald* (2 September 1905), a paper, since long identified as a paper of the domiciled Bengalis, while writing in praise of the boycott movement in Bengal was not surprised that the leaders of society in Bihar had not started the movement.

When it urged the Biharis, to join the Swadeshi movement,[141] it was rebuffed by the *Behar Times*. The paper (*Behar Times*, 19 October 1905) argued that whatever might be the result of the Swadeshi movement it would certainly not result in the withdrawal of the Partition proclamation. The paper also felt that it had spoilt all chances of Bengal being raised to a Governorship. It pointed out to the people the folly of following the Bengalis.[142]

The people expectedly followed advice of the *Behar Times*. No wonder the *Hindi Bangbasi* (18 November) in a long article, regretted the backwardness and indifference of the Biharis towards the Swadeshi movement.[143]

They had, however, chosen to remain indifferent. They were fortified with a hope that the Lieutenant-Governor, Andrew Fraser, would be sympathetic to their demands. In 1904 itself he had announced to the people of Patna that they would see more of him in future, in their midst as the government was acquiring a residence where he could always come and spend longer periods and be more accessible to the people.[144]

On a note of hope, Bihar and Biharis were to begin the year 1906.

NOTES

1. *General Report of the Census of India, 1901*, vol. I, pt. 1, Calcutta, 1901, p. 318.
2. C.J. Bishop, 'Sachchidananda Sinha and the Making of Modern Bihar: A Study in Constitutional Agitation at the Provincial Level, 1905-1919', unpublished Ph.D. thesis, University of Virginia, 1972, p. XII.
3. See Sachchidananda Sinha, *Some Eminent Behar Contemporaries* (henceforth *Behar Contemporaries*), Patna, 1944, pp. V-X.
4. Uma Shankar, *Mahesh Narayan: Ek Parichay* (Hindi), Dumka, 1963, pp. 6-8 and Sinha, *Behar Contemporaries*, p. 40.
5. See *The Beharee,* 5 August 1910 and Hans Kumar Tiwari and B. Varma (eds.), *Hindi Sahitya Aur Bihar* (Hindi) (henceforth *Hindi Sahitya*), vol. III, Patna, 1976, p. 366.
6. See *The Beharee*, 12 August 1910 and the *Bihar Bandhu* 19 August 1880.
7. Tiwari and Varma (eds.), *Hindi Sahitya,* vol. III, p. 366.
8. *The Beharee*, 12 August 1910.

9. A. Moin Zaidi and S. Zaidi (eds.), *The Encyclopaedia of the Indian National Congress*, vol. I: *1885-1890*, New Delhi, 1976, pp. 606-7.
10. Tiwari and Varma (eds.), *Hindi Sahitya,* vol. III, p. 366. Mahesh Narayan's Hindi poem 'Swapna' (Dream) was included in a book on *Khari Boli Padya,* ed. Pincott. See N.M.P. Srivastava, 'Behar Times, Beharee and Bihar', in *Prajna Bharati*, vol. VI, Patna, 1992, p. 239.
11. *The Beharee,* 6 August 1909 and 12 August 1910.
12. Annual General Report of the Patna Division for 1881-82, p. 19 in Bengal General (Miscellaneous) Progs, vol. 1 for 1882.
13. See *Report on the Administration of Bengal, 1885-86* which mentions the distinct identity of two papers. However, the Report of 1887-8 shows them together. See Annual Return of Presses worked and Newspapers published there at in the Bengal Presidency in the *Report on the Administration of Bengal, 1885-86*, Calcutta, 1887, p. CXCVII and *Report on the Administration of Bengal, 1887-88,* Calcutta, 1889, p. CXCVII.
14. N. Kumar, *Journalism in Bihar: A Supplement to Bihar State Gazetteer,* Patna, 1971, pp. 52-3.
15. N.M.P. Srivastava, 'Behar Times, Beharee and Bihar', p. 239.
16. Bishop, 'Sachchidananda Sinha and the Making of Modern Bihar', pp. 29-32 fns.
17. B.B. Majumdar, *Indian Political Associations and Reforms of Legislature (1818-1917)*, Calcutta, 1965, Appendix I, p. 403.
18. See *The Beharee*, 28 October 1910, which carried a life sketch of S. Sinha by Maheshwar Prasad, Professor of History and Economics, Muir Central College, Allahabad.
19. They are too numerous to be mentioned here but see his presidential speech at the *Beharee Students' Conference*, in B.N. Sinha, Compiled Volume of the *Presidential Addresses Delivered at the Beharee Students' Conference (1906-1923)*, Patna, 1931, pt. I, pp. 34-52.
20. *The Beharee*, 28 October 1910. It is worth mentioning that S. Sinha's return to India was not trouble-free. The Magistrate of Gaya noted that the Kayastha Sabha was much exercised on the question of 'readmitting into the caste Sachidanand a Kayastha of Shahabad, who has recently qualified as a Barrister-at-Law in England'. Annual General Report Patna Division, 1893-94, p. 82 in Bengal General (Miscellaneous) A Progs, November 1894, nos. 4-7.
21. David Thompson, *England in the Nineteenth Century, 1815-1914*, Harmondswoth, 1975, p. 231.
22. E.J. Hobsbawm, *Nations and Nationalism since 1780: Programme, Myth, Reality*, Cambridge, 1990, p. 105.

23. Thompson, *England in the Nineteenth Century*, p. 231. It should not surprise anyone that during the course of the abortive 1896 movement for the separation of Bihar which will be discussed later in the chapter, the *Bengalee,* a prominent Calcutta-based newspaper, did indeed write: 'So the separatist movement is not confined to England but the cry of separation has been raised in this country also.' See the *Bengalee*, 20 June 1896.
24. Sinha, *Behar Contemporaries*, pp. ii-iii. Glenn Bowman has drawn our attention to the existence of a similar feeling among the Palestinians. He argues that 'homeland' is 'itself a term already constituted within nationalist discourse; it is the place where the nationalist imagines his or her identity becoming fully realized. A domain wherein Palestinian identity is denied cannot be considered the Palestinians' homeland, even if it were the very same ground on which they imagine the future Palestinian nation will be built.' See Glenn Bowman, ' "A Country of Words": Conceiving the Palestinian Nation from the Position of Exile', in Ernesto Laclau (ed.), *The Making of Political Identities*, London, 1994, p. 139.
25. N.M.P. Srivastava, *Bihar Mein Rashtriyata Ka Vikas (1912-1947)* (Hindi), Patna, 1974, pp. 7-8.
26. Sinha, *Behar Contemporaries*, p. III.
27. Ibid.
28. Ibid.
29. Ibid., pp. II-III; Bishop, 'Sachchidananda Sinha and the Making of Modern Bihar', pp. 43-5, *The Beharee,* 28 October 1910.
30. Sinha, *Behar Contemporaries*, p. X.
31. Ibid., pp. VI-XI.
32. Ibid., p. XI., *The Beharee,* 28 October 1910.
33. See John R. McLane, *Indian Nationalism and Early Congress*, Princeton, 1977, pp. 309-17. See A.P. Jha, 'Political History of Bihar (1859-1912)', in K.K. Datta (ed.), *The Comprehensive History of Bihar* (henceforth *CHB*), vol. III, Part I, Patna, 1976, pp. 216-17.
34. General Administration Report of the Patna Division for 1893-94, p. 82, in Bengal General (Miscellaneous) A Progs, November 1894, File no. 5-R/16, sl. nos. 4-7.
35. Annual General Administration Report of the Patna Division, 1894-95, July 1895, p. 104, in Bengal General (Miscellaneous) Progs, volume for October-December 1895.
36. Annual General Administration Report of the Patna Division, 1895-96, pp. 88-9, in Bengal General (Miscellaneous) Progs, volume for January-September 1897.

37. *Annual General Administration Report of the Patna Division, 1896-97*, pp. 69-70, in Bengal General (Miscellaneous) Progs, volume for October-December 1897.
38. Sinha, *Behar Contemporaries*, p. xi.
39. The first English newspaper of Bihar the *Behar Herald* was essentially seen as an organ of domiciled Bengalis in Bihar. See Chapter 4.
40. M. Narayan and S. Sinha, 'The Partition of Bengal or the Separation of Behar? : An Ideally Perfect Alternative Scheme', Patna, 1906, p. 7. I have consulted its typescript copy at the Bihar State Archives Library, Patna.
41. Ibid., p. 7.
42. Ibid., p. 8.
43. Dipasri Banerjee, *Aspects of Administration in Bengal, 1898-1912*, New Delhi, 1980, pp. 9-10.
44. Ibid., pp. 15-16. See also B.B. Mishra, *The Unification and Division of India*, Delhi, 1990, p. 154.
45. India Home (Public) A Progs, April 1873, nos. 205-8.
46. Ibid., March 1896, nos. 175-82 and 1 K.W.
47. R.P. Cronin, *British Policy and Administration in Bengal: Partition and the New Province of Bengal and Assam, 1905-1912*, Calcutta, 1977, p. 4.
48. India Home (Public) A Progs, March 1896, nos. 175-82 and 1 K.W.
49. *The Hindoo Patriot*, 8, 26 and 27 January 1896.
50. *Report on Native Papers in Bengal* [henceforth *RNP(B)*], no. 6, 1896.
51. *The Bengalee*, 1 February 1896.
52. See for instance S. Sinha, *Behar Contemporaries*, p. XV; Narayan and Sinha, 'The Partition of Bengal or the Separation of Behar?', p. 8; and V.C.P. Chaudhary, *The Creation of Modern Bihar*, Patna and Darbhanga, 1964, pp. 55-6.
53. The *Pioneer*, 17 March 1896. The articles on the issue were believed to have been written by A. MacDonnell, a member of the I.C.S. See Sinha, *Behar Contemporaries*, p. XV.
54. Ibid. (The *Pioneer*).
55. Narayan and Sinha, 'The Partition of Bengal or the Separation of Behar?', p. 8.
56. See *The Pioneer*, 26 March 1896, which quotes the *Behar Times*.
57. Ibid.
58. See Annual General Administration Report of the Patna Division, 1895-96, p. 88 in Bengal General (Miscellaneous) Progs, volume for January-September 1897, and Sinha, *Behar Contemporaries*, XIII-XIV, *The Bengalee*, 18 April and 20 June 1896.

59. See later in the chapter.
60. *The Hindoo Patriot*, 10 July 1896 and Sinha *Behar Contemporaries*, p. XIV.
61. The *Pioneer*, 8 April 1896.
62. *The Bengalee*, 18 April 1896.
63. *RNP (B)*, no. 23, 1896.
64. The *Pioneer*, 6 June 1896.
65. *The Hindoo Patriot*, 8 June 1896.
66. Ibid., 9 June 1896.
67. Ibid., 15 June 1896
68. *RNP (B)*, no. 26, 1896.
69. Ibid.
70. See *The Bengalee*, 20 June 1896 and Chaudhary, *The Creation of Modern Bihar*, p. 60. Certainly Bihari leaders were not the only people to face this kind of accusation. Tom Nairn writing about the break-up of Britain has pointed out how new nationality movements tend to get condemned in this manner 'for opting out of an already achieved and workable progress on some larger scale; lapses into pettiness, self-condemned by a broader common sense. The notion surfaces to some degree in the commonplaces of the devolution debate: 'You could never manage on your own' ; 'Surely we're better all together. . . .' It's irrelevant to people's real problems'. He draws our attention to the mistake in this viewpoint which is the tendency to see the larger units of social organization as a kind of historical necessity. See Tom Nairn, *The Break-Up of Britain: Crisis and Neo-Nationalism*, London, 1977, pp. 74-5.
71. Annual General Administration Report of the Patna Division, 1895-96, p. 88. In Bengal General (Miscellaneous) Progs, volume for January-September 1897.
72. Ibid.
73. See McLane, *Indian Nationalism and the Early Congress*, p. 155. By this it is meant that very often different leaders demanded something from the government from public platforms but when presented with a chance to demand the same before a properly constituted authority they let the opportunity go by. For instance the Congress had for years demanded an enquiry into corruption in the police but when the Police Commission was constituted the party did not send either witnesses or evidence before it.
74. Sinha, *Behar Contemporaries*, p. XVI and Freedom Movement Papers (Region VII), File no. 6/2, p. 16.
75. *The Englishman*, 8 July 1896.

76. See ibid. It is worth mentioning that neither Mahesh Narayan and S. Sinha's pamphlet, 'The Partition of Bengal or the Separation of Behar' nor S. Sinha's *Some Eminent Behar Contemporaries* mentions what was actually demanded in the Address. Also the reply of the Lieutenant-Governor has been selectively quoted by them. See the pamphlet, p. 8 and Chaudhary, *The Creation of Modern Bihar*, p. 58 (fn.).
77. Annual General Administration Report of the Patna Division, 1895-96, p. 88. In Bengal General (Miscellaneous) Progs, volume for January-September 1897.
78. *The Englishman*, 14 July 1896.
79. Ibid., 16 July 1896.
80. Ibid., 17 July 1896.
81. *The Hindoo Patriot*, 11 July 1896.
82. Ibid., 20 July 1896.
83. Narayan and Sinha, 'The Partition of Bengal or the Separation of Behar', p. 6.
84. Sinha, *Behar Contemporaries,* pp. XVII-XVIII.
85. *RNP (B),* no. 38, 1896, and *Al Punch* (an Urdu weekly), vol. 12, August 1896, Issue 19. It also carried the poem. I am grateful to Zafar Alam, Reader, Dept. of Urdu, C.M. College, Darbhanga for having read the poem out for me.
86. Annual General Report of the Patna Division, 1896-97, p. 69. In Bengal General (Miscellaneous) Progs, volume for October-December 1897.
87. India Home (Public) A Progs, May 1897, nos. 204-324.
88. Chaudhary, *The Creation of Modern Bihar*, pp. 77-8.
89. See ibid., pp. 64-77.
90. Ibid., pp. 66-71.
91. Cronin, *British Policy and Administration in Bengal*, p. 4.
92. Ibid., p. 5 and Banerjee, *Aspects of Administration in Bengal,* p. 47.
93. S. Sarkar, *The Swadeshi Movement in Bengal, 1903-1908*, New Delhi, 1973, p. 10.
94. India Home (Public) A Progs, June 1903, no. 349.
95. Sarkar, *The Swadeshi Movement*, p. 10.
96. S. Gopal, *British Policy in India, 1858-1905*, Cambridge, 1965; Madras, 1984, p. 269.
97. S. Sarkar, *Modern India: 1885-1947*, Madras, 1983, p. 106.
98. India Home (Public) A Progs, February 1905, nos. 155-67.
99. Ibid.
100. *Report on Native-Owned English Newspapers in Bengal*, nos. 4, 5 and 6, 1904.

101. See ibid., nos. 4 and 6, 1904.
102. *RNP (B)*, no. 9, 1904.
103. *Report on Native-Owned English Newspapers in Bengal*, no. 9, 1904.
104. Sinha, *Behar Contemporaries*, p. XIX; and Banerjee, *Aspects of Administration in Bengal*, pp. 63-4.
105. See Chapter 3
106. India Home (Public) A Progs, February 1905, nos. 155-67.
107. Ibid.
108. Ibid.
109. Ibid.
110. Ibid.
111. Ibid.
112. Ibid.
113. Ibid.
114. Ibid.
115. Ibid.
116. Ibid.
117. *RNP (B)*, no. 11, 1904.
118. Sarkar, *Modern India*, p. 109.
119. India Home (Public) B Progs, January 1905, no. 116.
120. Narayan and Sinha, 'The Partition of Bengal or the Separation of Behar', p. 11.
121. See ibid., pp. 11-12.
122. *Report on Native-Owned English Newspapers in Bengal*, no. 4, 1905.
123. Ibid., no. 12, 1905.
124. Sarkar, *Modern India*, pp. 106-7.
125. Ibid., p. 107.
126. India Home (Public) A Progs, February 1905, nos. 155-67.
127. See ibid. Interestingly S. Sinha was to recall later that by not making a common cause with the leaders of Bihar and by not advocating the separation of Bihar as an alternative, the leaders of Bengal had failed to call the bluff of the government. See Sinha, *Behar Contemporaries*, p. 9. It needs to be pointed out that the leaders of Bihar too had committed the same mistake by not presenting their demand before the government.
128. India Home (Delhi) A Progs, December 1911, nos. 8-11. The despatch dated 25 August, Simla, 1911, from Government of India to the Secretary of State for India.
129. India Home (Public) A Progs, February 1905, nos. 155-67.
130. Ibid.
131. Ibid.
132. India Home (Public) A Progs, October 1905, nos. 163-98.

133. Ibid.
134. *RNP (B)*, no. 31, 1905.
135. Narayan and Sinha, 'The Partition of Bengal or the Separation of Behar', p. 45.
136. Ibid., p. 23.
137. *RNP (B)*, no. 31, 1905.
138. Narayan and Sinha, 'The Partition of Bengal or the Separation of Behar', p. 24.
139. Ibid., p. 25.
140. Ibid., p. 55.
141. *Report on Native-Owned English Newspapers in Bengal*, nos. 36 and 41, 1905.
142. Ibid., no. 42, 1905.
143. *RNP (B)*, no. 46, 1905.
144. *Report on Native-Owned English Newspapers in Bengal*, no. 33, 1904.

CHAPTER 6

Towards the Separation of Bihar

The years following the partition of Bengal witnessed significant developments in Bihar. Though the partition had left Bihar as the predominant partner in the old province of Bengal, her leaders continued their efforts to secure a distinct identity for the region. Pressure was put on the government to concede the demand both through ideological weapons and more direct political activity. In order to gather wider support from the people, Bihar's search for identity was justified both on ideological and pragmatic grounds. However, simultaneously pressure was also put on the government to satisfy other wants and aspirations of the province. New political organizations dedicated to the promotion of interests of the Bihari community came to be established and a significant political mobilization took place in the region, with Hindu and Muslim educated elites coming together in a big way and they, in turn, joining hands with the landholding elites.

In their bid to secure a sympathetic hearing from the government, the leaders of Bihar decided to follow a path of loyalty and the political activity, therefore, remained strictly confined within constitutional limits. The Bengal government remained extremely sympathetic to the demands of Bihari leaders especially till 1908. The fact of growth of regional consciousness in Bihar and the strength of the desire of the Biharis for a distinct political identity were recognized by officials who realized the need to respond to it positively. Therefore, when the Government of India decided to modify the partition scheme, Bihar and Orissa were constituted into a new province. The creation of the Province of Bihar and Orissa marked an important stage in the evolution of a regional identity. It also marked the beginning of a period since when the consciousness of a common identity began to spread to new groups. The present chapter looks into these political and administrative developments and discusses how these contributed to the emergence of a Bihari community.

IDEOLOGICAL PRESSURE

The leaders in Bihar got an early opportunity to mount political pressure on the government, though articulated in ideological terms, to modify the scheme of partition and give a separate political identity to Bihar. This opportunity came their way because of a series of political developments both in India and England, the mother country.

In India, the partition led to the emergence of a powerful Swadeshi movement and wide unrest in Bengal.[1] In August 1905 Lord Curzon resigned his post over a dispute with the Commander-in-Chief, Lord Kitchener[2] and was replaced by Lord Minto. In a further twist of events, within a fortnight of his arrival in Bombay in the month of November, general elections in England returned the Liberals to power[3] and John Morley who had a great liberal reputation was appointed the Secretary of State.[4] The resignation of Lord Curzon who had been the principal architect of the partition scheme and the coming into power of the Liberals gave birth to new hopes that the partition decision may be reconsidered.[5]

Two Bihari leaders, Sachchidananda Sinha and Mahesh Narayan seized this opportunity to put pressure on the government to modify the scheme of partition. This was done through a powerful pamphlet entitled, 'The Partition of Bengal or the Separation of Behar?: An Ideally Perfect Alternative Scheme',[6] brought out in January 1906, which by their own admission was for the purpose of 'educating our masters'.[7] In this pamphlet they presented an alternative scheme of territorial changes and put forward the arguments to prove why a separation of Bihar, Chota Nagpur and Orissa from Bengal and their constitution into a separate province was a better idea than truncating Bengal Proper. It was widely circulated in India and Britain and substantially influenced public opinion.[8]

In order to spread the ideas contained therein and gather wider support for the demand of separation, it was offered free in later years.[9]

The pamphlet tried to do many things. The 'Introduction' was utilized to put forward the initial justification for suggesting the separation of Bihar. Drawing attention to the unrest caused by the partition decision it sought to drive home the message to an 'alien' government to take note of the dissatisfaction of the people which was making difficult good governance of the affected area and take remedial measures. To suggest such a measure was the duty of all loyal citizens claimed the two pamphleteers.[10] So implicitly while demanding the separation of Bihar they were performing the duty of loyal citizens. Moving on, the primary reasons for demanding this were adduced. This time the harmful effects of Bengal connection were highlighted. This by now had become a staple theme of Bihari political leaders, their sympathizers and even some colonial officials. On this, they maintained 'Government in Calcutta is not always in touch with Behar problems'. Also as the surroundings of the Lieutenant-Governor were wholly Bengalee 'when our interests clash with those of Bengal it is unnecessary to say which of the two prevails'. They pointed out that with a government of their own many advantages would come their way. A local government would naturally be more solicitous of their welfare than any Calcutta-based government could ever be. A separate Bihar would mean that only the sons of the soil (Biharis) would be getting the clerical and provincial civil service jobs and the revenue of Bihar would entirely be spent there. The region would hope to have an Engineering and a Medical college and all this would give an impetus to local talent.[11]

However, the author duo was not to be satisfied with making these basic statements to demand the separation of Bihar. A foolproof case needed to be prepared and the pamphlet was essentially devoted to this task. The task was accomplished in three critical steps. The first step was to show the absolute necessity of redrawing the map of Bengal. The second step involved showing the demerits of the actual scheme carried out by the government, i.e. partition of Bengal and the third as also the final step was to demonstrate the superiority of the scheme that was proposed by the two authors.

The first step was easy to accomplish, as the Lower Province of Bengal was not only the largest of all the provinces of British

India both in area and population, as the figures showed, but in fact, was comparable in area with the United Kingdom, with a second Scotland added to it, while in population it was equal to the USA and Mexico combined.[12] The implied message was clear—the province was overblown and needed to be pruned. A territorial redrawing was further needed because the political limits of the provinces had been fixed in a haphazard way, governed by the exigencies of the times, as the British power advanced in the country without any regard to physical characteristic or the distinctions of race and language. This left homogeneous population split up under different administrations, while distinct and non-homogeneous people were brought together. The most glaring example of the phenomenon was the 'Lieutenant-Governorship of the Lower Provinces', as it 'included four distinct countries, viz., Bengal, Behar, Orissa and Chota Nagpore'.[13]

The second point was also easily made. The government had justified its partition decision on the ground that it would provide a definite western boundary corresponding with well recognized geographical, ethnological, social and linguistic characteristics and that it would concentrate in one province the Muslim population of Bengal with Dacca as the natural capital. These arguments were easy pickings for the authors. They argued that the creation of a river as a boundary did not mean that the two sides had different characteristics. Further, people on both sides of the river were Bengalis and spoke the same language. Lastly, even after partition a large Muslim population was still left in the old province.[14]

The final step was to give details of their own scheme and to establish its superiority over the scheme already carried out. The scheme envisaged the inclusion of Burdwan and the Presidency Divisions in the old province (thus unifying all of Bengal), transfer of Assam to Bengal, the separation of Bihar, Chota Nagpur and Orissa from Bengal and their formation into a second Lieutenant-Governorship. Under this scheme the area and population were more equitably divided than under the government scheme, which had left the old province with an area of approximately 1,35,697 sq miles and a population of 5,27,82,889 people while the new province had an area of 1,06,074 sq miles and a population of 3,13,03,282 people. Under their scheme the old province was to have an area of 1,33,202 sq miles with a population of 4,87,85,503 people while the new province of 'Behar (including Chote Nagpore) and Orissa' was to have an area of 1,09,682 sq miles and a population of 3,55,49,785 people. The argument was hammered, 'we presume it will be admitted that when we have got to divide a province into two parts, for the *purpose of better administration, the area and populations of the two divisions should be as far equal as possible*'[15] (emphasis added).

The two authors further claimed that the real superiority of their scheme was established when it was considered from the point of view of geographical, sociological and linguistic aspects. In this, special emphasis was put on proving the dissimilarity of Bihar (Chota Nagpur included) as also of Orissa from Bengal. The contrast in geographical characteristics, language, literature, physique and historical traditions between Bihar and Bengal obviously was played up. In a very clever move extensive use was made of official publications like Bengal Administration Reports and Census Reports to prove their point.

Thus, the most distinctive feature of Bengal was its network of rivers. The rivers, while of great utility in Bihar, did not occupy the position they did in Bengal. Food habits of the people, too, differed. The languages—Oriya, Bengali and Hindi—though having a common descent were not mutually intelligible to their speakers and the philological affinity between them 'no more makes those who speak them one people in the one case than the speakers of Italian, French and Spanish in the other'.[16]

The differences in the character of people came in for special emphasis. While the *Census Report* of 1872 was cited to argue that Biharis were Hindustanis, an unofficial though important Bengali source was used to prove that Bengalis, too, considered themselves distinct.[17] It was further argued that Bihar and Bengal were distinct entities historically too. Again strategically not only clever use was made of official sources but also the authority of R.C. Dutt, a distinguished Bengali intellectual, was used to prove their point. The whole exercise was also aimed at historical reconstruction of Bihar and assertion of Bihar's superiority over Bengal. Thus a quote from R.C. Dutt, 'There can be little doubt that Bengal was first colonized by Aryans from Behar, i.e. from the sister kingdoms of

Mithila and Magadha, and for the two thousand years Bengal received culture and knowledge from her western sister.' The point was hammered with quotes from Gait's *Report on the Census of Bengal*, 1901. 'Of the history of Bengal, "very little is known" as Mr. Gait rightly points out, "until the rise of Pal dynasty" during the 9th century. . . .'[18] The authors noted with some satisfaction, 'compared in fact with the hoary historic tradition of Behar, running far back into a distant past which takes us to the days of Gautama Buddha and Asoka those of Bengal are but of yesterday. . . .' The authors also pointed out that Bihar's connection with Bengal was of recent origin and was not to be treated as immutable or fixed. After thus showing that Bihar and Bengal had nothing in common, the authors asserted that 'the same arguments which tell against the dismemberment of Bengal apply *mutatis mutandis* in favour of the separation of Behar and Chota Nagpore'.[19]

The government was further told that while the Bengalis would acquiesce in this, Biharis would welcome it as a measure of political salvation. The Biharis were also called to arise and awake to work for the objective.

The pressure put by the Bihari leaders did not have any immediate impact though certain rumours were afloat in the early months of 1906 that Bihar, Chota Nagpur and Orissa were to be separated and formed into a new province. What had apparently given rise to the rumour was a rather small event—the visit of Governor-General, Lord Minto, to Patna who had come to the city in the month of February and held a Darbar there.[20] The visit was immediately interpreted as connected with a plan to make Bihar into a separate Lieutenant-Governorship.[21] Though these rumours turned out to be unfounded, the issue did not die down so easily and was again revived when C.J. O'Donnel, a British M.P., in a powerful pamphlet on the partition question pleaded unequivocally for the separation of Bihar.[22] This pamphlet repeated mainly the arguments put forward in the Bihari leaders' pamphlet,[23] but even this had no impact on the government. However, all these developments had an impact on the people of Bihar where by this time a wide unanimity had emerged on the separation issue.[24] But no further efforts were made for some time to achieve this objective and the issue was taken up again only in 1908. In the meantime political activities in Bihar got concerned with the more immediate needs of the region.

POLITICAL ACTIVITY AND STRATEGY

Simultaneously with the ideological pressure for separation, other issues of regional interest had also been taken up. A mere rumour that the post of Sanskrit Professor in Patna College was going to be filled by a Bengali Pandit raised the ire of a Bihari newspaper, the *Bihar Bandhu*, which felt that it would be an act of injustice to the local candidates.[25]

Till now Biharis were demanding jobs in Bihar for themselves, both on account of their educational backwardness and claim as being natives of the soil but in a new move, one Bihari paper the *Kayastha Messenger*, demanded jobs for Biharis on the basis of their population.[26] It is worth recalling that Biharis were the dominant group, population wise, in the Presidency. There certainly was a new mood of confidence among the people of Bihar which found its most vivid expression when the *Behar Times* changed its name to *The Beharee.*[27]

There was also a spurt in political activity with older organizations becoming more active and new organizations coming into being.

The Role of Bihar Landholders' Association

In championing the regional interests the role played by the Bihar Landholders' Association under the leadership of Maharaja of Darbhanga, Sir Rameshwar Singh, was very significant. As we have seen in Chapter 5, in 1896 the Association had stayed aloof from the agitation to separate Bihar and the then Maharaja of Darbhanga, Lakshmeshwar Singh, despite requests from some quarters, did not agree to lead the agitation though we do not know the precise reasons behind this decision. One possible reason could be that Guru Prasad Sen, a Bengali lawyer, journalist and landlord, who happened to be the secretary of the Association, was strongly against the separation demand. However, later, Mahesh Narayan, the most vocal champion of the separation demand became the assistant secretary and secretary of the Association[28] and it is reasonable to assume that he did play some role in making it play a more active role in furthering regional interests. The Maharaja and its other leaders, too, might have felt the need to do so. In the month of July 1907, a large and representative deputation of the members of the Association under the leadership of Maharaja Rameshwar Singh presented an 'Address' to the Lieutenant-Governor enumerating the various demands of the people of Bihar.[29]

The first issue taken up in the address was related to the representation of the Patna Division and Bihar Landholders' Association in the Provincial Council.[30] In fact, in January 1907 itself, *The Beharee* had pointed out that there was not a single Bihari on the Bengal Legislative Council and pleaded for the nomination of a member in case neither the District Boards nor the Municipalities nor the Bihar Landholders' Association could be called upon presently to elect a representative.[31] The issue was agitating thoughtful Biharis for some time and the Association took it up.

It went on to take up the issue of representation of Biharis in the government services. Their inadequate representation in the Education and Judicial Services was strongly raised. In fact, Rameshwar Singh in his presidential speech in the annual general meeting of the Association, held the day before the presentation of the address, had demanded that 'some means should be devised for making the Judges of the High Court better acquainted with a gentleman practising in Bihar and with the circumstances and aspirations of the Province.'[32] Demanding increased educational facilities for Bihar it pleaded for raising the status of Temple Medical School and Bihar School of Engineering to the level of colleges. Another demand was for an additional seat of government or a second capital of the province at Patna.[33] The address was significant because the Association, primarily an organization of landed aristocrats, had endorsed the demands hitherto put forward by the middle-class English-educated groups. The response of the Lieutenant-Governor, Sir Andrew Fraser, was more than encouraging, though he did not accept all the demands. The need of a representative from the Patna Division was readily conceded and the delegation was assured that one representative of the Division would fill the vacancy when it arose in September 1907. Fraser was also sympathetic to the demand of greater representation of Biharis in the Education and Judicial Services.[34]

The sympathetic reply of Fraser was not without reasons. Both the presidential speech and the resolutions passed in the meeting of the Association the previous day had been overtly pro-government. Fraser noted with happiness that the Maharaja of Darbhanga had clearly expressed his disapproval of seditious and inflammatory writings and speeches and of all acts of violence and lawlessness. Continuing, he also expressed happiness that the Association had also expressed with equal clarity its conviction of the loyalty of the landlords, of the educated classes and of the masses to the British rule, its abhorrence of violence and unconstitutional forms of agitation and its satisfaction that all classes of people of Bihar, Hindus and Muslims, under the guidance of their natural leaders had hitherto kept themselves aloof from such forms of agitation.[35] Fraser had clearly understood that a show of sympathy would ensure the continued support of Biharis in future. As events were soon to prove he was not to be disappointed.

POLITICAL MOBILIZATION

Thus while the landlords of Bihar were busy championing the various interests of the region, professional and educated elites who till now had performed the above role got busy trying to formally organize themselves so that sustained political activity could be undertaken. Conditions were perfectly conducive for the formation of a pan-Bihar association. As we have seen earlier in the study, the associations established in the 1870s had been localized affairs, both in terms of their activities and their area of influence, typical of a society that was just awakening into a new consciousness, with a poor state of physical and intellectual communication and a very limited number of people educated under the new system. But in the last thirty odd years things had changed a great deal. Largely through the efforts of these local associations, political consciousness had spread a great deal, state of communication had improved and there were a far greater number of those people who were receptive to new ideas and ideals. Also by this time every politically advanced province had a provincial association and conference of its own. Even the Central Provinces got its first provincial conference in 1905.[36] It was now realized that the time had come when Bihar should rise and equip herself to take her proper place in the 'Great National Federation'.[37] A sense of urgency was added to the desire as Bengali leaders renewed their efforts to befriend Biharis, probably with a hope to wean them away from their quest for a separate political identity. An attempt had been made in 1900 to associate Biharis in the affairs of the Bengal Provincial Conference by holding its session at Bhagalpur. On that occasion the response of the Biharis had not been heart-warming.[38] A fresh attempt was made in 1907 when a prominent Bihari leader, Deep Narayan Singh, was chosen to be the president of the Bengal Provincial Conference which was held at Berhampur.

Though Deep Narayan Singh did not shy away from referring to Bihar's movement for separation[39] even the fact that he had agreed to be the president of the Conference came in for sharp criticism in Bihar. *The Beharee* (12 April 1907) totally disapproved of his association with the Bengal Provincial Conference. It made clear that by associating him with it the Bengalis should not fancy that they have effected an improvement in the relations existing between Bengal and Bihar.[40] No wonder, Bihari leaders decided to have an organization of their own without any further loss of time. They moved fast. In the month of March 1907 the preliminary meeting to organize it was held under the presidency of Hasan Imam. Leading political figures of Bihar like Krishna Sahay, Shiv Shankar Sahay, Mahesh Narayan and Brahmdeo Narain were present on the occasion.[41]

As from the very beginning the association was conceived of as an all-Bihar organization the preliminary committee decided to have branches in every district in Bihar. These were to be called district associations and were to be treated as electorates to the central association. Steps were immediately taken to organize the district associations. Some persons, mostly being barristers having practised in the outlying districts, were appointed touring members of the Association. They, as also the provisional secretary, visited many districts and associations were formed in every district in Bihar except Shahabad and Champaran.[42]

There is detailed information regarding the establishment of district association at Bhagalpur. As soon as the scheme of the Association was received at Bhagalpur, Deep Narayan Singh invited Sachchidananda Sinha, who by this time had firmly established his credentials as a devoted worker in the public cause of Bihar, to come over to Bhagalpur in April and help in the formation of the District Committee. In fact, two committees were formed, one to take up political and the other to take up industrial and educational work.[43] It is important to note that along with the Bihar Provincial Association and in fact, as its offshoot, the Bihar Industrial and Educational Association was also established.[44] The progress of Bihar was thus not merely conceived in political terms.

The Beharee threw its weight in making the launch of the Association a successful venture. Its editor, Mahesh Narayan, had been one of the participants in the preliminary meeting of March 1907 and hence, the support of *The Beharee*. The paper (31 May 1907) reminded its readers, in view of the reluctance shown by the people in joining the political section of the Association, that it was the duty of the loyalists to participate in political movements and to temper them with moderation and wisdom instead of keeping aloof from them and allowing them to drift into the hands of the extremists. It assured the readers that there was no reason to suppose that the body would be hostile to government in any way.[45] This reminder of the paper was a veiled threat to the loyalist sections of the society that if they did not cooperate in the venture, it might come to be dominated by elements hostile to the government.

However, the Association did not come into being in a formal way in 1907. It was only in the month of December that year that the Preliminary Committee finally decided to hold the inaugural meeting of the proposed Association during the Easter holidays of 1908 and to organize this a reception committee was formed with Sachchidananda Sinha as the chairman and Brahmdeo Narayan as the secretary. The response of the public in Bihar was warm and enthusiastic. Finally, in 1908, in the month of April, a large assembly of a representative character gathered in Patna with delegates coming from all parts of Bihar. An indicator of the enthusiasm aroused by it was the fact that not only about 40 college students offered their services to act as volunteers to attend on the delegates but also some students like Girindra Mohan Mishra and Jayanath Pati attended it as delegates of one 'Deshbhakta Society' of Patna.[46]

After some discussion, this inaugural meeting was given the name of Bihar Provincial Conference[47] and the Bihar Provincial Association was founded by the first resolution of the Conference.[48] The Association set many ambitious tasks for itself. It wanted to equip and prepare Biharis to take up their proper place along with people of other provinces in the struggle for political, social, and industrial regeneration of India.[49] It also intended to promote the highest interests of the Bihari community in particular and of India in general, in cooperation as far as possible with other parts of India. It certainly was not intended to advance the interests of any particular class and was not a sectarian association. However, the rules of membership clearly point to the fact that it was not intended to be a mass organization either. According to these rules any Bihari who was not a minor and had passed the Entrance examination, legal or medical practitioners, engineers, zamindars, traders, bankers, teachers in private schools, authors or government pensioners could become its member.[50] However, limiting the membership to the upper and middle classes in the society did not mean that the interests of the common people were overlooked as became evident when it finally got going. The most significant aspect of the Association and one that gave it much strength and prestige was the fact that Hindus and Muslims participated in its affairs with equal enthusiasm and enjoyed similar control over it. In 1909, for example, the Executive Committee of the Association consisted of both prominent Muslims like Ali Imam, Hasan Imam, Mazahar-ul-Haque, Nasiruddin Hasan, and Hindus like Deep Narayan Singh, Parmeshwar Lal, Narayan Prasad, Brahmdeo Narayan, Sachchidananda Sinha, Langat Singh and others.[51]

The show of Hindu-Muslim unity was in full display from the first Bihar Provincial Conference itself, where a distinguished Muslim, Ali Imam, was chosen to act as the president. In his turn he not only paid a warm tribute to the Bihari Hindus for their cordiality towards the Muslims but also emphasized the need of sinking sectarian differences.[52] Its forum was used to put forward the major demands of the Biharis. As was to be expected from an organization of professionals and educated class people, demand was again made for larger employment of Biharis in the public services.[53] In a clear signal, however, that they were growing more ambitious and demanding, the Bihari leaders made it clear that no reform of the Provincial Council would be considered satisfactory which did not provide for the permanent representation of each district in the province.[54] Most significantly, a resolution on the separation of Bihar from Bengal and its constitution into a separate province was moved by M. Fakhruddin and supported by most of the district representatives.[55]

Now that the Bihari leaders had succeeded in organizing a conference of their own they were impelled to work more extensively and in depth for the welfare of the region. The Bihar Provincial Association began to intervene on behalf of the *ryots* in the Champaran district and drew attention to the unfair terms of indigo cultivation. It also planned to open a combined school and maktab in each district and also to start a cheap (in price) newspaper in Hindi. All these steps were calculated to reach out to the masses.[56] Obviously its vision was not narrowed down by the interests of upper and middle classes alone.

The Bihar Provincial Conference sessions became the chief medium through which the Association worked for the protection of various interests of Bihar. The sessions of the Conference, held at different places every year, became the principal agency of articulating and spreading regional consciousness. The momentum generated by the organization of the first Bihar Provincial Conference was maintained throughout the year and Bihar witnessed intense political activity. But before detailing that we need to specify the context in which these activities took place. It also needs to be mentioned that one of the constant notes of its activities was the manifestation of loyalty towards the colonial government, obviously in the hope of getting rewards for the region. This meant that Bihar continued to manifest anti-Swadeshi feelings.

The Manifesto of 1908

The region had been maintaining an anti-Swadeshi stance since 1905 itself. The initial reaction of Bihar seems to have been largely a product of two factors. The first was the existence of anti-Bengali sentiments among the educated classes in Bihar. Thus, almost as a rule, those Lieutenant-Governors who were sympathetic to the interests of Bengal were criticized in Bihar, as we have seen in the case of Alexander Mackenzie. On the other hand, George Campbell and Ashley Eden who were seen as being pro-Bihar were roundly condemned by the Bengal press.[57] This anti-Bengal sentiment was reflected in anti-Swadeshi attitude. The second factor was a feeling of anger among the Bihari leaders for their Bengali contemporaries, who had refused to make a common cause with them on the issue of Bihar's separation. At a later stage, it (anti-Swadeshi stance) would seem to be a deliberate tactic adopted by the Bihari leaders—tactic of acting as loyal subjects of the government—so that they may secure sympathetic treatment for the region from it. They hoped that it was bound to take notice of their loyal conduct. It is also worth noting that the Maharaja of Darbhanga, the biggest landlord in Bihar and the president of the Bihar Landholders' Association was also at this time actively engaged in organizing pro-government elements against the movement.[58]

The anti-Swadeshi front was opened by the Bihari newspapers as soon as the movement got underway. As early as 19 October 1905, while writing about the Swadeshi movement, the *Behar Times* pointed out the folly of following the Bengalis.[59] Biharis were not enthusiastic about it in any case. The same mood continued and began to permeate every section of Bihari society, for just two months later the *Al Punch* (28 December 1905) reported on an interesting conversation between a Muslim and his Bengali counterpart on the Swadeshi movement. The Muslim student felt that it would be very ungrateful on the part of Indians to show disloyalty to the British whose presence had been the cause of such a rapid progress of education among them. To drive the point further home the Bengali student was told that it was the English education which had placed the Bengalis in the forefront of the intellectual race.[60] The implications of this argument were clear and wanted to convey the message that the Bengalis were not very grateful people.

In an attempt to enlist support for the Swadeshi movement Surendra Nath Banerjee visited Bihar. However, his attempts were rebuffed. The leading Urdu paper of Bihar *Al Punch* (4 October

1906) noted with satisfaction that Biharis, both Hindus and Muslims, being intelligent people, flatly refused to lend their support to the turbulent and disorderly people (the Bengalis). Banerjee was advised not to waste his valuable time in Bihar trying to induce Biharis to join him so long as he did not come to encourage true Swadeshi spirit, dissociating it from political agitation.[61] *The Beharee* (2 November 1906) expressed similar opinions.[62] Even when extremism raised its head in the Punjab in 1907 and the government responded ruthlessly to it by deporting Lala Lajpat Rai and Ajit Singh and also by banning political meetings,[63] Bihar's reaction continued to be lukewarm. One government report noted, 'the educated Hindu community in Behar disapproves of recent action in the Punjab, but do not show any particular interest in the matter. The Muhammadan community in Behar, on the other hand, cordially approves of the action taken in the Punjab, but they consider that the home of the agitation is in Bengal.'[64] The presidential speech in the annual general meeting of the Bihar Landholders' Association in 1907 and the resolutions passed therein thus merely confirmed the general aversion felt in Bihar towards extremism. The articulation of such sentiments reached their high watermark in 1908 when, in the month of August, a Manifesto signed by about 6,000 people of 16 districts of Bihar and Chota Nagpur, containing their views on the existing political situation was presented to the Lieutenant-Governor at Patna.[65]

Through this overtly loyal document the 'educated and thoughtful Biharis',[66] to use the words of memorialists, sought to convince the government that they continued to deeply abhor all forms of violence, disapproved of the Extremist propaganda and condemned anarchism. It was also used to affirm their strong adherence to constitutional methods for securing reforms in the administration of the country.[67] Such strong affirmation of loyalty was not without a context. In the month of April, a bomb outrage had taken place at Muzaffarpur in Bihar. There two youths, Khudiram Bose and Prafulla Chaki, had thrown a bomb, which killed two European ladies, though it was intended to kill Mr. Kingsford, the District Judge of Muzaffarpur, who as Presidency Magistrate at Calcutta had repressed the nationalists.[68] Though *The Beharee* (9 May 1908) had lost no time in expressing its regret for the fact that the bomb outrage had taken place in Bihar and also extending its assurance to the government that the people of Bihar to a man dissociated themselves from such practices,[69] something more was needed to be done. The Manifesto did precisely that job. Though it was criticized by some persons of the younger generation who felt that it gave too much emphasis on people's duty to the state and not on state's duty to the people Sachchidananda Sinha valiantly rose to the defence of the Manifesto arguing that there was nothing in it to be ashamed of. He pointed out that it was not merely a condemnation of violence but also dealt with the question of ideals in Indian politics and the desirability of introducing reforms in the administration.[70]

Such an overt show of loyalty was not without any motives, for the Manifesto also laid down in unambiguous language that the people of Bihar also wanted it to be made known 'that they fully share with the vast bulk of their educated fellow subjects of other provinces, those reasonable and legitimate aspirations for reform and progress, which are the birthright of every British subject, aspirations which are the direct outcome of the great and beneficent system of state education which the Government of India has organized for the benefit of Indians'. It was made clear as regards the ideals that 'the Beharis hold that in politics there is and should be no goal except the highest public good realizable'.[71]

Very clearly the game of 'carrot and stick' was again being played. Only this time some of the decisions were being made by the Biharis. The government was informed that the aspirations of the Biharis needed to be met. The Manifesto had indicated a high degree of political mobilization where 6,000 people from 16 districts had been motivated to put their signatures to it, which undeniably would have involved a lot of coordinated effort. The momentum was maintained resulting in securing significant gains for Bihar.

Within a week of presenting the Manifesto, three leading pan-Bihar organizations, namely, the Bihar Landholders' Association, the Bihar Provincial Association and the Bihar Provincial Muslim League, representing both landed and professional elites of Hindu and Muslim communities, in a major display of concerted action for securing the region's interests, presented an Address to the Lieutenant-Governor, Sir Andrew Fraser, who was on his last official visit to Bihar, containing a summary of their grievances, needs and aspirations. The members of the deputation which presented the address were clear what they wanted, which was to see, 'our great Province, with its glorious traditions of which we are justly proud, rise once more in the scale of progress and to see it advance along lines of prosperity'.[72] Interestingly, of the three associations, two—the Bihar Provincial Association[73] and the Bihar Provincial Muslim League[74] had come into existence the same year, though the fact that Syed Ali Imam was the president of both must have made the task of forging a joint front relatively easier.

They put their best foot forward and informed the Lieutenant-Governor:

> . . . of all the Provinces of Northern India, Bihar is the only one where there is no such crucial problem as is known elsewhere by the name of the Hindu-Muhammadan question. *All of us in Bihar believe in mutual toleration and reasonable compromise as the true basis of political progress and our leaders—both Hindu and Muhammadan—have therefore always acted in harmony with one another in the furtherance of the cause of good administration and civic progress. Under these circumstances we hope that the expression of our opinion will naturally carry with it much greater weight than if it were of any one section, class or community.*[75] (emphasis added)

After reminding the Lieutenant-Governor thus of the strength behind their demands, the address enumerated them clearly. The demands largely reflected the concerns of Bihari elites. The first sought to set right the inadequate representation of Bihar in the Provincial Council. In an attempt to secure a strong position in the new power structure being created around the Councils, permanent representation in the Council was demanded for its four Divisions, Patna, Tirhut,[76] Bhagalpur and Chota Nagpur 'which constitute the Province of Bihar', in case separate representation of every district was found impracticable.[77] The insistence on Chota Nagpur being a part of the Province of Bihar thus indicated a larger conception of 'Bihar'. Even in the 1906 pamphlet, Chota Nagpur had been mostly seen as a distinct 'province' or 'country', though largely peopled by the Biharis. In an obvious bid to get the sympathy and support of the European planting community, who were important in the Tirhut Division, they demanded a permanent seat for the Bihar Planters' Association in the Provincial Council.[78]

Like the 1907 address of the Bihar Landholders' Association they demanded that Patna be treated as the second capital of the Lower Provinces on the analogy of Lucknow in the United Provinces, the sittings of the Provincial Council be held in Patna too, and the Lieutenant-Governor make a prolonged stay in Patna every year.[79]

A just share in the public services had always been a major demand of Biharis and it again found a prominent place in the address. It was prayed that rules for the appointment in the Provincial Civil Service and to the posts of munsifs be so altered that, all the posts open to Indians should come to be held in Bihar by the Biharis alone. Similarly, for appointments in Bihar especially in the services like education, police, post office, etc., the request was made for the appointment of competent Biharis. To encourage the study of engineering and medicine among them, the government was requested to give preference to Bihari graduates for appointments in Bihar. It was demanded that one of the judgeships in the Calcutta High Court should be invariably conferred upon a Bihari.[80] The jobs for Biharis in Bihar was demanded because they were 'children of the soil'. Interestingly they took care to exclude the Manbhum district of Chota Nagpur from Bihar as it was a 'purely Bengali district'.[81]

Educational demands were too important to be given a go by. Larger funds for education were demanded both on the grounds of its backwardness and its neglected condition in the past. Higher education remained a major priority. Thus, the demands included not only the maintenance of Patna College as a first class residential college and aid for private colleges in Bihar but also adequate representation of the Biharis on the Senate of the Calcutta University.[82]

The demands basically referred to the grievances, needs and aspirations of the upper and middle classes in the society. No attempts were made to voice the grievances of the ordinary people nor efforts were made to secure their support.

In his reply, Fraser conceded some of the major demands made in the address. He clearly expressed his opinion that 'the Provincial Civil Service and the Judicial Service ought in Bihar to be manned almost, if not quite exclusively, by Biharis, and that we ought to keep that ideal before us in the rules we make in regard to appointments in these services'. By doing so, he accepted, even if indirectly, the 'Bihar for the Biharis' demand.[83]

It was made clear that for appointments in Bihar, the mere fact of being a Bihari was not the only claim to be considered and other qualifications were needed but it was a claim 'which ought not to be ignored'. The reason was that 'A man is a better judge, he is a better executive officer, he is a better school-master, if he talks the vernacular of the people among whom he is working, if he understands them and sympathizes with them thoroughly'. While making it clear that it was necessary for the government to maintain this determination to do right he also wanted

> you ought to remain united in your determination to advance the interests of Bihar, and that you ought to be ready at all times, in a courteous and reasonable way, such as you have adopted at the present time, to lay your views before the Head of the Government and the officers who work amongst you.[84]

He was telling the Bihari leaders that they had to work unitedly in future if they wanted their region to progress.

Fraser's reply indicated a great sympathy for the major interests of the region. Joint political action on the part of Bihari leaders had thus secured a major victory in the shape of commitments made by the Lieutenant-Governor. These were considered significant enough to be termed as the *Magna Carta* of Bihar.[85] The later heads of government were to be reminded often of the promises made in 1908.

The strong Hindu-Muslim alliance that had been forged faced an acid test as the second Bihar Provincial Conference approached. A turbulent political situation was building up in India due to the Minto-Morley reform plan and the provisions of the proposed India Councils Act of 1909, which had conceded the demand of a separate electorate to the Muslims. It was seen by some people as having given excessive concession to the Muslims.[86] However, the Bihar Hindu-Muslim alliance, unmoved by developments elsewhere, stood firm and unshaken and Bihar's quest for a distinct identity and honourable place in India remained undisturbed as the proceedings of the Conference soon made clear.

The town of Bhagalpur, then the second most important town in Bihar, was the venue of the second Provincial Conference. How such conferences played a catalytic role in generating consciousness and a spirit of mutual goodwill can be understood from a newspaper report:

> The ever dull and paralyzed Bhagalpore has been pulsating with life these days. Only recently it was a mere pool of stagnant water, now it appears to be a living mountain of spiritualism and brotherly feelings. High and low, young and old, Hindus and Mohammedans alike seek to be animated with the happy advent of the Behar Provincial Conference.[87]

The Conference held in the month of April was attended by 106 delegates. Sachchidananda Sinha was elected president.[88] One notable feature of the Conference was the presence of Gopal Krishna Gokhale.[89]As pointed out earlier, the most important question facing the Conference related to the question of a separate electorate for the Muslims. Showing both courage and foresight and also a great spirit of mutual accommodation, it passed a resolution supporting the separate electorate for the Muslims and thus was able to effect a compromise on this very difficult issue.[90] It said:

> This Conference is of opinion that while it is necessary in the best interests of the country that all communities should continue at present to participate without distinction of race and creed in elections by general electorates, it is nevertheless essential in the present circumstances to secure full and adequate representation for so important a minority as the Mahomedans by the creation of special Mahomedan electorates. In the opinion of the Conference similar treatment, if necessary, be accorded to the Hindus where they are in a minority.[91]

It is significant that this resolution did not repudiate the basic ideal that there should be only general electorates and racial and religious distinctions should not be given any general recognition. It was obviously considered a temporary expedient. The excellent Hindu-Muslim relations in Bihar had made this noble gesture possible.

The resolutions passed in the Conference about Bihar reveal that the leaders were also concerned with the common people's welfare. Thus the people were asked to make honest efforts to settle petty civil and criminal differences by recourse to arbitration.

In a significant departure from the example set up the previous year, the Conference did not pass any resolution on the issue of separation of Bihar. But rather than being a signal that the desire of the Biharis for a separate identity was waning off, this departure was born out of two beliefs. First, that it was bound to take place. Second, that it was not immediately attainable. A careful reading of Sinha's presidential speech where the question was taken up makes all this abundantly clear.

He reaffirmed that the separation of Bihar and its formation into a distinct administration by the transfer of Presidency and Burdwan Divisions and the city of Calcutta to the Province of Eastern Bengal and Assam was desired by 'most of us'. He did not fail to remind the audience that the demand of the Biharis had received support from eminent Anglo-Indians, Indian administrators and politicians like Gokhale. His concluding remarks on the subject deserve to be quoted:

> I have not the least doubt that by reason of economic, no less than political difficulties, a modification of the partition and a readjustment of the provincial boundaries on some such lines as we Biharis desire, will become an inevitable necessity before long. But as it may be said that it is not at present within the range of practical politics, I do not think I shall be justified in taking up more of your time in a longer discussion of the subject at the present moment.[92]

Sinha's speech reveals the two major weaknesses from which the movement for the separation of Bihar suffered. The desire, as he said, was prevalent among 'the thoughtful and educated people'. Probably common people were indifferent. Why they were not mobilized behind the demand or why no systematic agitation was conducted to achieve this objective becomes easy to understand when one finds in Sinha's speech the reference that it was believed to be beyond the range of practical politics. Apparently, the willingness of the leaders to ask for or agitate for any issue was dependent on how they perceived what the reaction of the government was likely to be.

The third session of the Bihar Provincial Conference was scheduled to be held at Muzaffarpur, the headquarters of the Tirhut Division. Deep Narayan Singh was elected to preside over the Conference. Singh, like his two preceding presidents and interestingly like the succeeding president, i.e. Mazhar-ul-Haque, was a Bar-at-Law.

Appeals by *The Beharee* to leading men throughout the province to make special efforts to send as many delegates as possible and the election of delegates certainly helped in both spread of regional consciousness and politicization of the people. An appeal was also made to the landed magnates to join the Conference with enthusiasm. They were assured that it was strictly a loyal and constitutional body which sought 'the cooperation and guidance of the government and its officers in furthering the interests of Bihar'.[93]

The Conference met in the month of April 1910, and was attended by over 100 delegates, nearly half of them being Muslims.[94] The continued and equal participation by the Muslims showed, as one paper remarked, that it was the only institution among a number of such conferences in which both Hindus and Muslims merged their individual identities and joined together, with equal interest and enthusiasm in discussing questions of their common interest.[95] The Conference passed resolutions on the subject of the grievances of Indians in South Africa and on the introduction of free primary education. Regarding Bihar, a resolution on the poor representation of Biharis in the Provincial Service was also passed.[96]

The high point of the Conference was the presidential speech of Deep Narayan Singh where he attempted to meet the two criticisms directed at the Conference. The first referred to the very justification of a separate Bihar Provincial Conference, even while it was a part of Bengal and the question had been raised by the *Bengalee* in 1909. It had also been criticized, as we have seen above, for remaining indifferent to the Swadeshi and boycott movements.[97] He argued,

> It is because we believe Behar to be a distinct racial unit in the country—because her history and tradition are different from those of other provinces—because we are aware that our intellectual and economic conditions are not the same as those of our sister provinces . . . that we have decided to work out our own salvation on our own lines: hence the necessity for Behar Provincial Conference. It is for this and for no other purpose that we have established a separate political organization from that of our brothers in Bengal.[98]

He also justified Bihar's non-participation in the various movements taking place all around. While admitting that this had led some people to call Bihar a backward province, he justified this approach in the light of the fact that valuable lives had been lost in blind passion of self-sacrifice.[99] Showing concern for the masses he pointed out that universal primary education and the economic development of the masses would have to be the two chief planks in the work of nation-building in the immediate future.[100]

The fourth Provincial Conference, which also happened to be the last one before the separation of Bihar from Bengal and her constitution along with Orissa into a separate province was announced, was held in the month of November at Gaya.[101]

The Conference met at a time when rumours regarding a modification of the partition were rife. These rumours had started floating from the month of March. The Bengali papers like *Hindustan* began to talk of possible annulment of partition and separation of Bihar and Assam from Bengal.[102] As the rumours gained in strength, *The Beharee* (28 July) made it clear to the government that Bihar would oppose all modification of the partition that will partition Bihar or in any way make it play second fiddle to any other province. The only thing that could satisfy the Biharis, the paper warned, was to modify the partition in such a way that would make Bihar, including Chota Nagpur, with Orissa into a separate province with a Lieutenant-Governor with an Executive Council.[103] The mood of the Conference became evident when Nand Kishore Lal, the president of the Reception Committee, in his speech, advocated the cause of Bihar's separation.[104]

Though the Conference, like the previous years, did discuss the various problems facing Bihar and demanded larger funds for secondary schools and colleges in Bihar, raising of Patna College to the status of a model college, better representation of Biharis in the Senate and Syndicate of Calcutta University, but the most important resolution passed was on the issue of separation of Bihar. In a carefully worded resolution proposed by M. Fakhruddin it was said,

> That in view of the agitation for the modification of the partition of Bengal, this Conference is strongly of opinion that in case of any modification the government should be pleased to separate Bihar including Chota Nagpur from the Lower Province and constitute it into a separate local government with Councils.[105]

The presidential speech of Mazhar-ul-Haque made the demand even more clear. He emphasized,

> The modification of the partition is a different thing and there is no doubt that both the Bengalis and Biharis will accept and be satisfied with it. . . . In the new Lower Provinces as reconstituted, since the partition, Bihar occupied the position, both in area and population, of the predominant partner enjoying all the advantages which had accrued to it thereby, and this advantageous ground the Biharis were not prepared to lose, for any consideration whatsoever.[106]

It was explicitly argued that the Biharis only wanted modification. Neither did they want the *status quo* nor the cancellation of the partition. They wanted complete separation and creation of an independent Bihar.[107]

The four sessions of the Bihar Provincial Conference till 1911 gave a new direction to the politics of Bihar. They became the most important medium of spreading regional consciousness in Bihar. Till 1906 the various demands of the region or the assertion of her individuality were articulated mainly through the columns of papers. The Bihar Landholders' Association did start championing the interests of middle-class people after 1906 but the English-educated group, as such, did not have a separate organization of its own. Although the organization (i.e. the Bihar Provincial Association and the Bihar Provincial Conference, the former being the executive arm of the latter) was dominated by a rather upper crust of English-educated group and it too was a loyal body but its vision of Bihar and its sympathy for the masses were certainly of a higher order. It could also talk of peasants and free elementary education.

Regional consciousness in the meantime had been spreading among newer sections of the population. The students had been especially affected. A concrete expression was given to it when in 1906 they established the Beharee Students Association and launched under its aegis, the Beharee Students' Conference. The Conference was the brainchild of some Bihari students studying in Calcutta, who had already established an organization known as the Beharee Club. The object of the Conference was to supplement the education imparted in schools and colleges and to create an *espirit de corps* among the students. The Association had a network of branches in every district town and even some sub-divisional towns in Bihar.[108]

The Conferences were held at different places and were big annual affairs. The presidents were chosen from among the most distinguished of public figures in Bihar. The presidential speeches asked the students to be self-reliant and to take pride in the heritage and history of their province and the nation and to work for their good.

Deep Narayan Singh, in 1907 at the Bhagalpur session, exhorted the students not to be overwhelmed by the baneful material culture of the 'West'. Though it was good to assimilate the knowledge the West offered, they were also to remember 'that your own country and even your own Behar has played no mean part in the development of mankind'.[109] Two years later at the Gaya Conference in 1909, Hasan Imam appealed to the students 'Let the motherland be the first in your affections, your province the second, and your community wherever thereafter you choose to put it'.[110]

From the presidential chair thus patriotic feelings were sought to be inculcated. In a lengthy speech in 1910 Sachchidananda Sinha tried to justify the theory of subordinate patriotism.[111] The organization also made endeavours to advance the cause of industrial and technical education in Bihar.[112] It was through these conferences and associations that the people of Bihar were being made aware that they shared common interests and a common identity.

IDEOLOGICAL JUSTIFICATION: THE THEORY OF 'SUBORDINATE PATRIOTISM' AND FEDERAL NATIONALISM

The assertion of regional personality, which informed the activities of leaders and conferences in Bihar, and the desire of Bihar for a distinct political individuality, was justified by the theory of 'subordinate patriotism' and federal nationalism. Sachchidananda Sinha and Mahesh Narayan were the principal spokesmen of the idea of 'subordinate patriotism'. They felt that it was the bounden duty of the people of Bihar to advance first and foremost the cause of Bihar and the Biharis, by all legitimate means, while sharing jointly with the people of other Indian provinces those (duties) that devolved upon educated Indians in general. The idea was to develop among the people of Bihar, Sinha maintained, what was termed by Mr. Balfour as 'subordinate patriotism' akin to what Scotchmen felt for Scotland or Irishmen for Ireland, while sharing in a common patriotism (with the English and the Welsh) as Britons. The idea was thus based on the lines of American or German patriotism—first the state, and secondly the Republic or the Empire.[113]

Sachchidananda Sinha continued to propound and justify the idea further after Mahesh Narayan's death. Leading international authorities were quoted to prove the point. For instance, Viscount Milner who had argued that every 'German is familiar with the idea of a "narrower" and "wider" Fatherland. He is a patriotic Prussian, Saxon, Bavarian but he is a patriotic German to boot.'[114] It was argued that the ideal of a common nationality based on a common language, geographical associations and historic traditions was neither mistaken nor mischievous.[115]

Associated with this theory was what may be termed as a Federal Theory of Nationalism. Its detailed exposition came from Sachchidananda Sinha in his presidential speech in the Beharee Students' Conference of 1910.[116] This must be discussed in detail.

In a discussion of the evolution of an Indian nation and Indian nationality, he argued that merely by calling ourselves an Indian nation in our writings and speeches and by being as a kind of permanent opposition to His Majesty's Government, creation of an Indian nation was not possible. In his opinion the veneer of the political unity, as was possessed by the educated classes, was largely the outcome of a sense of common grievances against the authorities and a feeling of opposition to the constituted government. While this could help in the formation of a class or party it was bound to disappear with the disappearance of the latter. A true feeling of unity, which alone could be the basis of nationality, had to 'spring from within and derive its sustenance from the indigenous elements of the community'. Arguing further, he said that genuine unity could come only when an intellectual necessity was felt. And this could come into existence only when each unit or component part of a people realizes the fact that its individualization has reached a point in self-expression, when it is desirable, in the interest of further advance or progress, to merge itself with others. Thus before, there can be a true effort at nation building, the integral factors of the community must feel that their specialization has reached a point at which they may feel it to their advantage to merge their differences.[117]

It was in the light of these arguments that he chastized those who felt that 'the struggle by your own province, Behar, to realize its individualization—the condition precedent to the formation of a true nationality was an "anti-national" movement'.[118] The desire of Bihar for a separate political identity was not only desirable but it was also the duty of Biharis to work for this. No wonder, Sinha told the students,

> . . . if you are desirous to evolve a true Indian nationality, your duty is plain . . . your duty is to see that your province fully develops itself to the utmost in the struggle for existence and in its capacity to hold its own, till it becomes self-contained, so that when similar conditions have come to exist in the other provinces, the time shall have come for a recognition of the absolute necessity of unification and cooperation as the only course open for solving the conflicting problems which will then have arisen.[119]

By 1911, even before Bihar's separation was accomplished, one could hear voices regarding her duty towards Indian nationalism. These sentiments would grow stronger once Bihar got a distinct political identity. Early in 1911, *The Beharee* referred to this new duty. It argued that so long as Bihar contented herself with the idea of provincial advancement she encountered some difficulties which were, however, successfully overcome and she had her place assured in the group of Indian provinces but this had imposed on her greater responsibilities. Thus, 'From the responsibilities attaching to a programme of provincial patriotism, she now finds herself lifted on a higher plane, where the obligation of a higher and sublimer patriotism stares her in the face, the call of a loftier duty beckons to her.'[120] Bihar was fired by a lofty impulse, the paper said, to make the cause of Indian unity and Indian nationality a success. 'The goal may be far off but she will pursue it with the light of faith in her heart.'[121]

While Bihar was preparing herself for the new duty, circumstances were being created for the eventual fulfilment of her demand. It was fortunate that by this time Bengalis had become reconciled to the idea that if they wanted reunification of the two Bengals, they would have to lose Bihar, Chota Nagpur and Orissa. This was in sharp contrast to the attitude shown by them both in 1896 and 1905. While the Bengal press had made much fun of the Biharis' agitation of 1896 for the separation of the region, some going to the extent of terming them 'ignorant people', advising them to 'desist from mischievous course of action' and the Bengal leaders had refused to support the demand of Biharis at the time of partition, to ask for the separation of Bihar so that the two Bengals could remain united, time had taught them to respect other peoples' wishes.[122] No wonder, *Hitvarta* (16 November) now was prepared to admit that Bihar could not make satisfactory progress as she was bound up with advanced people,[123] and *Hitvadi* (17 November) now saw the Biharis as being practical when they demanded her separation. The popular leaders in Bihar,it said, were not 'babes' as to be influenced by Bengali leaders in speaking out against partition.[124]

However, all these observations were not of much consequence when the government began to think of making large scale territorial and administrative rearrangements in India.

THE MOVES OF THE GOVERNMENT

The desire of the Biharis to have a state of their own was going to be fulfilled rather sooner than later. A number of reasons prompted the Government of India to plan territorial rearrangement. One important reason was the continuance of political agitation, which had started after the partition of Bengal, and had been marked by the emergence of radical section within the Congress as also by a boycott of foreign goods, as a mark of protest, and finally growth of revolutionary terrorism. A deeply worried government wanted a settlement of the Bengal problem.[125]

The government came to realize that although in the initial phase sentiments had played a role (in the movement) but after the enlargement of the Legislative Councils and especially of the representative element in them, the grievances of the Bengalis had become much more real and tangible, as they found themselves in a minority in the Councils of both the provinces into which Lieutenant-Governorship of Bengal had been partitioned, being outnumbered in the one by the Biharis and Oriyas and in the other by the Muslims of Eastern Bengal and the inhabitants of Assam. Thus, they could not exercise in either province the influence to which they considered themselves entitled by reason of their numbers, wealth and culture. It was also felt that with an increase in the representative character in the Councils and of its powers, the resentment of the Bengalis would increase.[126] The realization that the partition had been partly responsible for the growing estrangement between the Hindus and Muslims in many parts of the province made the government hope that its modification would in some degree 'alleviate this most regrettable antagonism'.[127]

But it was also understood that the partition could not be simply undone and reversion to *status quo* was impossible on political and administrative grounds. The old province was unmanageable. It was realized that any solution must provide convenient administrative units, while the legitimate expectations of the Bengalis had to be fulfilled and the interests of the Muslims of Eastern Bengal had also to be safeguarded. The solution had to be clearly based on broad grounds of political and administrative expediency. It was part of this principle that the Government of India decided,

> To create a Lieutenant-Governorship-in-Council to consist of Behar, Chota Nagpur and Orissa with a Legislative Council and a capital at Patna. The area of the province would be approximately 113,000 square miles and the population about 35,000,000.[128]

The government made clear that some alternatives like the transfer of Chota Nagpur or of Orissa to the Central Provinces, and the creation of a Chief Commissionership rather than a Lieutenant-Governorship for Bihar, Chota Nagpur and Orissa were considered but none of them seemed to deserve more than passing consideration.[129] Elaborating the proposal it was said in the despatch,

> We now turn to the proposal to create a Lieutenant-Governorship-in-Council for Behar, Chota Nagpur and Orissa. We are convinced that if

the Governor of Bengal is to do justice to the territories which we propose to assign to him, and to safeguard the interests of the Mahomedans of his province, Behar and Chota Nagpur must be dissociated from Bengal. *Quite apart, however, from that consideration, we are satisfied that it is in the highest degree desirable to give the Hindi-speaking people now included within the Province of Bengal a separate administration. These people have hitherto been unequally yoked with the Bengalis, and have never therefore had a fair opportunity for development. The cry of Behar for the Beharis has frequently been raised in connection with the conferment of appointments, an excessive number of offices in Behar having been held by Bengalis. The Beharis are a sturdy loyal people, and it is a matter of common knowledge that, although they have long desired separation from Bengal, they refrained at the time of partition from asking for it, because they did not wish to join the Bengalis in opposition to Government. There has, moreover, been a very marked awakening in Behar in recent years, and a strong belief has grown up among the Beharis that Behar will never develop until it is dissociated from Bengal. That belief will, unless a remedy be found, give rise to agitation in the near future, and the present is an admirable opportunity to carry out on our own initiative a thoroughly sound and much desired change. The Oriyas, like the Beharis, have little in common with the Bengalis, and we propose to leave Orissa (and the Sambalpur district) with Behar and Chota Nagpur.*[130] (emphasis added)

The above passage greatly explains the reasons why the Government of India decided to separate Bihar and constitute her along with Chota Nagpur and Orrisa into a new Province.

It should be admitted, though, that one feeling among the colonial officials like Harcourt Butler was that the 'uniting of Bengal would isolate the province from the rest of India and reduce its influence, for ever'. Butler wrote to Minto, the ex-Viceroy, 'it was better on the whole to reunite them (the two Bengals) and sever Behar, and let the two Bengals stew in their own juice instead of affecting the whole of India'.[131] By the first week of November, Lord Crewe, the Secretary of State for India, gave his approval to the proposals of the Government of India. He was clear that the complete administrative severance of Bihar, Chota Nagpur and Orissa would involve no hardship to the Presidency. He took due notice of the desire of hardy and law-abiding inhabitants of Bihar for a clearer expression of their local individuality.[132]

The Government of India was informed that at the Durbar (to be held in Delhi) on 12 December 1911, His Imperial Majesty, the King-Emperor would declare, apart from some other declarations, the transfer of capital from Calcutta to Delhi and the creation of a Lieutenant-Governorship-in-Council administering the areas of Bihar, Chota Nagpur and Orissa.[133] On the appointed day the announcement was duly made by King George V. Interestingly, even at this stage Chota Nagpur was being treated as a distinct entity.

The Biharis had finally got a province of their own, the creation of which, by the self-admission of its most prominent separatist leaders, had appeared to be beyond the range of practical politics as late as 1909. No wonder, the announcement was received with a burst of joy, rarely seen before, in Bihar.

Meetings were held at different places like Muzaffarpur, Bhagalpur, Purnea and Ranchi to thank King George V for granting separate provincehood for Bihar.[134] The Bihari Press which had been in the vanguard of the movement for the separation of the region poured out its feelings of thankfulness for the government.

While *The Beharee* (15 December) was happy that the despatch had admitted and recognized the various disadvantages under which Bihar was labouring because of its connection with Bengal,[135] the *Shiksha* (21 December) felt that Bihar would not be looked down upon anymore and would be able to enjoy the rights and privileges which were its just dues. More concretely, it not only expected a High Court for Bihar in due course but also hoped that Biharis would secure seats in it. Patna, the ancient capital, it felt, would regain its lost glory.[136] The expectations of Biharis were certainly running high. It was not that only Patna-based papers were celebrating in joy. Far more important for the future unity of the province was the fact that even a Darbhanga-based paper like the *Mithila Mihir* joined in the celebrations. It not only referred to the unbounded joys of Biharis on account of separation but also maintained that modern Bihar would have the Delhi Durbar as its starting point.[137]

However, this expression of joy was soon followed by a war of words between Bihari papers regarding the capital of the new province. Disregarding the fact that Patna had already been selected as the capital of the province, the Gaya-based *Kayastha Messenger* (18 December) demanded that Gaya be made the capital,[138] while the *Young India* pleaded the case of Bhagalpur.[139] But their proposals came in for sharp criticism from the *Mithila Mihir* (30 December) and *Bihar Bandhu* (30 December).[140] However, these verbal skirmishes should not be seen as undermining the identity of Bihar, which, in fact, got more concretized through them.

THE PROVINCE OF BIHAR AND ORISSA

The King's announcement had merely referred to the creation of a Lieutenant-Governorship-in-Council administering the areas of 'Behar, Chota Nagpur and Orissa'.[141] Neither the name of the province was yet decided nor the boundary fixed. Bihar was still a geographical expression. The first question was, however, taken up in 1911 itself. A. Earle, Home Secretary, on the issue of the name of the new province pointed out 'The term "Bengal, Bihar and Orissa" is historical. Possibly, the name of the new province, *if not Bihar, might be "Bihar and Orissa"*. Possibly, Chota Nagpur would be content to be included in "Bihar" '[142] (emphasis added).

M.S.D. Butler, Deputy Secretary, in his note of 24 December 1911 on this, suggested,

> See pages 171-172 of volume VIII of the Imperial Gazetteer for a history of Bihar, pages 249-250 of volume XIX for Orissa, and page 328, volume X for Chota Nagpur. Both Bihar and Orissa claim antiquity from the dawn of history. The Chota Nagpur district has no such ancient history of its own. The people of Orissa will no doubt resent if the name of their province is omitted from the territorial designation. As Secretary suggests, the name of the new province should be "Bihar and Orissa" on the analogy of the United Provinces of Agra and Oudh.[143]

The Governor-General-in-Council on 25 January 1912 finally decided to accept the name of the new province as the 'Province of Bihar and Orissa'.[144]

In this way, Chota Nagpur was included in Bihar. History, or the lack of it, came to play a major role in the merger of Chota Nagpur into Bihar. The christening of the new province had been done without any hassles. However, for a number of reasons, the second question—that of defining the boundaries of the province—was more difficult to solve. For one thing, the colonial government had never properly defined 'Bihar', as we have seen above in the study. Very generally, Patna and Bhagalpur Divisions were seen to be constituting Bihar.[145] But the government had not always stuck to this view. One telling instance was provided in 1905 when the Government of India, while discussing a plan of forming a Chief Commissionership of Bihar, maintained that apart from including certain other areas it could include 'possibly the districts of Monghyr and Bhagalpur'.[146] The districts of Purnea and Bhagalpur posed special problems as since the days of Francis Buchanan's survey in the early years of the nineteenth century who had drawn attention to the fact that the two districts contained parts of both the provinces of Bengal and Bihar,[147] a common sense view had developed that they belonged to both the provinces. It was no wonder then that both the provincial leaders and masses especially of these districts were greatly interested and involved in the boundary question as any adverse decision was likely to impact their future a great deal. The district of Santhal Parganas and parts of the Chota Nagpur were also likely to become bones of contention between Bengal and Bihar.

As the government got busy with the task at hand, the two contending parties began campaign for the inclusion of areas seen by them as 'theirs'. While the leading Bengali newspapers like the *Bengalee* felt that there were important reasons why a part of Bhagalpur should go to Bengal,[148] the *Ananda Bazar Patrika* (11 January 1912) showed greater ambition and argued for the inclusion of whole of Orissa, half of Bhagalpur Division and parts of Chota Nagpur into Bengal.[149] As was to be expected, this Bengal campaign came in for severe criticism in the Bihar papers. The *Shiksha* (11 January) decrying the agitation for the inclusion of Santhal Parganas and Purnea in Bengal pointed out that the contention of the Bengalis that the language of the majority of the people there was Bengali was not supported by the census returns which showed that their number was not even 5 lakh. The paper went on to comment 'The selfishness of the Bengalis makes the Biharis hate them'.[150] In a bid to ease off the situation some prominent Bihari leaders like Sachchidananda Sinha, Deep Narayan Singh, Nand Kishore Lal, Parmeshwar Lal and Md. Fakhruddin put forward a comprehensive method for the division of territories between the two provinces. In a joint letter to the *Bengalee* they suggested that in accordance with the resolution of the last Congress the sound principle would be that all Bengali-speaking tracts be brought under the Government of Bengal and all Hindi-speaking tracts under the Lieutenant-Governor of Bihar. As per the arrangement, they pointed out the portions of Purnea and Maldah, to the east of the river Mahananda, 'which is the ethnic boundary between Bengal and Bihar', should go to Bengal and the western portions to Bihar. A similar method of division was suggested for the Santhal Parganas. As for Chota Nagpur Division they suggested the transfer of the entire Manbhum district and Pargana Dalbhoom of Singhbhum district to Bengal, while the rest of the Division, being Hindi-speaking, was to remain in Bihar.[151] Simultaneously with this press campaign, Bihari leaders and common people also began to mount pressure on the government to give Bihar a proper boundary.

In this connection a very important meeting of the Bihari elites and leaders took place in Calcutta. In the meeting held at the residence of Maharaja of Darbhanga large landed estates like Banaily, Hathwa, Gidhaur and Tekari were represented. Also present were the prominent provincial leaders of Bihar like Sachchidananda Sinha, Deep Narayan Singh, Syed Hasan Imam and Mazhar-ul-Haque and many others. The Maharaja of Darbhanga in his presidential speech expressed the hope that the new province would have a High Court of its own in its capital city. He demanded that Bhagalpur and Purnea should be allowed to remain in Bihar as they were at that time and because existent relationships conclusively showed that this was a most desirable end to be kept in view. A resolution was also passed maintaining that no portion of Bhagalpur except Darjeeling should be severed from it.[152] This meeting was significant because of the fact that after 1908 it was only now that the landed and professional elites had come together to fight for Bihar's interests.

Another important meeting was held at Bhagalpur on 8 January. It was attended by over 1,500 people, including lawyers, merchants, zamindars and officials and was presided over by Abdul Mazid, Bar-at-Law. It too passed resolutions, strongly condemning the Bengali agitation to dismember Bihar by demanding transfer of Bhagalpur to Bengal and praying for the retention of Bhagalpur Division in Bihar. It totally disapproved its (Bhagalpur's) suggested affinity with Bengal.[153]

However, the most striking developments took place in the Purnea district, where large meetings were organized by groups of villages. In these meetings demand was made for retention of whole Purnea district in Bihar. Thus, a public meeting held at Alta Hat, in the Kishanganj subdivision, attended by about 4,000 people passed a resolution to the effect that the inhabitants of almost all the villages in Thana Bahadurganj prayed to the Government of India that no portion of their district as then constituted be severed and that the entire district of Purnea be placed under the Lieutenant-Governor of Bihar.[154]

Similarly, a meeting of the inhabitants of almost all the villages of Thanas Islampur and Chopra on the 18 January, held at Islampur, requested the Governor-General 'not to dismember the district and to place the entire district under the Lieuteneant-Governor of Behar'. It was made clear that any partition would greatly affect their interests and would not serve any useful purpose.[155] A similar request to keep the whole of Purnea district in Bihar was made in a meeting held at Kasba which was attended by about 2,000 people.[156]

Even more significant were the meetings held at Salamari and Barsoi, as these fell on the eastern side of the Mahananda River, and were thus supposed to be ethnically similar to Bengal. In these meetings, people prayed to the government that the district of Purnea, without any division, should remain in Bihar.[157]

It was through these momentous meetings that Bihar was being finally defined by the people themselves. Till now common people had largely been bystanders, as the educated elites worked for the creation of a separate province of Bihar but now they entered the game themselves. Bihar was getting ready for the mass movements of the Gandhian era. The Government of India, almost at the same time, was engaged in the similar task of defining Bihar. The Bengali leaders had not yet given up hope of getting included parts of Bihar and Assam into Bengal. They made an indirect effort. Bhupendra Nath Basu through a question in the Imperial Legislative Council wished to know if it was the intention of the government to include in Bengal (a) Sylhet and Manbhum, (b) any portions of Bhagalpur, Purnea and the Santhal Parganas where Bengali may be the prevailing language. The government in reply made it clear that it had no such intention. What is of real interest in this episode is the fact that this version of the question was even allowed to be raised only after being modified. The official proceeding does not carry the original version of the question, which undoubtedly was problematic enough for the government to make the Law Member of Viceroy's Executive Council, Ali Imam, observe that it was designed to tie-up the hands of the government in matters of territorial distribution. He felt that the 'agitatiors' of Calcutta have gathered from the terms of the despatch dealing with the Delhi announcement that the Muhammadans in the new province of Bengal would be given a majority of about 2 million over the Hindus. 'They have set up their sail accordingly and raised these questions with the sole object of securing a majority for themselves, which can be obtained in no other way than the inclusion of areas from Assam and Bihar.'[158] The Bengali move had been checkmated, the Bihari Law Member playing a critical role in the process.

The government, as pointed out above, was also grappling with the question of defining Bihar. The question came up when parliamentary Bills for constituting new provinces were being discussed. In a note W.H. Vincent observed that 'the expression 'Bihar' is somewhat vague and it might be doubtful how far it would include districts like the Santhal Parganas and Purnea.'[159]

S.A. Imam, the Law Member, too felt the same. He pointed out, 'there is no such territory known to me as "Behar District". The sense in which the word "district" is accepted in India will hardly coincide with what is meant in the English draft. A more definite expression is needed which can be had by means of a schedule as is pointed out by secretary.'[160] Acting on such advice, on 7 February 1912 the Viceroy informed the Secretary of State that 'the expression "districts of Bihar, Chota Nagpur, Orissa and Assam" in the Bill is unsuitable, as these are not "districts" but comprise districts'. It was then suggested that a schedule be adopted, specifying as to what districts of the Bhagalpur Division, Patna Division (whole of it), etc., were to be incorporated.[161]

The advice was acted upon and a proclamation was prepared. By this Proclamation dated 22 March 1912, the Province of Bihar and Orissa was constituted out of the districts of Bhagalpur,

Monghyr, Purnea and the Santhal Parganas of the Bhagalpur Division, the whole of Patna and Tirhut Divisions, the Chota Nagpur Division (comprising the districts of Hazaribagh, Manbhum, Palamau, Ranchi and Singhbhum) and the Orissa Division.[162] It meant that both Purnea and Santhal Parganas were included in Bihar in their entirety. The new province was to come into being on 1 April 1912 and Sir C.S. Bayley was to be the first Lieutenant-Governor.[163]

The quest of Bihar for a distinct political identity had come to a successful end. It was time to look beyond. *The Beharee*, the mouthpiece of educated elites of Bihar, in an article 'Behar and her New Life' pointed out where the duty lay. It said:

> The next session of the Indian National Congress meets in our own town (Patna). . . . The best and the readiest way which has commended itself to our publicmen of celebrating the resuscitation of the ancient, though departed, glory of their province is by extending an invitation to our great national Assembly to meet at the headquarters of the province. . . . The first thought which Behar entertains on the occasion of her opportunities for perfect self-expression and development is in respect of her duty to the great motherland, of which she is now an important unit. This is a most gratifying and auspicious indication. It is well . . . that the new-born energy and newly awakened self-consciousness of our province should automatically respond to the stirrings of national life.[164]

The period 1906 to 1912 proved a fruitful one for Bihar. During this period, at least till 1908, the Government of Bengal under Andrew Fraser remained extremely sympathetic to the demands of Bihar, which had already become the predominant partner in the Bengal Presidency. Two important political developments also took place during this period. The landed aristocracy came out to support the demands of those groups whose status in the society mainly derived from their educational attainments, i.e. the English-educated groups. The second development was that Hindu and Muslim leaders succeeded in forging a stronger political bond than before. Its outcome was the establishment of the Bihar Provincial Association and organization of the Bihar Provincial Conference. This show of solidarity made it difficult for the government to ignore the claims of Bihar in various fields. Increased pressure was mounted on the government to separate her. It would be naïve to suggest that the separation of Bihar and her constitution into a separate province along with Orissa was brought about by the efforts of Biharis alone but it is true that they made the government realize that Bihar could no longer be forced to play second fiddle to any province. Hence when the government began rethinking on the issue of territorial reorganization of India, especially on the issue of Bengal partition, the separation of Bihar and her formation into a province was an idea that suggested itself.

NOTES

1. S. Sarkar, *Modern India: 1885-1947*, Madras, 1983, pp. 106-24.
2. See S. Gopal, *The British Policy in India, 1858-1905*, Cambridge, 1965; Madras, 1984, pp. 275-95. *The Behar Herald* (26 August 1905) referred in *Report on Native-Owned English Newspapers in Bengal*, no. 35, 1905. The paper pointed out that the news was not received with that outburst of pleasure and rejoicing with which it was received in Bengal.
3. M.N. Das, *India under Morley and Minto: Politics Behind Revolution, Repression and Reforms*, London, 1964, p. 48.
4. Sarkar, *Modern India*, p. 112.
5. Das, *India Under Morley and Minto*, p. 34.
6. Mahesh Narayan and Sachchidananda Sinha, 'The Partition of Bengal or the Separation of Behar?: An Ideally Perfect Alternative Scheme', Patna, 1906. I have consulted its typescript copy at the Bihar State Archives Library, Patna.
7. Sachchidananda Sinha, *Some Eminent Behar Contemporaries*, (henceforth *Behar Contemporaries*); Patna, 1944, p. xx. Sachchidananda Sinha in February 1904 had written an article in the *Hindustan Review* entitled 'The Partition of Lower Province: An Alternative Proposal' and Mahesh Narayan wrote with the same title in the *Hindustan Review* of August 1905. Both these were combined in the pamphlet, see N.M.P Srivastva, *Bihar Mein Rashtriyata ka Vikas (1912-1947)* (Hindi), Patna, 1974, p. 10. It needs to be pointed out that the pamphlet covered events till the end of 1905.
8. Sinha, *Behar Contemporaries*, p. xx.
9. *The Beharee* in its different issues of 1909, 1910, 1911 ran its advertisements; one could get it by sending an application with a half *anna* postage stamp.
10. Narayan and Sinha, 'The Partition of Bengal or the Separation of Behar', pp. 1-2.

11. Ibid., pp 3-5.
12. Ibid., pp. 16-18.
13. Ibid., p.18.
14. Ibid., pp. 21-3.
15. Ibid., pp. 20-31.
16. Ibid., pp. 32-41.
17. Ibid., pp. 43-5.
18. Ibid.
19. Ibid., pp. 45-9.
20. Sinha, *Behar Contemporaries*, p. XXII.
21. *Sanjivani* (1 February) and *Orissa Vasi* (1 February) referred in *Report on Native Papers in Bengal* [henceforth *RNP (B)*], no. 7, 1906.
22. India Home (Public) Progs, December 1906, no. 4, 'Deposit'.
23. For instance, the differences between the Bengalis and the Biharis. They were more widely different than the 'Celts and the Teutons in race origin, in language, in marriage customs and even in food.' He also argued that the idea of separating Bihar in order to give relief to the overworked 'Government of the Lower Provinces' had the highest official approval till Lord Curzon came to upset everything. Patna's superiority over Dacca was asserted. Patna was an ancient city, 'the capital of all India, in centuries before Christ'. It was easy of approach, healthy and centrally located. A very important reason in favour of the Bihar separation lay in the fact that it was most keenly desired by its people. The Bihar solution 'breaks no racial ties and recognizes ethnical and linguistic frontiers that have existed from the dawn of history, and which even the Muslim conquerors never disturbed.' See ibid.
24. The *Kayastha Messenger* of Gaya (3 December 1906) in a reply to the *Amrita Bazar Patrika's* assertion that there was no unanimity among the Biharis on the issue of separation made it clear that the entire community with the exception of a few 'Bengalised Biharis' were in its favour. See *Report on Native-Owned English Newspapers in Bengal,* no. 49, 1906.
25. *RNP (B),* no. 9, 1906.
26. *Report on Native-Owned English Newspapers in Bengal,* no. 37, 1906.
27. Sinha, *Behar Contemporaries*, p. XXIII.
28. See the *Bihar Bandhu*, 15 October 1901 and S.N. Pandey, *Education and Social Changes in Bihar (1900-1921),* Varanasi, 1975, p. 208.
29. Bengal General (Education) B Progs, December 1907, File no. 4A/23, Sl. nos. 134-7.
30. Ibid.
31. *Report on Native-Owned English Newspapers in Bengal,* no. 4, 1907.

32. Bengal General (Education) B Progs, December 1907, File no. 4A/23, Sl. nos. 134-7.
33. Ibid.
34. Ibid.
35. Ibid. The Maharaja had said 'We are only voicing the sentiments of the vast majority of our own countrymen in expressing our disapprobation of seditious and inflammatory writing and speech and all acts of violence and lawlessness, acts which, if indulged in, will, with inevitable certainty, retard those reforms we all earnestly desire to see accomplished.' See Das, *India Under Morley and Minto*, p. 111.
36. John R. McLane, *Indian Nationalism and the Early Congress*, Princeton, 1977, p. 147.
37. See the extract from *The Beharee*, 3 May 1907 in History of Freedom Movement Papers (henceforth F.M. Papers), Region VII, vol. II, File no. 2/2.
38. See speech of Deep Narayan Singh, Chairman of the Reception Committee in the *Bengalee*, 21 April 1900 where he tried to explain the reasons for poor Bihari presence at the conference and obliquely criticized Bengali leaders and press of not espousing the interests of Bihar.
39. See Sudeshna Basak, *Socio-Cultural Study of a Minority Linguistic Group: The Bengalees in Bihar*, Delhi, 1991, Appendix I, Extract from *The Beharee*, 9 April 1907, which had carried an extract from the presidential speech.
40. See *Report on Native-Owned English Newspapers in Bengal,* nos. 15 and 16, 1907.
41. See *The Beharee*, 10 September 1909. It gives the year of this meeting as 1909, which is obviously a printing error, because Mahesh Narayan, who was present in the meeting died in 1907 itself. *The Beharee* of (3 May 1907) talks about the tentative scheme of the association which had formally been launched in 1908. See its extract in F.M. Papers Region VII, vol. II, File no. 2/2.
42. Ibid. (*The Beharee,* 10 September 1909).
43. See [Extract from] *The Beharee*, 3 May 1907, in F.M. Papers, Region VII, vol. II, File no. 2/2. The political committee was headed by Deep Narayan Singh and had in all 19 members while the second committee was headed by Tilakdhari Lall and had 14 members in all.
44. See Bengal Municipal Department, A Progs, February 1909, File no. M 17-A/3, Sl. nos. 4-9.
45. *Report on Native-Owned English Newspapers in Bengal,* no. 23, 1907.
46. See *The Beharee*, 10 September 1909 and Girindra Mohan Mishra

Kicchu Dekhal Kicchu Sunal (Maithili), Darbhanga, Shaka 1894, pp. 32-3.

47. Ibid. (*The Beharee*, 10 September 1909).
48. Ibid. It is rather strange that it has been suggested by one scholar that the first session of the Bihar Provincial Conference held in 1908 under the presidentship of Ali Imam was convened by the Bihar Provincial Congress Committee, which too was formed in 1908. See K.K. Datta, 'Freedom Movement in Bihar', in K.K. Datta (ed.), *The Comprehensive History of Bihar* (henceforth *CHB*), vol. III, pt. I, Patna, 1976, p. 260. The fact is that the Provincial Congress Committee was formed later in 1908.
49. See *The Beharee*, 4 June 1909.
50. Bengal Political (Political) A Progs, September 1911, nos. 20-31.
51. *The Beharee*, 29 January and 13 August 1909.
52. The *Bengalee* of 17 April 1908 referred in *Report on Native-Owned English Newspapers in Bengal,* no. 17, 1908.
53. Ibid.
54. See India Home (Public) A Progs, October 1908, nos. 15-17.
55. Sinha, *Behar Contemporaries*, p. xxiv. Also see Pandey, *Education and Social Changes in Bihar*, p. 103.
56. See *The Beharee,* 30 September 1909.
57. See Chapters 3 and 4.
58. See Das *India under Morley and Minto*, p. 110. The Maharaja had said 'I think it would be well for us on this occasion, in view of the unrest that has lately manifested itself in various quarters of the land, to record in a very definite and emphatic manner that the Hindu population of India, the aristocracy, the middle classes as well as the masses of people are all sincerely loyal to the British rule in India.'
59. *Report on Native-Owned English Newspapers in Bengal,* no. 42, 1905.
60. *RNP (B)*, no. 2, 1906.
61. *RNP (B)*, no. 41, 1906.
62. *Report on Native-Owned English Newspapers in Bengal*, no. 46, 1906. Sumit Sarkar has also referred to a similar kind of attitude in Orissa citing Utkal Union Conference's example, see his *Modern India*, p. 125.
63. Sarkar, *Modern India*, pp. 128-9.
64. India Home (Political) B Progs, July 1906, Prog. no. 78 in Prog. nos. 39-177.
65. Bengal Political Department B Progs, August 1908, File no. M/49/ 1-2, Sl. nos. 301-2.
66. See India Home (Public) A Progs, October 1908, nos. 15-17.

67. See the Presidential Speech by S. Sinha at the Bihar Provincial Conference in 1909 in *The Beharee*, 16 April 1909.
68. See Datta, 'Freedom Movement in Bihar', p. 261.
69. *Report on Native-Owned English Newspapers in Bengal,* no. 20, 1908.
70. See *The Beharee*, 16 April 1909.
71. Ibid.
72. See India Home (Public) A Progs, October 1908, nos. 15-17.
73. See above in this chapter.
74. The Provincial Muslim League was set up in March 1908. Syed Ali Imam was the President and Mazhar-ul-Haque, the Secretary. See Syed Sharfuddin Pirzada (ed.), *Foundations of Pakistan: All India Muslim League Documents, 1906-1947*, vol. I, New Delhi, Indian edn., 1982, p. LIII.
75. India Home (Public) A Progs, October 1908, nos. 15-17.
76. Tirhut Division was created in 1908. It consisted of the districts which lay in the north of the Ganges and were earlier part of the Patna Division.
77. India Home (Public) A Progs, October 1908, nos. 15-17.
78. Ibid.
79. Ibid.
80. Ibid.
81. Ibid.
82. Ibid.
83. Ibid.
84. Ibid.
85. See *The Beharee*, 8 December 1911.
86. See Sarkar, *Modern India,* p. 142 and F. Robinson, *Separatism among Indian Muslims: The Politics of United Provinces' Muslims, 1860-1923*, Cambridge, 1974, pp. 152-9.
87. *The Beharee*, 9 April 1909.
88. Ibid., 16 April 1909.
89. Ibid.
90. Ibid.
91. Ibid., 23 April 1909.
92. Ibid.
93. Ibid., 8 April 1910.
94. Ibid., 22 April 1910.
95. Ibid.
96. Ibid.
97. Ibid.
98. Ibid.
99. Ibid.

100. Ibid.
101. See ibid., 17 November 1911.
102. See *RNP (B)*, no. 12, 1911.
103. See *Report on Native-Owned English Newspapers in Bengal*, no. 31, 1911.
104. See *The Beharee*, 17 November 1911.
105. Ibid.
106. V. A. Narayan, 'Bihar Provincial Congress Committee (1908-1928)', in P.N. Ojha (ed.), *History of Indian National Congress in Bihar, 1885-1985*, Patna, 1985, p. 84.
107. Ibid.
108. See the compiled volume of the *Presidential Addresses Delivered at the Beharee Students' Conference*, compiled by B.N. Sinha, Patna, 1931, pt. I. Also see the Foreword by Rajendra Prasad, p. 1. However, Girindra Mohan Mishra who had been actively associated with the conference since its inception presents a different account of its origin. According to him in 1906 one student Ayodhya Prasad of Chapra wrote to Rajendra Prasad, who had topped in B.A. regarding the organization of Beharee Students' Conference. Rajendra Prasad through letters encouraged the students of Patna to act in the matter and they met under the presidentship of Muhammad Yunus, Bar-at-Law and decided to organize it. A reception committee, under a student Muhammad Khalilur Rahman was formed for the purpose. See Girindra Mohan Mishra, *Kicchu Dekhal Kicchu Sunal*, pp. 18-19. It needs to be mentioned that anti-Bengali sentiments got reflected even in this noble venture of the Bihari students. Their decision to name it as the Beharee Students' Conference and by implication to exclude Bengali students from any active participation in its affairs, came in for strong censure from the president of the first conference, Syed Sharfuddin. See the compiled volume of the *Presidential Addresses Delivered at the Beharee Students' Conference*, pp. 2-3.
109. Ibid. (*Addresses*), p. 10.
110. Ibid., p. 26.
111. Ibid., pp. 46-8.
112. Ibid., p. 9.
113. See *The Hindustan Review*, Allahabad, New Series, vol. 16, no. 96, August 1907, pp. 177-8. Sachchidananda Sinha edited the journal. And also see Sinha, *Behar Contemporaries*, pp. 40-1. Interestingly, Balfour and Miner belonged to a select group of men in England who showed insight into the question of nationality. See Benjamin Akzin, *State and Nation*, London, 1964, p. 18.

114. Ibid. (*Hindustan Review*, vol. 16, no. 96, August 1907), pp. 177-8.
115. Ibid.
116. See the volume of the *Presidential Addresses Delivered at the Beharee Students' Conference*, pp. 46-8.
117. Ibid.
118. Ibid., p. 47.
119. Ibid., p. 48.
120. *The Beharee,* 17 February 1911.
121. Ibid.
122. See Chapter 5.
123. *RNP (B),* no. 47, 1911.
124. Ibid.
125. R.C. Majumdar, H.C. Raychaudhari and K.K. Datta, *An Advanced History of India*, rpt., Madras, 1985, p. 924.
126. India Home (Delhi) A Progs, December 1911, nos. 8-11. The despatch dated 25 August, Simla, 1911, from Government of India to the Secretary of State.
127. Ibid.
128. Ibid.
129. Ibid.
130. Ibid.
131. See Chaudhary, *The Creation of Modern Bihar*, pp. 170-1 for the full quotes from Harcourt Butler's letters dated 21 November 1911 and 13 May 1912 to Minto.
132. India Home (Delhi) A Progs, December 1911, nos. 8-11.
133. Ibid.
134. See *The Beharee,* 22 and 29 December 1911.
135. *Report on Native-Owned English Newspapers in Bengal,* no. 51, 1911.
136. *RNP (B)*, no. 1, 1912.
137. Ibid.
138. *Report on Native-Owned English Newspapers in Bengal,* no. 1, 1912.
139. See *RNP (B)*, no. 2, 1912.
140. See *RNP (B)*, nos. 1 and 2, 1912.
141. India Home (Delhi) A Progs, December 1911, nos. 8-11.
142. Ibid., February 1911, no. 45.
143. Ibid.
144. Ibid.
145. See Chapter 3.
146. See Chapter 5.
147. See M. Martin, *The History, Antiquities, Topography and Statistics of Eastern India* (1838), Indian rpt. Delhi, 1976, vol. II, p. 1 and vol. IV, p. 1.

148. See *The Beharee*, 12 January 1912.
149. *RNP (B)*, no. 3, 1912.
150. Ibid.
151. *The Beharee*, 12 January 1912.
152. See Bihar and Orissa Political Department Special Section Progs 1911, File no. 346/11. No other details. Also see *The Beharee*, 12 January 1912.
153. Ibid. (The Proceedings).
154. Ibid.
155. Ibid.
156. India Home (Delhi) B Progs, January 1912, nos. 75-8.
157. Ibid.
158. See India Home (Public) A Progs, April 1912, no. 53.
159. India Home (Delhi) A Progs, February 1912, nos. 71-80.
160. Ibid.
161. Ibid.
162. See India Home (Public) A Progs, April 1912, nos. 127-8, and *Report on the Administration of the Territories now Included in the Province of Bihar and Orissa, 1911-12*, Patna, 1913, p. ii (summary).
163. Ibid.
164. *The Beharee*, 12 January 1912.

CHAPTER 7

Conclusion

The region of Bihar got a distinct politico-administrative identity of its own in 1912, marking the end of a quest which had its origin in the growth of regional consciousness around the symbol of 'Bihar' during the last three decades of the nineteenth century. Its separation from Bengal and constitution along with Orissa into the Province of Bihar and Orissa also marked the end of a phase in the evolution of people of Bihar into a distinct Bihari community. This study tried to understand as to how and why the consciousness of a common identity emerged around the symbol of Bihar, why it led to the movement for a separate politico-administrative identity for the region and what were the reasons which prompted the government to concede this demand. The study has identified four major factors, which acting separately and in concert with one another made this entire process possible. The first of these factors was that the region possessed the objective attributes which marked it off from other parts of the Bengal Presidency. The second important factor was the colonial rule, its accompanying effects, its perceptions and policies. The third factor was the inner process of change occurring within the Bihar society and its resultant effects. The last such factor was the movement for the creation of a separate province of Bihar, which though itself an outcome of growing regional consciousness was, in turn, to contribute significantly to the further growth and strengthening of this consciousness.

The presence of the markers of distinctiveness—the objective bases—was absolutely crucial to the fashioning of a regional identity in Bihar. These markers lay essentially in the historical traditions of the region, its linguistic characteristics and ethnic attributes of the people. The historical tradition dated back to the ancient period of Indian history and counted among its sons some of the most legendary names in Indian history such as Mahavira, the 24th

Tirthankar of Jains, Chandragupta Maurya, Ashoka and Sher Shah. This tradition had been appropriated in the name of Bihar when the region was constituted as a suba (suba Bihar) by Akbar with its capital at Patna (ancient Patliputra). The British through their gazetteers and other official reports further strengthened Bihar's claim of having a distinct and glorious tradition dating back to ancient times. It is no wonder, then, that the Bihari political leaders made full use of this history in demanding a separate politico-administrative identity for the region and were sincere in their belief that in so doing they were merely trying to resuscitate the lost glory of the region. As much as history, languages also separated Bihar from other parts of the Presidency, especially, in this context, Bengal. During two hundred years of Mughal rule those associated with administration learnt to use Persian while at a more popular level people spoke Hindi and its allied languages and dialects as also Urdu or Hindustani. The British also through the decision to introduce Hindi as the official vernacular language of Bihar helped in strengthening this linguistic exclusiveness of the region. It was as a Hindi-speaking region that Bihar was separated from Bengal.

Ethnically, people of Bihar were believed both by themselves as also outsiders as being far more largely of the Aryan stock than those of Bengal Proper. However, these objective bases of identity would have remained of no importance but for the arrival of the British on the scene. It was the initial impact of the colonial rule on Bihar which created the context which made it imperative to give a new salience and meaning to these objective characteristics. Bihar was made a part of the Presidency of Bengal and thus its distinct political status as a suba got obliterated. Also, the colonial intrusion in course of time started hurting local interests. Among these interests the most important was the decreasing opportunities for the natives of Bihar in getting government jobs. In their attempt to improve the standard of officials the colonial rulers made English education compulsory for official employment. However, the poor progress of English education in Bihar till around 1870 provided opportunities to better-educated Bengalis to come and occupy not only important public offices to the exclusion of native people but also to establish a very strong position in the professions of law and medicine. The presence of the Bengalis, speaking a different language and having a very heightened sense of their distinct identity coupled with a display of superior attitude towards the less well-educated and by implication less cultured people of Bihar impacted them in different ways. On the one hand their material prospects were affected, on the other their sense of self-esteem was hurt. The agitation launched by them for the exclusion of Bengalis from local posts was just one, though very significant, aspect of this feeling of resentment, which was also manifested by their desire to pronounce certain letters differently from Bengalis, their reluctance to translate even Bengali textbooks into Hindi, their refusal to patronize Bengali-dominated newspapers and their decision of excluding even the Bengali students from associating with the Beharee Students' Conference, even though their interests as students did not conflict with each other. Bengalis were the significant 'Other' against whom they largely perceived their own distinctiveness, emphasized their markers and constructed their identity.

The factor which finally made it both possible and imperative to assert the regional distinctiveness of Bihar was the emergence of an educated class and new social groups following the spread of English education since about 1870. The new professional groups like those of lawyers and journalists, not constrained by restrictions imposed on government servants, took the lead in the espousal of regional interests and dissemination of the idea of a common identity. A factor of special significance was the more than equal participation of Muslims both in English education and hence public services and professions which made possible the assertion of rights and claims of Bihari people as a whole. The spread of literacy made available a large number of people among whom the idea of a common identity could be disseminated.

In the growth of regional consciousness in Bihar and in establishing a distinct Bihari political identity colonial perceptions and policies played a key role. From around 1870s the British became more and more aware of the distinctive needs of the region and its people. Their language policy was born out of a view that Hindi and not Urdu was the language of the common people in Bihar. Though there were differences within the bureaucracy on the soundness of the opinion, the final decision aided the process of finally establishing Bihar as a Hindi-speaking region. The British employment policy, product of a desire to balance and rule by ameliorating the perceived imbalance of one group *vis-à-vis* another group (in this case the imbalance of Biharis in the race of employment as against Bengalis) strengthened the consciousness among the people of Bihar that it was 'their' region and they had a greater right over government jobs there than any outside community. This indirectly encouraged people to agitate for effective implementation of this policy and its extension to other areas seen to be constituting 'Bihar'. It needs to be mentioned that 'Bihar for Biharis' demand was made after this policy was put in place.

The voluntary associations and newspapers which started emerging from around 1870 through their activities and articulations contributed immensely to the growth of a regional consciousness and kept alive the demand for Bihar's separation from Bengal. Though the growth of education and emergence of English-educated groups was greatly instrumental in their launch, the increased urbanization and improvements in the communication system was no less significant. Divisional towns like Patna and Bhagalpur and district towns like Muzaffarpur, Monghyr, Gaya and others became magnets attracting people from neighbouring areas in search of education and employment, enabling men from different backgrounds to interact and associate with each other and to discover concerns and problems which were social and common rather than personal. 'Bihar' was the symbol around which all their activities revolved. While the early voluntary associations were mainly concerned with non-political issues, trying to work for educational and social improvement of the people of Bihar, the pan-Bihar associations established in the twentieth century like the Bihar Provincial Association and Bihar Provincial Conference were overtly concerned with articulation and achievement of political and non-political goals for the people of Bihar. The newspapers unlike the early associations were from the very beginning far more radical in their approach. They first pointed out the incongruity of Bihar's union with Bengal and the harms resulting from this union. In this, special emphasis was laid on the issue of employment with Bihari papers demanding that employment in Bihar should be given to Biharis only. The 'Bihar for Biharis' movement which contributed immensely to the making of a Bihari community was conducted mainly through the columns of newspapers.

After two decades of growing regional consciousness in Bihar, the political climate began to change at a quicker pace in the 1890s. A number of new leaders like Mahesh Narayan, Sachchidananda Sinha, N.K. Lal, Ali Imam and Hasan Imam emerged. Some like S. Sinha and Imam Brothers came from a common social background, had studied in England around the same time to get into the same profession and forged strong friendship ties cutting across religious lines. Having been witness to the rising tide of nationalist aspirations in Europe, it is not surprising that they were hurt by the absence of a distinct political identity for Bihar.

They also believed that the region and its people would not flourish unless Bihar was separated from Bengal. The new leaders did not share the inhibitions of the older leaders, inhibitions emerging out both on account of their close contact with Calcutta and a sincere belief that the colonial government would not agree to a separation of Bihar, and decided to make determined efforts to achieve this goal. To open up the government to this possibility and to secure a fair deal for Bihar in different matters, they launched an English journal—*The Behar Times* in 1894. Rather sooner than later a golden chance came their way to press their case. In 1896 the government made a move to transfer Chittagong Division to Assam to ease the workload on the Lieutenant-Governor of Bengal. Bihar leaders, buoyed up by the support extended by the influential Anglo-Indian paper, the *Pioneer*, launched a movement to demand its separation. The educated classes in Bihar in a series of meetings decided to put pressure on the government to concede this demand which was largely articulated by the *Behar Times* and backed up by some other newspapers. The demand was made on the ground that Bihar was a homogeneous tract, its people wanted separation from Bengal as they were different from Bengalis in every way, their requirements were different and they needed a different treatment from the government, which implicitly was possible only after it was given a separate political identity. The major political argument was that it would give a greater amount of relief to the Lieutenant-Governor of Bengal than any other scheme of territorial redistribution. The movement collapsed once the Lieutenant-

Governor indicated that government was not even prepared to think over the proposal. The movement, at no stage, could draw the support of the common people behind this demand, nor the leaders made any attempts to reach out to them. However, it needs to be mentioned that modern politics in India till this period was mainly an affair of the elites and educated classes of the people. Masses were yet to enter the political scene.

The next attempt in this direction was made at the time of the partition of Bengal. Though no public movement was launched to secure Bihar's separation, the case was put forward by newspapers and publicists. Efforts were made to seek cooperation of Bengal leaders so that a joint demand could be made before the government that if it wanted to reduce administrative burden on the Bengal government it should separate Bihar rather than partitioning Bengal Proper. However, the Bengal leaders showed no inclination to support this proposal and hence attempts at forging a joint front could not succeed. One offshoot of the government's transfer proposals was that the consciousness of a common Bihari identity spread to Chota Nagpur Division too. Till this period articulation of this consciousness had been made by the people of Patna and Bhagalpur Divisions only but when faced with the threat of being transferred to the Central Provinces the elites and common people of Chota Nagpur proclaimed their Bihari identity.

After the partition of Bengal, Bihar became the predominant partner in the old province but still efforts to secure a distinct political status for the region continued. After 1906 the tactics of the leaders underwent a subtle change. Thwarted by the Bengali leaders in their bid to forge a joint front against the government, they decided to openly follow the path of loyalty. The British were sought to be convinced that Biharis, if the government met their wishes, would not betray them. It was not a matter of surprise that they consistently stayed away from the Swadeshi agitation.

During this period the region witnessed a new kind of political mobilization. While the professional and other English-educated groups formed the Bihar Provincial Association and organized the Bihar Provincial Conference to articulate the different demands of the region, the Bihar Landholders' Association showed an unprecedented zeal in taking up various issues of regional interest. Finally in 1908 the landholding elites joined hands with the professional groups. Bihari Hindus and Muslims had always been working *in tandem*. Thus a formidable political coalition emerged by 1908 in Bihar and succeeded in securing major commitments from the government. All through this period ideological justification for Bihar's demand was made through various means. The Bihari leaders believed in the existence of both a plurality and hierarchy of social attachments. They did not see love for the region and for the nation in terms of binary opposition. Rather the very effort of nation-building, in their view, implied that every constituent unit should be allowed the fullest opportunity to realize its individual identity and develop its potential, both material and intellectual, to the fullest.

The demand for Bihar's separation from Bengal was made on occasions and no opportunity was lost to keep the ideal alive. It was made clear to the government that in any future scheme of territorial rearrangement, Bihar's separation should find a place. Though it would be naïve to suggest that its separation was achieved only through the efforts of its leaders, it would not be incorrect to say that they kept the issue alive till it was resolved to their satisfaction. As our evidences suggest the consciousness of a common identity had been confined mainly to the educated and upper classes of Bihari society but the creation of the Province of Bihar and Orissa proved the moment from when this consciousness began to spread among the masses, when in meetings, held at different places they gathered in thousands to thank the government for separating Bihar and also when they came together to protest against the proposed transfer of certain areas to Bengal. The making of Bihar had also been the making of Biharis.

That Bihar's desire and efforts for a distinct identity was never an anti-national gesture was proved soon enough. In the very same year of its separation from Bengal, i.e. 1912, the annual session of the Indian National Congress, met at Patna and Bihar whole-heartedly joined the mainstream of national politics and when the Gandhian era of the national movement began it emerged as one of the strongest centres of this movement.

The creation of a new province did not, however, mean the solution of all the problems of the region. It was not yet endowed with a High Court of its own. The Maharaja of Darbhanga had already expressed the hope and the implied wish of the people of Bihar of having a High Court for the new province. The leading newspaper of Bihar *The Beharee* pressed on with the request, 'The policy of Provincial Autonomy which is to be the pathway of future progress in Indian administration, requires before all else the formation of self-contained provinces with their own executive, judiciary and legislature.'[1] Also the economic situation of the region had been deteriorating for the last twenty years. While the number of people dependent on agriculture had increased, the number of people engaged in production and trade for local market had decreased considerably.[2] The total number of literates was just over 4 per cent in the Province of Bihar and Orissa.[3] Apart from these problems new sources of tension like casteism and communalism were rearing their ugly heads. But opportunity to chart out a new course, to take Bihar forward in every walk of life had been provided. Hope was still alive in 1915 when Nand Kishore Lal, who had been actively associated with Bihar's struggle for a distinct identity, while reminding the younger generation of the efforts made for securing Bihar's separation, asked them to carry on the task of taking the province forward so that the senior leaders may have the consolation that their

> Visions have not come to nought
> Who saw by lightning in night
> The deeds they dreamed are being wrought
> By those who work in clearer light.[4]

NOTES

1. Annual Report on Indian Newspapers in Bihar and Orissa for 1912 in Bihar and Orissa Political (Special) Progs 1913, File no. 32, Sl. nos. 1-6.
2. Nirmala Banerjee, 'Modernization and Marginalization', in *Social Scientist,* October-November 1985, vol. 13, no. 10/11, pp. 48-71.
3. S.N. Pandey, *Education and Social Changes in Bihar (1900-1921)*, Varanasi, 1975, p. 172.
4. See Nand Kishore Lal's Presidential Address at the Bihar Provincial Conference in 1915, The Freedom Movement (F.M.) Papers, Region VII, File no. 6/2, p. 53 (201).

Bibliography

PRIMARY SOURCES

OFFICIAL RECORDS

Unpublished Documents

National Archives of India

India Home Proceedings
- Archaeology
- Books and Publications
- Delhi
- Education
- Establishment
- Judicial
- Political
- Public

Freedom Movement Papers Region VII

Bihar State Archives

Bengal Appointment Proceeding.
Bengal General (Education) Proceedings
Bengal General (Miscellaneous) Proceedings
Bengal Judicial Proceedings
Bengal Municipal Proceedings
Bengal Political (Political) Proceedings
Bihar and Orissa Political (Special) Proceedings.

Patna Commissioner's Record in Bastas

General Department
Revenue Department
Judicial Department

OFFICIAL PUBLICATIONS

Appointment in Bengal and Their Holders About the Year 1850 down to 1902, Calcutta, 1903.

Buchanan, Francis, *An Account of the Districts of Bihar and Patna in 1811-1812*, 1st edn., Patna 1934; rpt. New Delhi, 1986.

———, *Journal of Francis Buchanan Kept During the Survey of the District of Shahabad in 1812-13*, ed. with notes and introduction by C.E.A.W. Oldham, Patna, 1926.

———, *Journal of Francis Buchanan Kept During the Survey of the District of Bhagalpur in 1810-11*, ed. with notes and introduction by C.E.A.W. Oldham, Patna, 1930.

Byrne, J., *Bengal District Gazetteers, Bhagalpur*, Calcutta, 1911.

Datta, K.K., *Annual Report of the Ad Hoc Regional Records Survey Committee, Bihar (1950-51)*.

———, *Annual Report of the Ad Hoc Regional Records Survey Committee Bihar (1951-52)*.

———, *Annual Report of the Ad Hoc Regional Records Survey Committee Bihar (1952-53)*.

———, *Report of the Regional Records Survey Committee Bihar, 1957-58.*

———, *Report of the Regional Records Survey Committee Bihar, 1959-60.*

———, *Report of the Regional Records Survey Committee Bihar, 1960-61.*

———, *Report of the Regional Records Survey Committee Bihar, 1961-62.*

District Census Reports 1891, Bhagalpur Division (no other details).

———, *Chota Nagpur Division.*

———, *Patna Division.*

Education Commission: Report by the Bengal Provincial Committee with Evidence Taken Before the Committee and Memorials Addressed to the Education Commission, Calcutta, 1884.

General Report of the Census of India, 1901, vol. I, pt. I, Calcutta, 1901.

Grierson, G.A., *Linguistic Survey of India,* vol. V, *Indo-Aryan Family (Eastern Groups)*, pt. II, *Bihari and Oriya*, 1st published 1903, rpt., Delhi, 1990.

———, *The Administration of the Lower Provinces of Bengal from 1882-83 to 1886-87. Being a Supplement to Annual General Administration Report for 1885-86*, Calcutta, 1887.

Hamilton, W., *The East India Gazetteer* (1828), vol. I, rpt., Delhi, 1984.

Hunter, W.W., *A Statistical Account of Bengal*, 20 vols., London; 1875-7, Indian rpt., Delhi, 1976.

Imperial Gazetteer of India (Provincial Series) Bengal, Clacutta, 1909; rpt., New Delhi, 1984.

Jha, J.S., *Report of the Regional Records Survey Committee Bihar (1965-1976)*, Patna, 1978.

———, *Report of the Regional Records Survey Committee Bihar (1976-1980)*, Patna, 1982.

Kumar, N., *Bihar District Gazetteers, Patna*, Patna, 1970.

———, *Image of Patna: A Supplement to Patna District Gazetteer*, Patna, 1971.

———, *Journalism in Bihar: A Supplement to Bihar State Gazetteer*, Patna, 1971.

Martin, Montgomery, *The History, Antiquities, Topography and Statistics*

of Eastern India (1838), in 4 vols., Indian rpt., Delhi, 1976.
O'Donnell, C.J., *The Lower Provinces of Bengal and their Feudatories: The Report. Census of India, 1891*, vol. VIII, Calcutta, 1893.
———, *The Imperial Gazetteer of India*, vol. III, London, 1881.
O'Malley, L.S.S, *Bengal District Gazetteers, Muzaffarpur*, Calcutta, 1907.
———, *Bengal District Gazetteers, Patna*, Calcutta, 1907.
———, *Bengal District Gazetteers, Monghyr*, Calcutta, 1909.
———, *Bengal District Gazetteers, Santhal Parganas*, Calcutta, 1910.
———, *Bengal District Gazetteers, Singhbhum, Saraikela Kharsawan*, Calcutta, 1910.
———, revised by R.E. Swanzy, *Bihar and Orissa District Gazetteers, Champaran*, Calcutta, 1907; Patna, 1938.
Report on Native Papers in Bengal, 1870-1912 (weekly).
Report on Native-Owned English Newspapers in Bengal, 1901-1912 (weekly).
Report on Public Instruction in Bengal, 1865-66 to 1891-92. These were also entitled *General Report on Public Instruction in Bengal.* These annual reports were published from Calcutta.
Report on the Administration of Bengal, 1869-70 to 1906-07. These annual reports were published from Calcutta.
Report on the Administration of the Territories now Included in the Province of Bihar and Orissa, 1911-12, Patna, 1913.
Review of Education in Bengal (1892-93 to 1896-97): First Quinquennial Report, Calcutta, 1897.
Review of Education in Bengal (1897-98 to 1901-02): Second Quinquennial Report, Calcutta, 1902.
Risley, H.H., *The Tribes and Castes of Bengal*, vol. I, Calcutta, 1891.
Roy Chaudhary, P.C., *Bihar District Gazetteers, Gaya*, Patna, 1957.
———, *Bihar District Gazetteers, Muzaffarpur*, Patna, 1958.
The Calcutta Gazette (weekly).
The Durbar List, 1905.
Thornton, E., *A Gazetteer of the Territories under the Government of East India Company*, 1858; rpt., Delhi, 1984.

UNOFFICIAL SOURCES

Contemporary Newspapers and Journals

The Beharee
The Englishman
The Pioneer
The Bengalee
The Hindustan Review
The Hindoo Patriot

The Bengal Times
Bihar Bandhu (Hindi)
Motichoor (Hindi)
Shiksha (Hindi)
Vidya-Vinod (Hindi)

Memoirs and Pamphlets

Sinha, Sachchidananda, *Some Eminent Behar Contemporaries*, Patna, 1944.

Narayan, Mahesh and Sachchidananda Sinha, 'The Partition of Bengal or the Separation of Behar?: An Ideally Perfect Alternative Scheme', Patna, 1906.

SECONDARY SOURCES

Books, Articles and Unpublished Thesis

Ahmad, Aziz, *Studies in Islamic Culture in the Indian Environment*, London, 1964

Ahmad, I.A., 'Medieval Bihar', *Bihar: Past and Present*, Patna, 1987.

Ahmad, Q., *The Wahabi Movement in India*, Calcutta, 1966.

——— (ed.), *Patna Through the Ages*, Delhi, 1988.

Ahmad, Q. and J.S. Jha, *Mazahrul Haque*, New Delhi, 1969.

Akzin, Benjamin, *State and Nation*, London, 1964.

Alam, Muzaffar, 'Eastern India in the Early Eighteenth Century "Crisis": Some Evidence from Bihar', in *The Indian Economic and Social History Review*, 28, I, 1991.

Aloysius, G., *Nationalism Without a Nation in India*, New Delhi, 1997.

Anderson, Benedict, *Imagined Communities: Reflections on the Origin and Spread of Nationalism*, London, 1983.

Askari, S.H., *Aspects of the Cultural History of Medieval Bihar*, Patna, 1984.

Askari, S.H. and Q. Ahmad (eds.), *The Comprehensive History of Bihar*, vol. II, pt. I, Patna, 1983.

———, *The Comprehensive History of Bihar*, vol. II, pt. II, Patna, 1988.

Banerjea, Surendranath, *A Nation in Making*, Calcutta, 1st published 1925, 1963.

Banerjee, Dipasri, *Aspects of Administration in Bengal, 1898-1912*, New Delhi, 1980.

Banerjee, Nirmala, 'Modernization and Marginalization', in *Social Scientist*, October-November 1985, vol. 13, nos. 10/11, pp. 48-71.

Basak, Sudeshna, *Socio-Cultural Study of a Minority Linguistic Group: The Bengalees in Bihar*, Delhi, 1991.

Basu, Aparna (ed.), *Imperialism, Nationalism and Regionalism in Canadian and Modern Indian History*, New Delhi, 1989.

Basu, M.K., 'Regional Patriotism: A Study in Bihar Politics', *Indian Historical Review*, vol. III, no. 2, 1977.

Basu, Sajal, *Regional Movements: Politics of Languages, Ethnicity, Identity*, New Delhi, 1992.

Bayly, C.A., *The Local Roots of Indian Politics: Allahabad, 1880-1920*, Oxford, 1975.

———, *Rulers, Townsmen and Bazaars: North Indian Society in the Age of British Expansion, 1770-1870*, New Delhi, 1997.

Beams, John, *Memoirs of a Bengal Civilian*, London, 1961.

Bishop C.J, 'Sachchidananda Sinha and the Making of Modern Bihar: A Study in Constitutional Agitation at the Provincial Level, 1905-1919', unpublished Ph.D. thesis, University of Virginia, 1972.

Bose, Sugata and Ayesha Jalal, *Modern South Asia: History, Culture, Political Economy*, New Delhi, 1998.

Bottomore, T.B., *Elites and Society*, Harmondsworth, 1966.

Bradley-Birt, F.B., *Chota Nagpore: A Little Known Province of the Empire*, London, 1903, 2nd edn. 1910.

Brass, Paul R., *Language, Religion and Politics in North India*, Cambridge, 1974.

———, *Ethicity and Nationalism: Theory and Comparison*, New Delhi, 1991.

Breuilly, John, *Nationalism and the State*, Manchester, 1982.

Broomfield, J.H., 'The Partition of Bengal: A Problem in British Administration, 1830-1912,' IHCP. 23 (1961), Indian History Congress Proceedings.

Buckland C.E., *Bengal under Lieutenant-Governors*, vols. I and II, Calcutta, 1901, rpt. New Delhi, 1976.

Campbell, George, *Memoirs of My Indian Career*, vol. 1, London, 1893, ed. C.E. Bernard.

Carroll, L., 'The Kayastha Samachar', *The Indian Economic and Social History Review*, July-September 1973.

Chandra, Bipan, *Communalism in Modern India*, New Delhi, 1984.

———, *Modern India*, Delhi, 1971.

Chandra, Satish et al. (eds.), *Regionalism and National Integration*, Jaipur, 1977.

Chandra, Sudhir, *The Oppressive Present: Literature and Social Consciousness in Colonial India*, Delhi, 1992.

———, 'Regional Consciousness in 19th Century India', *Economic and Political Weekly*, vol. 17, no. 32, August 1982.

Chatterjee, P., 'Bengal: Rise and Growth of a Nationality', *Social Scientist*, August, 1975, vol. 4, no. 1.

———, *The Nation And Its Fragments: Colonial and Post Colonial Histories*, New Delhi, 1993.

Chatterji, P.C. (ed.), *Self-Image Identity and Nationality*, Shimla, 1989.

Chattopadhyaya, H., *Internal Migration in India: A Case Study of Bengal*, Calcutta, 1987.

Chaudhary, R.K., *History of Bihar*, Patna, 1958.

Chaudhary, V.C.P., *The Creation of Modern Bihar*, Patna and Darbhanga, 1964.

Christian, J., 'Names of Places in Behar', *Calcutta Review*, vol. XCII, 1891.

———, *Bihar Proverbs*, London, 1891.

Chunder, Bholanath, *The Travels of a Hindoo to Various Parts of India, Bengal and Upper India*, London, 1869.

Cohn, Bernard S., *Colonialism and Its Forms of Knowledge: The British in India*, New Delhi, 1997.

Cotton, H.J.S., *New India or India in Transition*, London, 1904.

Crane, R.I. (ed.), *Aspects of Political Mobilization in South Asia*, Syracuse, New York, 1976.

———, *Regions and Regionalism in South Asian Studies: An Exploratory Study*, Duke University, Durham, 1966.

Cronin, R.P., *British Policy and Administration in Bengal: Partition and the New Province of Bengal and Assam, 1905-1912*, Calcutta, 1977.

Dalton, D. and A.J. Wilson (eds.), *The States of South Asia*, New Delhi, 1982.

Das, A.N., *The Republic of Bihar*, New Delhi, 1992.

Dasgupta, Jyotirindra, *Language Conflict and National Development: Group Politics and National Language Policy in India*, Berkeley, 1971.

Dasgupta, Uma, 'The Indian Press: 1870-1880', *Modern Asian Studies*, vol. 11, no. 1, 1977.

Das, M.N., *India under Morley and Minto: Politics Behind Revolution, Repression and Reforms*, London, 1964.

Datta, K.K., *Freedom Movement in Bihar*, 3 vols., Patna, 1957.

——— (ed.). *The Comprehensive History of Bihar*, vol. III in two pts., Patna, 1976.

———, *Survey of India's Social Life and Economic Conditions in the Eighteenth Century, 1707-1813*, New Delhi, 1978.

Desai, A.R., *Social Background of Indian Nationalism*, rpt., Bombay, 1989.

Deutsch, Karl W., *Nationalism and Social Communication: An Inquiry into the Foundation of Nationality*, Cambridge, Massachusetts, 1953, rpt. 1966.

———, *Nationalism and its Alternatives*, New York, 1969.
Diwakar, R.R. (ed.), *Bihar Through the Ages*, Calcutta, 1959.
Dutt, R.P., *India Today* (rpt.), Calcutta, 1989.
Dutta, Prabhat K., *Politics of Region and Religion in India*, New Delhi, 1991.
Emerson, Rupert, *From Empire to Nation: The Rise of Self Assertion of Asian and African Peoples*, Boston, 1962.
Finkle, Jason L. and Richard W. Gable, *Political Development and Social Change*, New York, 1982.
Fox, Richard G. (ed.), *Realm and Region in Traditional India*, New Delhi, 1977.
Frankel, Francine R. and M.S.A. Rao (eds.), *Dominance and State Power in Modern India*, vol. I: *Decline of a Social Order*, Delhi, 1989.
Fraser, A.H.L., *Among Indian Rajahs and Ryots: A Civil Servant's Recollections and Impressions of Thirty-Seven Years of Work and Sport in the Central Provinces and Bengal*, London, 1912.
Geertz, Clifford (ed.), *Old Societies and New States*, New York, 1963.
Gellner, Ernest, *Nations and Nationalism*, Oxford, 1983; New Delhi, 1986.
———, *Culture, Identity and Politics*, Cambridge, 1987.
———, *Encounters with Nationalism*, Blackwell, Oxford, 1994.
Gopal, S., *British Policy in India, 1858-1905*, Cambridge, 1965; Madras, 1984.
Gopal, Surendra, *Patna in the Nineteenth Century*, Calcutta, 1982.
———, 'Social Changes in Bihar in the Second Half of the 19th Century', *Man in India*, vol. 47, no. 2, April-June 1967.
Gour, Prabhu Narayan (ed.), *Sachchidananda Sinha Commemoration Volume*, Patna, 1947.
Grierson, G.A., *Bihar Peasant Life*, Calcutta, 1885.
Gupta, Partha Sarathi, 'Identity-Formation and Nation-States: Some Reflections', Presidential Address, Indian History Congress, Fifty-ninth Session, Patiala, 1998.
Gupta, Shaibal, 'Non-development of Bihar: A Case of Retarded Sub-Nationalism', *Economic and Political Weekly*, vol. 16, no. 37, September 1981.
Habib, Irfan, 'Emergence of Nationalities', *Social Scientist*, August 1975, vol. 4, no. 1.
———, *An Atlas of the Mughal Empire*, Delhi, 1982.
Hamilton, W., *A Geographical, Statistical and Historical Description of Hindostan, and the Adjacent Countries*, London, 1820.
Hand, J.R., *Early English Administration of Bihar*, Calcutta, 1894.

Hardy, P., *The Muslims of British India*, Cambridge, 1972.

Hastings, Adrian, *The Construction of Nationhood: Ethnicity, Religion and Nationalism*, Cambridge, 1997.

Henningham, Stephen, *A Great Indian Estate and Its Landholders in Colonial India: Darbhanga 1860-1942*, Delhi, 1990.

Houlton, John, *Bihar: The Heart of India*, Calcutta, 1941.

Hobsbawm, E.J., *Nations and Nationalism since 1780: Programme, Myth, Reality*, Cambridge, 1990.

Hobsbawm, E.J. and T. Ranger (eds.), *The Invention of Tradition*, Cambridge, 1983.

Ignatieff, Michael, *Blood and Belonging: Journey into the New Nationalism*, London, 1993.

Israel, Milton (ed.), *National Unity: The South Asian Experience*, New Delhi, 1983.

Jenkins, Brian and Spyros A. Sofos (eds.), *Nation and Identity in Contemporary Europe*, London and New York, 1996.

Jha, Hetukar, *Nation-Building in a North Indian Region (The Case of Mithila)*, Patna, 1976.

———, *Colonial Context of Higher Education in India (Patna University from 1917 to 1951): A Sociological Appraisal*, New Delhi, 1985.

Jha, J.C. and J.N. Sarkar, *A History of Patna College, 1863-1963*, Patna, 1963

Jha, J.S., *The Beginnings of Modern Education in Mithila*, Patna, 1972.

———, *Education in Bihar (1813-1859)*, Patna, 1979.

———, *Early Revolutionary Movement in Bihar*, Patna, 1977.

———, *Aspects of the History of Modern Bihar*, Patna, 1988.

———, 'History of Darbhanga Raj', in *The Journal of the Bihar Research Society*, vol. XLVIII, July-December, pts. I-IV, Maharajadhiraj Dr. Kameshwar Singh Memorial Volume, Patna, 1962.

Jha, Shashisekhar, *Political Elite in Bihar*, Bombay, 1972.

Jha, Sureshwar, M.M. Thakur and B. Thakur (eds.), *Dimensions of Society and Culture of Bihar: Essays in Honour of Dr. Madaneshwar Mishra*, Dr Madaneshwar Mishra Felicitation Volume, Darbhanga, 2003.

Karat, Prakash, 'Problem of National Unity: Historical and Economic Roots of Regionalism', in *Social Scientist*, September 1984, vol. 12, no. 9.

Kellas, James G., *The Politics of Nationalism and Ethnicity*, London, 1991.

Kopf, David (ed.), *Bengal Regional Identity*, Michigan, 1969.

Kumar, Dharma (ed.), *The Cambridge Economic History of India*, vol. II: *c. 1757-c.1970*, Cambridge, 1982; Hyderabad, 1984.

Laclau, Ernesto (ed.), *The Making of Political Identities,* London, 1994.

Leach, E. and S.N. Mukherjee (eds.), *Elites in South Asia,* Cambridge, 1970.

Leonard, John G., 'Politics and Social Change in South India: A Study of Andhra Movement', *Journal of Commonwealth Political Studies*, vol. 5, no. 1, March 1964.

MacDonald, Ellen, 'The growth of Regional Consciousness in Maharashtra', *The Indian Economic and Social History Review*, vol. 5, no. 3, September 1968.

Mahto, S., 'Progress and Development of Language by European Missionaries among the Tribals of Eastern India (Chota Nagpur, 1845-1918)', *Indian History Congress Proceedings Volume*, 41st Session, Bombay, 1980.

Majeed, Akhtar (ed.), *Regionalism: Developmental Tensions in India*, New Delhi, 1984.

Majumdar, B.B., *Indian Political Associations and Reform of Legislature (1818-1917)*, Calcutta, 1965.

Majumdar, R.C., H.C. Raychaudhari and K.K. Datta, *An Advanced History of India,* rpt., Madras, 1985.

Mehrotra, S.R., *The Emergence of the Indian National Congress*, Delhi, 1971.

McLane, John R., *Indian Nationalism and the Early Congress*, Princeton, 1977.

Mishra, Govind, *History of Bihar*, New Delhi, 1970.

Mishra, P.K., *The Political History of Orissa, 1900-1936*, New Delhi, 1979.

Mishra, Madhu Sudan, *Politics of Regionalism in India with Special Reference to Punjab*, New Delhi, 1988.

Misra, B.B., *The Unification and Division of India*, Delhi, 1990.

———, *The Bureaucracy in India: An Historical Analysis of Development up to 1947*, Delhi, 1972.

———, *The Indian Middle Classes: Their Growth in Modern Times*, London, 1961; Delhi, 1978.

Mohanty, Nivedita, *Oriya Nationalism: Quest for a United Orissa 1866-1936*, New Delhi, 1982.

Mohapatra, Bishnu N., ' "Ways of Belonging": The *Kanchi Kaveri* Legend and the Construction of Oriya Identity', *Studies in History*, 12, 2, n.s. (1996).

Nairn, Tom, *The Break-Up of Britain: Crisis and Neo-Nationalism*, London, 1977.

Natesan, G.A. (ed.), *Eminent Mussalmans*, Madras, n.d.

Ojha, P.N. (ed.), *Studies in Indian History and Culture*, vol. I (*1985-86*), Patna, 1987.

——— (ed.), *History of Indian National Congress in Bihar, 1885-1985,* Patna, 1985.

Pandey, B.N. (ed.), *A Centenary History of the Indian National Congress*, vol. I, New Delhi, 1985.

Pandey, G., *The Ascendancy of the Congress in Uttar Pradesh, 1926-34: A Study in Imperfect Mobilization*, Delhi, 1978.

Pandey, S.N., *Education and Social Changes in Bihar (1900-1921),* Varanasi, 1975.

Panikkar, K.N., 'Culture and Ideology', *Economic and Political Weekly*, vol. 22, October-December 1987, no. 49.

——— (ed.), *Studies in History*, Special Number on Intellectual History of Colonial India, vol. 3, no. 1, January-June 1987.

———, *Culture, Ideology, Hegemony: Intellectuals and Social Consciousness in Colonial India*, New Delhi, 1995.

Pant, A.D. and S.K. Gupta (eds.), *Multi Ethnicity and National Integration*, Allahabad, 1985.

Pirzada, Syed Sharfuddin (ed.), *Foundations of Pakistan: All India Muslim League Documents, 1906-1947*, vol. I, New Delhi, Indian edn., 1982.

Prasad, Rajendra, *An Autobiography*, Bombay, 1957.

Puri, Balraj, 'Sub-National Identities and National Integration' *Economic and Political Weekly*, vol. 11, no. 26, 26 June 1976.

———, Politics of Ethnic and 'Communal Identities', *Economic and Political Weekly*, vol. 25, no. 14, 7April 1990.

Ramakant (ed.), *Regionalism in South Asia*, Jaipur, 1983.

Rao, K.V. Narayan, *The Emergence of Andhra Pradesh,* Bombay, 1973.

Raychaudhuri, Tapan and Irfan Habib (eds.), *The Cambridge Economic History of India*, vol. I: *c. 1200-c. 1750,* Cambridge, 1982; Hyderabad, 1984.

Report of a Monster Meeting at the Town Hall on the Education Question held on 2nd July 1870, Calcutta, 1870.

Richards, John F., *The Mughal Empire*, Cambridge, 1996.

Robb, P.G., *The Evolution of British Policy Towards Indian Politics, 1880-1920: Essays on Colonial Attitudes, Imperial Strategies and Bihar*, New Delhi, 1992.

Robinson, Francis, *Separatism among Indian Muslims: The Politics of the United Provinces' Muslims, 1860-1923*, Cambridge, 1974.

Roy Chaudhary, P.C., *Inside Bihar*, Calcutta, 1962.

Said, E.W., *Orientalism*, London, 1978, rpt. by Penguin Books (1985).

Sarkar, S., *The Swadeshi Movement in Bengal, 1903-1908,* New Delhi, 1973.

———, *Modern India: 1885-1947*, Madras, 1983.

———, *Writing Social History*, New Delhi, 1997.

Seal, Anil, *The Emergence of Indian Nationalism: Competition and Collaboration in the Later Nineteenth Century*, Cambridge, 1968.

Seligman, Edwin. R.A. (ed.), *Encyclopaedia of the Social Sciences*, vol. XIII, New York, 1924.

Shrivastava, N.M.P., 'Behar Times, Beharee and Bihar', in *Prajna Bharati*, vol. VI, Patna, 1992.

Singh, Upendra Narayan, *Some Aspects of Rural Life in Bihar: An Economic Study, 1796-1833*, Patna, 1980.

Sinha, B.N., Compiled Volume of the *Presidential Addresses Delivered at the Beharee Students' Conference (1906-1923),* pt. I, Patna, 1931.

Sinha, B.P., *Sachchidanand Sinha*, New Delhi, 1969.

Sinha, Sachchidananda, *A Memorandum to be presented to the Hon'ble the President of the Constituent Assembly of India, by the representatives of Bihar in the Constituent Assembly, As a Rejoinder to a Note submitted by the Representatives of West Bengal in the Constituent Assembly, On the Question of the Amalgamation of certain Districts or parts of Districts of Bihar with West Bengal* (n.d.).

Sitaramayya, B. Pattabhi, *The History of Indian National Congress in (1885-1935)*, Madras, 1935.

Smith, A.D. *Theories of Nationalism*, London, 1971.

Smith, W.C., *Modern Islam in India: A Social Analysis*, Lahore, 1943.

Stalin, J., 'Marxism and the National Question', *Works*, vol. II, Moscow, 1953.

Stokes, Eric, *The English Utilitarians and India*, Oxford, 1959; Delhi, 1982.

Strachey, John, *India: Its Administration and Progress*, 1st edn., 1888; rpt. New Delhi, 1977.

Suntharalingam, R., *Politics and Nationalist Awakening in South India, 1852-91*, Jaipur and Delhi, 1979.

Taylor, David and Malcolm Yapp (eds.), *Political Identity in South Asia*, London, 1979.

Temple, R., *Men and Events of My Time*, London, 1882.

Thakur, Upendra, 'Bihar: A Geographical Introduction and a Historical Review', in *Bihar: Past and Present*, Patna, 1987.

Thapar, Romila, *A History of India*, vol. 2, Harmondsworth, 1966.

Thompson, David, *England in the Nineteenth Century, 1815-1914*, Harmondsworth, 1975.

Vanaik, Achin, 'Is There a Nationality Question in India?', *Economic and Political Weekly*, vol. 23, no. 44, 29 October 1988.

Wallace, Paul (ed.), *Region and Nation in India*, New Delhi, 1985.

Weber, Eugen, *Peasants into Frenchmen: The Modernization of Rural France, 1870-1914*, London, 1977.

Weiner, Myron, *Sons of the Soil: Migration and Ethnic Conflict in India*, New Delhi, 1978.

———, *Political Change in South Asia*, Calcutta, 1963.

Wilson, Minden, *History of Behar Indigo Factories, Reminiscences of Behar, Tirhoot and Its Inhabitants of the Past, History of Behar Light Horse Volunteers*, Calcutta, 1908.

Yang, Anand, *The Limited Raj: Agrarian Relations in Colonial India: Saran District, 1793-1920*, Berkeley, 1989.

Zaidi, A. Moin and S. Zaidi (eds.), *The Encyclopaedia of the Indian National Congress,* vol. I: *1885-1890*, New Delhi, 1976.

———, *The Encyclopaedia of the Indian National Congress,* vol. II: *1891-1895*, New Delhi, 1976.

HINDI AND MAITHILI WORKS

Bhatta, Keshav Ram, *Sajjad Sumbul*, Calcutta, 1904.

Lal, Bansidhar, *Bhartenduugeen Hindi Patrakarita*, Kanpur, 1986.

Mall, Jawahir, *Upalambha or Mata Ke Putra Prati Upadesh*, Patna, 1886.

'Manohar', Ramji Mishra, *Dastanne Patliputra*, New Delhi, 1989.

Mishra, G.M., *Kicchu Dekhal Kicchu Sunal* (Maithili), Darbhanga, Shaka 1894.

Mishra, Ram Dahin (ed.), *Bihar Ke Ratna*, Bankipur, n.d.

Prasad, Devi, *Rameshwar-Yatra*, Muzaffarpur, n.d.

Prasad, Sadhu Charan, *Bharat Bhraman*, vol. III, Kashi, 1902.

Prasad, Shiv, *Bhugol Hastamalak*, Calcutta, 1855.

Sahay, K.S., *Hindi Ka Sansmaran Sahitya*, Varanasi, 1982.

Sahay, Shivpujan, *Hindi Sahitya Aur Bihar*, vol. I, Patna, 1960.

Sahay, Shivpujan and B. Varma (eds.), *Hindi Sahitya Aur Bihar*, vol. II, Patna, 1963.

Singh, Ramdeen, *Bihar Darpan* (1st published in 1882), rpt., Darbhanga, 1996 under the editorship of Dhirendra Nath Singh under the Kameshwar Singh Heritage Series.

———, *Hitopadesh*, Patna, 1896.

Shukla, Ramchandra, *Hindi Sahitya Ka Itihas*, Kashi, Samvat 2038.

Srivastava, N.M.P., *Bihar Mein Rashtriyata Ka Vikas (1912-1947)*, Patna, 1974.

Tiwari, Bhola Nath, *Hindi Bhasa*, Allahabad, 1986.

Tiwari, Hans Kumar and B. Varma (eds.), *Hindi Sahitya Aur Bihar,* vol. III, Patna, 1976.

Tripathi, Ram Naresh, *Kavita Kaumudi*, pt. II, Prayag, Samvat 1977.

Uma Shankar, *Mahesh Narayan: Ek Parichay*, Dumka, 1963.

———, *Mahesh Narayan: Vyaktitwa Aur Krititwa,* Dumka, 1965.

Varma, B. and K. Sharma 'Nayan' (eds.), *Hindi Sahitya Aur Bihar*, vol. IV, Patna, 1984.

Vyas, Ambika Dutt, *Ashcharya Vritanta*, Bhagalpur, Samvat 1950.

———, *Upadesh Lata*, Bhagalpur, 1892.

———, *Ishwarechcha*, Kashi, 1898.

———, *Bat-Bat Me Bat,* Banaras, Samvat 1945.

Index